Collected Writings of the Communist Party of the Philippines

Contents

Rectify Errors, Rebuild the Party! PG 3

Program for a People's Democratic Revolution 79
Urgent Tasks 106
Reaffirm our Basic Principles 182

Marxism-Leninism-Mao Zedong Thought as a guide to the Philippine Revolution 235

Rectify Errors, Rebuild the Party!

Ratified by the Congress of Re-Establishment of the Communist Party of the Philippines

I. MAO TSETUNG THOUGHT IS OUR GUIDE TO SELF-CRITICISM AND PARTY REBUILDING

Mao Tsetung Thought is the highest development of Marxism-Leninism in the present world era of the impending collapse of imperialism and the world triumph of socialism. A genuine proletarian revolutionary party must, in the present era, constantly strive for the integration of Mao Tsetung Thought and revolutionary practice in order to achieve thoroughgoing victory.

Mao Tsetung Thought is the supreme guide in analyzing and summing up the experience of the Communist Party of the Philippines. Our Party has been committed from the very beginning to Marxist-Leninist theory and its creative application to the concrete conditions in the Philippines in fighting US imperialism, feudalism and bureaucrat capitalism. Availing itself of the constant advance of the theory and practice of the international communist movement, our Party is consequently committed to the theory and practice of Mao Tsetung Thought which is now the highest development of Marxism-Leninism.

We are at the stage of world history and of the international communist movement when all parties and cadres of Marxist-Leninist standpoint are re-examining their experience in accordance with Mao Tsetung Thought. Communist parties like the Communist Party of the Philippines, which so far have not established proletarian revolutionary power, are confronted with the question of pursuing Mao Tsetung Thought or otherwise. This urgent question is sharpened by the emergence and worldwide campaign of modern revisionism.

Mao Tsetung Thought sets the demarcation line dividing the proletarian revolutionaries from the false pretenders to the title of revolutionaries in this period of great upheaval, great division and great reorganization of political forces. Mao Tsetung Thought now guides all proletarian revolutionary movements that are inflicting mortal blows on US imperialism, modern revisionism and all reaction. The continuing failures of old parties that are not guided by Mao Tsetung Thought only prove that without its guidance and faithful application the revolution cannot be won and consolidated. The experience of revisionist parties the world over provides more than sufficient proof. The history of our own Party is marked by failures on account of serious errors and weaknesses that need to be rectified now in accordance with Mao Tsetung Thought.

As modern revisionism is being fostered and spread by the modern revisionist clique with its headquarters in the Soviet Union, all proletarian revolutionaries are impelled to express themselves and act in accordance with Mao Tsetung Thought which is the acme of Marxist-Leninism in this world era. Two steps forward are now being made with Mao Tsetung Thought. Under the direct leadership of Chairman Mao, the People's Republic of China has become the central base of the world revolution. It is the center of gravity of the world's countryside encircling the cities of the world.

In a Philippines that is not yet liberated from US imperialism and feudalism, revisionist currents are bound to develop as they have. Currents of opportunism, with the local petty bourgeoisie and bourgeoisie as their fountainhead, serve as the basis for the superimposition of modern revisionism from its world center in Moscow. If modern revisionism is not effectively combatted with correct theory and practice, then US imperialism, domestic feudalism and bureaucrat capitalism can persist in Philippine society.

II. SUMMING UP OUR EXPERIENCE AND DRAWING REVOLUTIONARY LESSONS

It is our urgent task to analyze and sum up our experience as a Party. The sole reason for this analysis and summing up is to draw revolutionary lessons, to identify errors and weaknesses, in order to enable us to rectify them, strengthen ourselves and rebuild a proletarian revolutionary party that is guided by Mao Tsetung Thought.

When we criticize errors and weaknesses, it is "to learn from past mistakes to avoid future ones" and "to cure sickness to save the patient". In the scientific spirit of Marxism-Leninism, we make our criticism in order to rebuild the Party on stronger foundations and build up revolutionary power. As the nucleus of proletarian dictatorship, the Communist Party of the Philippines must consolidate itself through the process of rectification.

Our Party has existed for the last 38 years and yet it has not won revolutionary power. The failures it has incurred should be clearly analyzed in accordance with Mao Tsetung

Thought so as to enable the proletarian revolutionaries of today to act correctly.

Only the broad outlines of Party history can be herein presented with the end in view of showing its dialectical development. This summing-up cannot possibly incorporate all the details that may be available. It is for further discussions among Party cadres to do this. However, our trusted comrades, old and new, have already engaged during the last three years in thorough discussions concerning the problems of the Party.

At the outset, let it be stated that in our summing-up, the handling of the three main weapons of the Philippine revolution assumes prime consideration. These are: the building up of a Marxist-Leninist party, armed struggle, and the national united front.

Also in our summing-up, we shall cover the fields of ideology, politics, military and organization. As a matter of fact, the main body of this discussion is divided into these four aspects. However, before dealing with these, let us trace briefly the history of the Communist Party of the Philippines.

III. BRIEF HISTORICAL REVIEW

A. Founding of the Party and its Illegalization

The national democratic movement in the Philippines entered a new stage when on November 7, 1930, the Communist Party of the Philippines was founded in Manila. The founding of the Party served to signify that the Filipino working class had advanced ideologically, politically, and organizationally, and had started to seek class leadership in the Philippine revolution. Thus, the era of the new-democratic movement was ushered in with the emergence of a working class party committed to the integration of Marxist-Leninist theory and Philippine practice.

As a newly founded working class party, the Communist Party of the Philippines was immediately based in the city among the most advanced workers represented by Crisanto Evangelista. Without sufficient consideration of and safeguard against the oppressive and coercive character of the US imperialist regime and the domestic ruling classes, the Party was publicly launched on the 13th anniversary of the October Revolution. Within a short period, on May 1, 1931 and subsequently, the reactionary authorities took punitive actions against the Party. Cadres and members of the Party were arrested and imprisoned. Mass organizations under the leadership of the Party were banned. In 1932, the Supreme Court formally outlawed the Party and its mass organizations and meted out prison sentences to their leading members.

At the time that the first line of Party leaders was incapacitated, no reliable second line of Party leaders had yet been developed to carry on Party work. Nevertheless, by 1935, there were already some elements who established Marxist study groups among the petty bourgeoisie in Manila. Some of these elements had their political education under the Right opportunist Browderite leadership.

In the period that the Communist Party of the Philippines was outlawed, the Socialist Party headed by Pedro Abad Santos was building up strength on the basis of a loose mass organization of peasants and agricultural workers in Central Luzon.

B. Merger of the Communist Party and the Socialist Party

A merger was made between the Communist Party of the Philippines and the Socialist Party on November 7, 1938 after the leadership of the former was given conditional pardon by the Commonwealth government in accordance with the anti-fascist Popular Front policy. This merger came about with the assistance of James Allen, representative of the Communist Party of the USA. During this period, the Communist Party of the Philippines continued to be closely associated with the Browderite leadership of the Communist Party of the USA.

The open leadership elected by the merger congress was represented by Crisanto Evangelista as chairman, Pedro Abad Santos as vice-chairman and Guillermo Capadocia as general secretary.

The secret second line of leadership was represented by Vicente Lava whose time was mostly devoted to his full-time government employment at the Bureau of Science and whose political work was limited to leading a small progressive petty-bourgeois organization, the League for the Defense of Democracy. Lava epitomized Party members of petty-bourgeois origin who were under the influence of the Right opportunist Browderite leadership of the Communist Party of the USA. Other members of the secret second line of leadership were those who had had limited success in urban Party work, especially among petty-bourgeois elements, during the period that the Party was outlawed.

The Communist Party (merger of the Communist Party and Socialist Party) under the Evangelista leadership worked hard for a city-based anti-fascist movement, which advocated the boycott of Japanese goods and the creation of "labor battalions" under the auspices of a united labor front, the Collective Labor Movement, and with the cooperation of the Commonwealth government. Political work among the urban petty bourgeoisie was carried on by Vicente Lava. With the aid of Communist cadres, the erstwhile Socialist leaders tried to raise the political consciousness of peasants in Central Luzon, but this was given only secondary importance. The main bulk of Party work was done in the city by a city-based and city-oriented Party.

C. The Party During the Japanese Occupation

When the Japanese invaders occupied Manila in January 1942, the Party leadership took no steps to leave the city in an organized way so that soon after, the first line of leadership was easily arrested by the Japanese fascists. The second line of leadership and the mass of Party members who had also been concentrated in the city spontaneously fled to the countryside in various directions. Nevertheless, the majority of Party members fled to various towns in Central Luzon but without coordination.

The Central Luzon Bureau Conference was held on February 6, 1942 to discuss Party policies in the face of the grave situation. It was at this conference that the decision to organize a guerrilla army was taken and the ascendance of the second line of leadership to the central leadership was formalized. Vicente Lava, who became general secretary, was elected in absentia as he had fled to Rizal province. Over a month later on March 29, the Hukbalahap (Hukbo ng Bayan Laban sa Hapon) or the People's Anti-Japanese Army was established in Barrio San Lorenzo in Cabiao, Nueva Ecija.

Meanwhile, two principal leaders of the Party who had been arrested, Abad Santos and Capadocia, agreed to cooperate with the Japanese in convincing Party members to desist from resistance. However, the former was incapacitated by illness and the latter was arrested by the Party when he attempted to implement his compromise. Later on, however, Capadocia was re-educated by the Party.

The Party and the army was based in the Mount Arayat area. It did not take long for the Japanese to pinpoint the area as the seat of the Party and in 1943 the Japanese launched the so-called March Raid which resulted in the capture of many leading Party cadres and members.

During the encircling raid, the people in the vicinity of Mount Arayat dispersed and tried to slip through in small groups; in the process, many leading cadres and members were captured. In an attempt to minimize losses from the enemy offensive, the Vicente Lava leadership adopted the "retreat for defense" policy.

The "retreat for defense" policy meant the breaking up of all Hukbalahap "squadrons" (of company strength) and other units of platoon strength into minuscule units of three to five fighters. It promoted tactical passivity and helplessness in the face of the enemy. It fell in line with the "lie-low" policy of the USAFFE.

It was only as late as the Bagumbali Conference of late September 1944, when the Party declared the "retreat for defense" policy incorrect, that the Hukbalahap "squadrons" were regrouped to take the offensive against the enemy. After a policy of active resistance was taken and implemented, the strength of the people's armed forces increased by leaps and bounds. But while this policy was adopted, the US air force had already started to bombard the Philippines, preparing for massive landing by the US imperialist military forces.

While the "retreat for defense" policy in particular was corrected and Vicente Lava was demoted from the general secretaryship, he retained his membership in the Central Committee to promote together with others a Right opportunist line. The Bagumbali Conference decided to prepare the establishment of the Democratic Alliance for parliamentary struggle upon the return of US imperialism and the Commonwealth government.

D. The Party Upon the Return of US Imperialism

It was in the course of conducting a people's war during the Japanese occupation that the Communist Party of the Philippines gained real political power in certain areas, thus proving the great thesis of Comrade Mao Tsetung that "political power grows out of the barrel of a gun".

Nevertheless, an erroneous position was taken with regard to the central question of keeping the people's armed power in the face of the return of US imperialism and the concomitant reinstatement of landlordism in those areas where the people had asserted their own armed power. Among Party members and their mass following, the aggressive nature of US imperialism was not thoroughly exposed. Neither was the armed peasantry under the leadership of the Party mobilized on the basis of the new democratic stage of the Philippine revolution of which the peasantry is the main force. In areas where the leadership of the Party had been established, the anti-national and anti-democratic links between US imperialism and feudalism were not exposed and denounced for the guidance of the people.

Aside from deficiency in ideological mobilization and in grasping the mass line with regard to US imperialism and the agrarian revolution, the Communist Party of the Philippines did not succeed in developing a Party organization and armed force of a national scale even while developing its main force in Central Luzon. To a much lesser extent, it was only in the Southern Tagalog region where Party units and armed units outside of Central Luzon were established towards the end of the anti-Japanese war.

At the end of World War II, the Party leadership decided to shift its headquarters and the center of its political activity from the countryside to the city. Relying on the word of US military agents, Party leaders took the Rightist line that the main form of struggle had changed into the parliamentary form, that the people were tired of war, that they could participate in bourgeois elections under conditions of "democratic peace". Thus, the central organs and newspapers of the Communist Party of Philippines were shifted to the city.

In the countryside, the Huk Veterans League and the Pambansang Kaisahan ng Magbubukid (National Peasant Union) were set up as legal mass organizations to supplant the Hukbalahap and the BUDC (Barrio United Defense Corps). In the city, the Congress of Labor Organizations and other urban organizations were established. The Party and these mass organizations were to engage in legal and parliamentary struggle through the Democratic Alliance. Within the Democratic Alliance, the Party itself was merely one of the organizations subordinate to the bourgeois personalities leading the alliance.

The policy of disarming and disbanding armed units of the people's army was adopted and implemented. The political power that had been gained by the people's armed forces was, therefore, broken when arms became separated from the men who had wielded them. The Party leadership, however, nurtured the illusion that whereas the "democratic peace" line of making a token surrender of arms to the Military Police was merely a "propaganda line", the "true line" was that the Party was actually keeping caches of arms. Little was it realized that the enemy would not be fooled by a token surrender of arms and that the gap between the "propaganda line" and the "true line" merely confused the massses more than it misled the enemy. The basic fact was that armed units were disarmed and disbanded even as the enemy massacred entire "squadrons" of the Hukbalahap (like "Squadrons 77 and 99) and took other forms of repressive measures against the masses and the Hukbalahap.

Under the direction of US imperialism, the Military Police and civilian guards gave armed protection to the landlords to enable them to recover control over their lands in Central Luzon and even to exact excessive demand, such as the collection of arrears on land rent, on the past years of the Japanese occupation. These subsequent developments proved the bankruptcy of the counter-revolutionary line of welcoming the US imperialists and abandoning the armed struggle.

During the period that the Chinese Communist Party under the leadership of Comrade Mao Tsetung was setting the example of heightening its armed struggle and capability at a time that the US imperialists were maneuvering a Kuomintang-controlled "coalition" government, the leadership of the Communist Party of the Philippines nurtured the illusion that it could engage in bourgeois parliamentary struggle through the Democratic Alliance and it did field its own candidates in the few areas where it held great political influence. Soon after the Party had taken the legal forefront in fighting against the Bell Trade Act and Parity Amendment and other imperialist-landlord measures, Party-supported members of Congress who had been elected in the 1946 elections were unjustly ousted from Congress, thus exposing once more the bankruptcy of the policy of relying mainly on bourgeois parliamentarism.

During the early post-war period, the Right opportunist trend dominated the Party. Vicente Lava was most articulate and active in providing ideological support to this trend within the Party Central Committee. However, the Party general secretaryship was left to Pedro Castro who wanted to develop a mass open party for purposes of bourgeois parliamentary struggle, and then to Jorge Frianeza who advocated a united front with the reactionary Roxas administration. The 1946 Constitution of the Party, like the 1938 merger Constitution, advocated parliamentary struggle as the main form of struggle. The counter-revolutionary revisionist line within the Party was aggravated by petty-bourgeois careerism, regionalism and by individual acts of flightism which seriously undermined the Party.

E. The Party in the Period of Military Adventurism

It was in 1948 that the question of armed struggle was firmly raised by revolutionary Party cadres and the revolutionary masses in the face of fascist abuses perpetrated by the puppet government of Roxas against the Communist Party, Hukbalahap, democratic mass organizations and their leaders and the broad masses of the people. The question of armed struggle was, however, interpreted by the Jose Lava leadership mainly on the basis of external conditions. There was the one-sided expectation by the Party leadership that the near-violent split in the ruling classes due to the election frauds of 1949, the revolutionary victory of the Chinese people, the Korean War and the economic recession in the United States would absolutely open the way for the victory of the people's army in the Philippines, notwithstanding the internal weakness of the Party and the people's army due to previous Right opportunist errors. External conditions were interpreted as the very reasons for a quick military victory.

The Party leadership represented by Jose Lava failed to provide the most essential reasons for engaging in armed struggle, like a programme of armed struggle against US imperialism and its local running dogs and for agrarian revolution among others, and equally it failed to recognize that armed struggle under the conditions existing in the Philippines would have to be protracted. Against the superficial reasons provided by the Lava leadership to justify the policy of striving for a quick military victory, the Right opportunists took the line of converting the Communist Party of the Philippines into a big open mass party for purposes of the parliamentary form of struggle and took the narrow view that the trade unionists should automatically prevail in the Party leadership.

Both opposing sides failed to consider extensively whether the Party's headquarters and center of political gravity should be the city or the countryside. Both Right opportunists and "Left" opportunists agreed that the Communist Party of the Philippines remain an urban Party.

Despite its advocacy of armed struggle, the Jose Lava leadership decided to command the People's Liberation Army (Hukbong Mapagpalaya ng Bayan) from the city. Although it assumed the policy of armed struggle, the Jose Lava leadership did not lay down the correct theoretical and political basis for its organizational and military efforts. For this reason, it inconsistently allowed Luis Taruc as commander-in-chief of the people's army to negotiate for amnesty with the Quirino government.

The Politburo conference of January 1950 assumed a purely military viewpoint and drew up the "PB Resolutions" which maintained a line of rapid military victory. The Jose Lava leadership adopted a two-year timetable for seizing political power in the cities, without an all-sided and dialectical appreciation of the strength of the Party and the people's army on the one hand and the strength of the enemy on the other.

An adventurist military policy was initiated by a city-based Party leadership which was called the Secretariat or the Politburo-In. Instead of advancing in a series of waves within a protracted period of time, the people's army in the countryside was ordered to make simultaneous over-extended attacks on the enemy at widely separated points in Central Luzon and Southern Luzon as part of the plan to prepare for the seizure of Manila. The military objectives were big military camps, cities and provincial capitals. This was done in a spirit of haste on March 29 and then on August 26, 1950 in accordance with the "PB Resolutions" of January 1950, without any thought of the forthcoming counter-attack by the enemy with massive campaigns of "encirclement and suppression" and also without any serious thought of the necessity of being able to concentrate the forces of the people's army in order to deal with the subsequent enemy counter-attack.

Over-extended and inadequately armed units were also adventuristically disposed on the "gates" of Manila to bolster the illusion that the seat of reactionary rule was "soon" to fall. On the other hand, the headquarters of the Politburo-Out was snuggled in the unpopulated vastness of the Laguna portion of the Sierra Madre, isolated from the main force of the people's army. As the Secretariat or the Politburo-In (the main Party leadership) was separated physically from the Politburo-Out, so was the latter physically far separated from the people's armed forces that it was supposed to command upon orders of the Politburo-In. Military operations and the supply and communication lines were excessively stretched out over unreliable areas.

In October 1950, the Politburo-In was totally smashed in the city, with other Party members, sympathizers and couriers apprehended. A big harvest of Party documents, which included lists of members and tactical plans, was made by the enemy and this helped the enemy destroy the Party organization in the city and smash the people's armed forces in the countryside.

F. The Party In the Period of Continued Military Defeat

After the capture of the Secretariat or the Politburo-In in Manila, the Politburo-Out organized a Central Committee conference in February and March of 1951 in order to discuss the new situation. As clear proof of the increasingly desperate situation of the Party, the conference itself was under heavy military pressure by a massive enemy encirclement. With only a negligible armed force for protection, the conference could only depend on mere physical concealment within the encirclement.

The Central Committee conference failed to pose and criticize the adventurist errors of the Jose Lava leadership organizationally, politically and ideologically. The Jesus Lava leadership elected by the conference was essentially a part of the previous leadership; the Politburo-Out merely replaced the apprehended Politburo-In as the main leading body. At the most, the capture of the entire Politburo-In was narrowly adduced to tactical errors like negligence of security particularly in the city. The Central Committee failed to make a profound and systematic self-criticism as basis for a rectification movement.

The CC Resolutions of 1951 merely reiterated mechanically with the same over-confidence as that of the Jose Lava leadership the PB Resolutions of 1950. Grossly ignorant of the strategy and tactics of people's war, the Jesus Lava leadership could not state categorically that the people's army was on the strategic defensive; instead it muddle-headedly considered the incumbent stage of armed struggle as strategic "counter-offensive". As in previous stages of the Party history, a new situation within the Party developed due to grave errors of a previous Party leadership and yet no rectification movement was launched to correct the basic mistakes and weaknesses in ideology, politics, organization and armed struggle.

The errors of the Jose Lava leadership were obscured by the inner-Party struggle which arose between Jesus Lava and the Taruc brothers on fragmented issues. In this regard, the Jesus Lava leadership resorted mainly to organizational maneuvers to cover up for the adventurist errors of the Party leadership and to combat the capitulationist ideas of the Taruc brothers.

As a result of the unrectified ideological and political weaknesses, and as a result of the disastrous military adventures of the Jose Lava leadership, capitulationism started to set in the ranks of the Party leadership and was represented by the disgruntled and traitorous Luis Taruc who surrendered to the reactionary puppet government of Ramon Magsaysay in 1954. The outright capitulationist trend was aggravated to become the principal current by successive military defeats and by the chronic incorrect handling of cadres and the sectarian and liberal manipulation of cadres to perpetuate the clannish chain of Lava leadership.

Upon its assumption of office, the Jesus Lava leadership was buffetted from one military defeat to another. After the 1951 Central Committee conference, the Party headquarters, with its complement of staff members and security force, divided itself into several smaller groups and these were in blind flight within the massive enemy encirclement that enveloped the Sierra Madre from Laguna to Nueva Ecija and on both sides of Quezon. At a time that the Party leadership needed to concentrate its armed forces and smash or break through the weak points of the enemy encirclement, there was no sufficient number of men it could command. From this time on, the Jesus Lava leadership was never in effective control of any sizeable armed force because the strongest regional command (Reco 2) closely associated with Luis Taruc became disaffected with the Lava leadership and all other forces had been fragmented because of the over-extended dispersal of armed units during the adventurist leadership of Jose Lava.

During the period of 1951-1954, many principal leaders of the armed struggle fell under the massive encirclement campaigns in Southern Tagalog, Central Luzon, Bicol and Panay. It was during this period that roving rebel tendencies developed in the HMB because of ineffective central command and the slicing-off tactics of the enemy.

Under the impact and conditions of military defeat, the Jesus Lava leadership decided to adopt parliamentary struggle as the main form of struggle in 1955, thus falling into the same capitulationist line of Luis Taruc. The policy of armed struggle was abandoned and those who had opposed this policy before became gleeful, wrongly feeling vindicated by the adventurist error of the Jose Lava leadership and by the Right opportunist about-face of the Jesus Lava leadership.

The Jesus Lava leadership went as far as de-activating armed units that were accessible to its command, and these were converted into so-called organizational brigades. Under the impact of the world revisionist campaign that was being waged by the Khrushchev revisionists, the Jesus Lava leadership in succeeding years felt more justified in its wrong policy. Around 1958, he disbanded his own security men and fled from the countryside to the city to start the life of a city fugitive, isolated from the masses. This pattern of flight from the countryside to the city resulted in the capture of the principal leaders of the Party in the Greater Manila area. It signified the utter failure of the series of Lava leaderships in the Communist Party of the Philippines.

Living the life of a city fugitive, Lava wrote political transmissions and directives and made appointments without the benefit of collective Party discussions. It was during this period that Jesus Lava acting alone decided to adopt the liquidationist "single-file" policy. This policy required one Party member to be in contact with only one other Party member. The whole Party organization was, at first, reduced to a few one-way files until the loss of only one member in a single file would result in the automatic disconnection of several others from the Party or the complete dissolution of the entire file. This process led to the grave disorganization of the Party. After a few more years, Jesus Lava was to lose contact with both legal and armed cadres of the Party.

It was during this liquidationist period that the Party fell behind, even behind the national bourgeoisie and urban petty bourgeoisie which were raising the banner of nationalism of the Recto brand as early as 1957 and more strongly in 1961. Until new Party cadres emerged and some Party members were reactivated, the Party fell too far behind the events of the day. Meanwhile, Jesus Lava made decisions for the Party all by himself as Party discussions would now reveal. In May 1964, Jesus Lava was finally arrested in Sampaloc, Manila under circumstances which clearly showed that he surrendered himself. In the first place, he had deliberately, by his own Right opportunism, one-man flightism and liquidationism, placed himself into the urban mouth of the reactionary whale.

IV. MAIN ERRORS AND WEAKNESSES

A. Ideological Weaknesses

The main ideological weakness of all previous leaderships of the Communist Party of the Philippines has been subjectivism, appearing in the form of dogmatism and empiricism, and resulting in Right and "Left" opportunist lines. The Philippines, being a semi-colonial and semi-feudal country, has a large petty bourgeoisie which serves as the historical and social basis for subjectivism. Since the Party exists in this kind of society, it is liable to reflect subjectivist trends from without and from within if it is not alert and careful in its Marxist-Leninist ideological building which is the first requirement in Party building.

The Party could be penetrated by a considerable number of Party members of petty-bourgeois orientation (middle peasants, intellectuals, handicraftsmen and other petty producers) who fail to remould their world outlook and methods of thinking in accordance with Marxism-Leninism and who fail to integrate revolutionary practice with dialectical materialism and historical materialism.

Although the first Party members were mainly from the working class represented by Comrade Crisanto Evangelista, the Party leadership erroneously put much reliance on open, legal, parliamentary and urban political activity which resulted in the paralyzation of the Communist Party of the Philippines once it was outlawed by the US imperialists and their running dogs. A revolutionary and thoroughgoing proletarian world outlook would have made the Party recognize the dialectics of the whole Philippine situation and would have enabled it to adopt the correct methods of legal and illegal struggle.

It was around 1935, however, while the Party was still outlawed by its class enemies when a considerable number of Party members of petty-bourgeois class status crept into a fluid underground Party that was deprived of a definite central leadership and tried to carry on political work, bringing with them their unremoulded petty bourgeois and bourgeois ideas. At the helm of this petty bourgeois element within the Party were those who were greatly influenced by the empiricist and Right opportunist current spread by Browder. At this time, the Communist Party of the Philippines, under the auspices of the Communist International, was assisted by the Communist Party of the USA by seeing to it that cadres like Vicente Lava who became its leading representative would carry on Party work.

Subjectivism of the empiricist type was manifested by major political policies and developments such as the principal importance given to urban Party work before the outbreak of the Pacific war; the merger of the Socialist Party and the Party which artificially increased the membership of the latter; the Rightist preamble in the merger constitution; capitulationism towards US imperialism and the Commonwealth government; the absence of any plan to shift the Party headquarters from the city to the countryside; the adoption of the "retreat for defense" policy of 1943 and the belief of Vicente Lava that there could be no proletarian leadership in the countryside; the purely anti-Japanese line during the war period and the shift of the Party central organs to the city after the anti-Japanese war and the blatantly Right opportunist policies of Vicente Lava, Jorge Frianeza and Pedro Castro during the period of 1945-1948.

Empiricism grows on a static underestimation of the people's democratic forces and on a static overestimation. of the enemy strength. Party work becomes dictated by the actions of the enemy instead of by a dialectical comprehension of the situation and the balance of forces. Revolutionary initiative becomes lost because of a static, one-sided, fragmented and narrow view of the requirements of the anti-imperialist, anti-feudal and anti-fascist struggle.

Thus, there is the overconcentration on urban political work because of the subjectivist and opportunist desire to compete or collaborate with bourgeois parties and groups, and beg for "democratic peace" from the US imperialists and local reactionaries in their own urban citadel. The countryside is grossly underestimated and thus, revolutionary initiative, the indispensable mass support of the peasantry, and a wide area for maneuver are ignored. There is also the personal desire of the petty bourgeois to enjoy the comforts and prestige of city life.

There is, however, the other side of the coin of subjectivism. Between 1948 and 1955, subjectivism of the dogmatist type prevailed during the first two years of the Jose Lava leadership and the first five years of the Jesus Lava leadership. This dogmatism grew on an overestimation of the people's democratic forces and an underestimation of the enemy strength, without taking into full account the painstaking process of a protracted people's war. Under the Jose Lava leadership, the strategic view was adopted that, in a brief period of two years, the Party was certain to seize power. The Jose Lava leadership did not take into full account the necessity of a concrete and extended process of Party building, building of a people's army and the building of a revolutionary national united front.

The Jose Lava leadership was fond of "Left" jargon so unrelated to the whole basic situation, a manifestation of subjectivism of the dogmatist type. This leadership took the style of confounding comrades with book knowledge and some supposedly special knowledge about the world situation and about the inner circles of the enemy. On the basis of such knowledge it took decisions that over-strained the Party and the masses beyond their capability and understanding. It did not care for painstaking work among the masses in the development of a protracted people's war.

On the other hand, subjectivism of the empiricist type manifested by the Vicente Lava leadership and the Jesus Lava leadership was the cowardly reaction to the incumbent military superiority of the enemy. These leaderships took the line of passivity both strategically and tactically. They lost sight of the possible development of revolutionary principles and policies correctly adopted and applied on the basis of the internal laws of development of Philippine history and society. They simply went with the tide of defeat, without trying to seize revolutionary initiative.

Empiricism and dogmatism are two sides of the same petty-bourgeois coin. A twirl of the coin of subjectivism will abruptly show this or that side. The subjectivist errors of the Vicente and Jose Lava leaderships were mainly empiricism and dogmatism, respectively. These errors spring from the same petty bourgeois disease of subjectivism that has afflicted the Party and that has wrought havoc to the revolutionary movement.

Reversals from empiricism to dogmatism and from dogmatism to empiricism are peculiarly common to those who still retain the petty-bourgeois world outlook. Nevertheless, when one is the principal aspect of a subjectivist stand, the other is bound to be the secondary aspect and the secondary aspect becomes the principal aspect at another moment. That is the dialectical relationship of empiricism and dogmatism. Comrades should not wonder why under a dogmatist leadership there should be cases of empiricism; what is common between dogmatism and empiricism is the use of narrow and limited experience as the basis for over-all subjectivist decisions. Also, comrades should not wonder why a leadership with the same petty-bourgeois orientation should swing from empiricism to dogmatism and back to empiricism, and so on and so forth. All subjectivists fail to grasp the laws of dialectical development and so they are volatile and erratic.

In 1951, the Jesus Lava leadership continued to carry the dogmatist line of the Jose Lava leadership. But after a few years, subjectivism of the empiricist type started to dominate because of military defeats. The Jesus Lava leadership started to overestimate the strength of the enemy and it adopted parliamentary struggle as the main form of struggle, took flight from the countryside and then took up the so-called "single-file" policy based on its narrow individual experience.

In summing up the series of subjectivist leaderships, we can state that Vicente Lava, Jose Lava and Jesus Lava were responsible for the petty-bourgeois disease that has long afflicted the Communist Party of the Philippines. The black bourgeois line of the Lavas continues to promote revisionism in the Philippines. It is essentially the inability to grasp proletarian revolutionary ideology and apply this on the concrete conditions of Philippine society. The usurpation of the Party leadership by the Lavas during the last more than 30 years accounts for the fact that the Communist Party of the Philippines is still weak. Although the political errors of each Lava leadership became exposed in the wake of far-reaching damage, no thoroughgoing rectification movement had ever been conducted to expose and correct the basic errors in ideology.

Despite the fact that Vicente Lava's subjectivism as expressed by his "retreat for defense" policy had resulted in great damage to the Party, there was no subsequent rectification movement that could have prevented the Right opportunist errors of the subsequent early post-war years. Also, despite the serious errors of the Lava leadership, the subsequent leadership did not engage in any serious rectification movement. Until now, despite the grave errors of the Jesus Lava leadership and those of other previous leaderships, there has been strong resistance to ideological, political, and organizational rectification. The Party flounders from error to error when there is no systematic and objective evaluation of each error ideologically, politically and organizationally.

The fact that Party leadership was passed from one blood brother to another, a singular phenomenon in the entire international communist movement, could be taken as a magniloquent symptom of the subjectivism that had predominated within the Party.

The black bourgeois line of the Lavas is careerism on a grand scale within the Party. A dangerous pattern has been established wherein Party responsibilities are apportioned to blood relatives on the basis of personal trust rather than on the basis of ideological and genuine Party trust. In this manner a mechanical and slavish artificial majority could always be depended upon to elect the Lava brothers as general secretaries of the Party in a series.

The evil of subjectivism is still persistent within the Party and must be eradicated. It still appears in the form of sentimentalism on the part of elder cadres who had received their ideological training from the previous leaderships. Sentimentally, they recognize the personal sacrifices of the Lava brothers but at the same time they do not see how many lives of people and cadres have been sacrificed at the altar of subjectivist errors and failures and they do not see that the so-called personal sacrifices of the Lava brothers were the very product of their subjectivist errors and failures.

This sentimentalism has become a hindrance to the rectification of ideological, political and organizational errors. It is combined with a subjectivist awe for high bourgeois academic degrees that some cadres have. It also appears in the form of personal trust for those who have had ideological training from and those who enjoy the sanction of the series of Lava leaderships.

The black bourgeois line of the Lavas as it has developed on the basis of subjectivism now nourishes the growth of modem revisionism in the Philippines. Since we are determined to rebuild the Party, the black bourgeois line of the Lavas and all errors of subjectivism must be resolutely opposed and weeded out by a thoroughgoing rectification movement. In conducting such a movement it is not so much the persons of the Lava "dynasty" that we are after; what we are after is the rectification of subjectivist errors. If no rectification movement is to be undertaken, if no ideological consolidation of the Party is to be made, then modern revisionism would flourish to disarm and undermine the people's democratic revolution.

Lava revisionism has been persistent for decades within the Party only because rectification, as demonstrated by Comrade Mao Tsetung in the Chinese Communist Party, has never before been conducted as we have decided to do. A rectification movement within the Communist Party of the Philippines, the nucleus of the proletarian dictatorship, should be conducted in the Marxist-Leninist way that a cultural revolution is conducted under the proletarian state in order to combat Right opportunism and modern revisionism.

The preponderant form of subjectivism that has characterized the Lava leadership is empiricism. The dogmatist leadership of Jose Lava and, partially, of Jesus Lava was approximately a seven-year "Left" interregnum in what is more than 30 years of empiricism carried out mainly by the Vicente Lava and Jesus Lava leaderships. Empiricism in philosophy results in Right opportunism in politics. Empiricism and Right opportunism in turn provide the basis for modern revisionism which is persistently advocated by the neo-bourgeois and revisionist renegade clique in Moscow. At present, modern revisionism is futilely trying to gain ground. The Communist Party of the Philippines must combat it thoroughly and seriously, especially now that Party rebuilding is being undertaken.

B. Political Errors

Right opportunism and "Left" opportunism have been committed in the history of the Communist Party of the Philippines. These political errors have emanated from the subjectivist world outlook. They have restricted the building of a Marxist-Leninist party that is firmly and closely linked with the masses on a national scale, that has a correct style of work and conducts criticism and self-criticism, that implements a programme of agrarian revolution and that makes use of the national united front to broaden its influence and support in its struggle against US imperialism, feudalism and bureaucrat capitalism.

The urban, parliamentary and open character of the Communist Party of the Philippines during the early months of its existence in 1930 and 1931 was mainly responsible for the political disaster and difficulties that it soon suffered. During this early period, the Party leadership was given to the use of "Left" language in public against the entire bourgeoisie, and illegal work was not effectively carried out together with legal work.

The Party did not arouse and mobilize the peasantry as the main force of the revolution. Even when the principal leaders of the Party and its mass organizations were banished to different provinces, they were not conscious of the significance of planting the seeds of the new democratic revolution in the countryside. The idea of the national united front was not also immediately taken up and adopted. Even the urban petty bourgeoisie was not given serious attention as a class ally and as a source of cadres.

However, during the period that the Party was outlawed, cadres of petty-bourgeois origin crept into the Party and by 1935 their presence therein became marked. Because of their continued petty-bourgeois social status and their failure to remould their outlook, these cadres restrained the putting of emphasis on Party work among the toiling masses, especially in the countryside. In the trade unions, Party cadres working illegally could be counted on one's fingers. As late as 1937, only a few cadres were working among the peasants in a few towns of Central Luzon. It was the Socialist Party of Pedro Abad Santos, however, which had a large but loose mass following in the countryside. A few activists of this reformist party actually read Marxist literature but were lacking the discipline of Communist cadres.

It was through the merger of the Communist Party of the Philippines and the Socialist Party in 1938 that the black bourgeois line of revisionism became formalized. The constitution of the merger party contained in its preamble the clause that it "defends the Constitution (of the US-puppet commonwealth government) and the rights proclaimed therein..." and in Section I of Article III, the statement it "opposes with all its power any clique, group, circle, faction or party which conspires or acts to subvert, undermine, weaken or overthrow any or all institutions of Philippine democracy whereby the majority of the Filipino people have obtained power to determine their own destiny in any degree." Getting the good wishes of Quezon in the Popular Front preoccupied most of the Party leaders then.

The necessity of preparing and developing rural bases in the face of the growing threat of fascism was not fully grasped by the Party leaders; and even if it were so surmised, no adequate preparations for armed struggle were made. The international situation that was already clearly pointing to the imminence of World War II was not fully related to the Philippine situation. From 1938 to 1942, the first and second lines of leadership agreed on the principal importance of urban Party work and overconcentrated on defending "civil liberties" while minimizing the importance of Party building and army building among the peasants. It was simply assumed that the merger of the Communist Party and the Socialist Party would enmass the peasantry to the side of the Party. Under the banner of the Popular Front and under the auspices of the commonwealth government, leading Party cadres ran for electoral offices in the reactionary government especially in Greater Manila and in some few provinces and they did not pursue what was principal revolutionary work in the countryside.

At the outbreak of World War II, the Party submitted a memorandum to commonwealth president Manuel L. Quezon for arms support from the bourgeois government; but the latter, sure of his class interests, refused despite the Popular Front. Instead of putting the main stress on the revolutionary work of arousing and mobilizing the peasant masses, the Party leadership chose to put the main stress on the secondary, which consisted of legal and urban work under the banner of the Popular Front. It was misled by the false prospect of arms support from a puppet government under US imperialist control

When the Japanese imperialists invaded Manila, the first line of leadership was apprehended in the city and the rest of the city cadres did not exactly know where to retreat. At this point, we can see the error of Right opportunism as having grown within the Party without having been the object of critical exposure and thoroughgoing rectification.

Focusing Party work on parliamentary struggle, the merger party failed to make the most essential preparations for the anti-fascist armed struggle. The city cadres who fled to the countryside at the time of the Japanese invasion were unable to withdraw in an organized way, thus exposing the failure of the Crisanto Evangelista leadership to build up the Party with deep foundations among the peasant masses on the basis of their struggle for land which is the main content of the people's democratic revolution. There was no rural base prepared for waging a people's war against the Japanese fascists.

Taught nevertheless by the immediate situation, the Party leadership held the Central Luzon Bureau Conference and soon after organized the People's Army Against the Japanese (Hukbalahap) to lead the popular resistance against the Japanese invaders and the puppet government. With the Hukbalahap under its command, the Party began to build political power in the countryside.

But the Right opportunist political line persisted and when the Party and the Army met their first serious setback in the anti-Japanese struggle during the "March raid", the Vicente Lava leadership promoted Right opportunism by adopting the "retreat for defense" policy. It was a policy that contravened the Marxist-Leninist principle that Red political power could be built only by waging armed struggle. This policy was nothing but a variation of the USAFFE "lie low" policy of avoiding armed struggle with the Japanese invaders. This Right opportunist line restricted the rise of people's democratic power not only in the short run but even long after it was declared an erroneous policy.

The spontaneous resistance of the masses exposed the bankruptcy of the "retreat for defense" policy and the Bagumbali Conference declared this policy erroneous. Although the conference resulted in the demotion of some Right opportunists and in the regrouping of Hukbalahap "squadrons" for intensified resistance, the Right opportunist error was not thoroughly rectified and the Right opportunists still retained a big say in the Central Committee. Furthermore, the "Socialists" who had automatically become "Communists" by virtue of the 1938 merger were not provided by the Party leadership with the correct Marxist-Leninist education and were always susceptible to Right opportunism. The capitulationist and renegade Luis Taruc would remain to be the general representative of a great many of them who failed to advance to the level of Marxist-Leninists.

The abandonment of the "retreat for defense" policy resulted in some limited successes for the Party and the army. In a few months' time, the area and the population covered by both increased to the extent that the greater part of Central Luzon came under the effective leadership of the Party and that the people's army could send out sizeable units to establish or reinforce armed bases in the Southern Tagalog area.

However, at the end of the anti-Japanese struggle when the US imperialists landed to reconquer the Philippines, the Right opportunist line would again strikingly emerge as the main line. There arose the illusion that the people were tired of war and that the Party could strive for the realization of its principles under conditions of "democratic peace" granted by US imperialism and the landlords. Against this illusion were the brutalities committed by the military police, the civilian guards and all kinds of American agents against the people and the unjust arrest and incarceration of the principal leaders and fighters of the Hukbalahap. Thus, a strategic dual line was adopted with the so-called "propaganda" line differing from the so-called "true" line. The "propaganda" line was that the Party was publicly desirous of "democratic peace", of participating in bourgeois politics through the Democratic Alliance; and the "true" line was that it was actually keeping its armed power in the form of concealed arms caches. The Party leadership ordered the disbanding of the majority of Hukbalahap "squadrons" and token arms surrender were made. It shifted back the center of its political activity to the city under the banner of bourgeois parliamentarism.

With the adoption of this strategic dual line, deception was idealistically intended as an essential component of the strategic line. But while the enemy was not fooled by the token surrender of weapons by the Hukbalahap, confusion was introduced into the ranks of the cadres and masses. The Party leadership failed to establish the correct mass line as it adopted a strategic dual line and lost its grip on the gun.

The 1946 constitution of the Party continued to carry the black bourgeois line of revisionism by stating in its Article VIII, Section 2, "Affiliation with or participation in the activities of any group, class, faction or party which aims or acts to destroy, weaken or overthrow the democratic Constitution of the Philippines shall be punished with immediate ouster from the Party".

Until May 1948, when the Jose Lava leadership assumed central responsibility, the Party experienced the blatant reign of Right opportunism or revisionism. During the early post-war period, the Right opportunist influence of Vicente Lava, Pedro Castro and Jorge Frianeza prevailed. The Pedro Castro leadership was denounced and replaced for Right opportunism and tailism and for advocating the development of a mass and open Party that was supposed to engage solely in bourgeois elections. But the errors of this leadership were never consistently rectified ideologically and politically all throughout the Party although drastic organizational measures were taken against those who took sides with Pedro Castro without so much as an explanation to the masses of Party members. Jorge Frianeza replaced him and was soon removed from the secretaryship and expelled for Rightism but again no thoroughgoing rectification movement was conducted to weed out the persistent roots of the errors.

Without clarifying the ideological, political and organizational grounds for a protracted people's war, the Jose Lava leadership merely took advantage of the Party's and the people's clamor that armed struggle was necessary on account of the fascist attacks against them and a number of duly-elected representatives in Congress who opposed the Bell Trade Act and the Parity Amendment. This leadership automatically expected revolutionary triumph on the basis of external conditions.

Because of the absence of a thoroughgoing rectification movement against the previous Rightist leadership being conducted aside from organizational and administrative measures, Right opportunism could still persist as a strong undercurrent or secondary aspect of opportunism even under the "Left" opportunist leadership of Jose Lava. Soon after its assumption of office and adoption of the line of armed struggle, it actually permitted Luis Taruc to negotiate the terms of surrender and amnesty for the people's armed forces with the Quirino government. This was another instance of an opportunist line that undermined the revolutionary will of the masses more than it deceived the enemy. No genuine Marxist-Leninist party leadership would ever consider surrendering to or seeking amnesty from the enemy. To do so would be to betray the fighting masses, promote capitulationism and serve the enemy.

The Jose Lava leadership committed mainly the error of "Left" opportunism by dogmatically assuming that the class enemies of the proletariat were weakening and splitting up all the way on a straight line and that the Party could seize power within a very short period. There was a failure to recognize that in a semi-colonial and semi-feudal country, a protracted people's war would have to be waged with due regard to the strength of the enemy.

The Party could depend only on the people in areas covered by the Hukbalahap and the Barrio United Defense Corps during the anti-Japanese struggle. Because of previous failure to distribute cadres to important parts of the country other than Central Luzon, Manila, Rizal and Southern Tagalog and because of the Right opportunism of previous years, the Party and the people's army were not able to build up on a national scale and, therefore, were not able to unite with the people on a national scale. It would require a protracted period of time for the Party to convert into a revolutionary advantage the initial disadvantage of fighting for people's democratic power in an archipelago like the Philippines.

The "Left" opportunist leadership of Jose Lava failed to understand comprehensively the requirements of a people's democratic revolution. It failed to see the necessity of solid party building, the development of armed rural bases on the basis of an agrarian revolution and the national united front. If it recognized the necessary combination and correct use of these weapons, then it could have easily taken the view that people's war is protracted and painstaking.

During this period, the notion became prevalent that the establishment of rural bases was a strange and utopian idea "because the Philippines is a small country and an archipelago having no rear adjacent to and contiguous with a big friendly country". Jose Lava as general secretary dismissed arrogantly the concept of rural bases as a grandiose idea. Little was it realized that the rural base was itself the center of gravity or great rear of guerrilla zones. The camp of the Politburo-Out in the Laguna portion of the Sierra Madre depended merely on a hidden physical base instead of a rural base where the people's support is strong by virtue of armed struggle and agrarian revolution.

A protracted revolutionary armed struggle should have been waged in combination with an agrarian revolution and the development of rural bases. The people's army should have advanced in a series of waves from stable base areas but a petty-bourgeois leadership was too much in a hurry, too impetuous to capture within so short a period the bourgeois state power centered in Manila. This petty-bourgeois leadership never realized that the Party could fight the bourgeois state by establishing the people's democratic power in the countryside. At the height of the adventurist folly, Party leaders would bid each other good-bye in public with: "See you in Malacanang!" This infantile talk reflected the adventurist desire of the Jose Lava leadership to move the people's army to the city gates within a short period of time without first developing the armed power of the masses and then advancing in a series of waves from well-consolidated rural bases.

The Central Committee plenary session which was held by the Politburo-Out under the Jesus Lava leadership in February-March of 1951 after the capture of the Politburo-In failed to clarify fully the building and wielding of the three weapons of the Philippine revolution; namely, party building, armed struggle and the national united front. It obscured the basic errors of the Jose Lava leadership by superficial rationalization such as "carelessness" of the captured Party leaders and the tactical errors of lower cadres and commanders and the rank and file. A rectification movement would have unfolded the ideological and political basis of the failure of the Jose Lava leadership and thus removed the danger of opportunism continuing in its Right or "Left" form.

Jesus Lava's assumption of the Party leadership did not mean an immediate reversal of Jose Lava's "Left" opportunist political line. It was when the Jesus Lava leadership lost effective central command over all units of the people's army and was further burdened by the series of military difficulties exerted by the enemy and by the capitulationism and splittism of Luis Taruc and his Titoite cohorts that it swung to the Right opportunist line. Its Right opportunism became most evident in the formal adoption of parliamentary struggle as the main form of struggle in 1955 and in the disbandment of armed units under its command. This Right opportunism would continuously be further borne out by the subsequent one-man flights of principal leaders of the Party from the countryside to the city. This one-man flightism resulted in the worst policy of the Jesus Lava leadership, the "single file" policy, which meant the liquidation of the collective life of the Party and the dissolution of practically all Party units and armed units, thus defeating even the Right opportunist objective of engaging mainly in parliamentary struggle.

The militant resurgence of the Communist Party of the Philippines has been on account of the emergence of new Party cadres and reactivated Party cadres who are now guided by today's highest development of Marxism-Leninism, Mao Tsetung Thought.

At the present moment, however, the black bourgeois line of the Lavas remains a pernicious influence within the Party. Afflicting the Party for an exceedingly long period, without having been profoundly criticized before this present stage of the development of our Party, this black bourgeois line cannot be defeated within a few weeks, months or years. It cannot be removed from the Party even if its direct representatives are overthrown from their positions of Party authority unless we combat the ideological and political roots of their errors. Considering the present circumstances, the dangers of Right or "Left" opportunism will always confront us. But those who hold on to the living study and application of Mao Tsetung Thought and to the correct mass line of the Party will always maintain and heighten their revolutionary strength and courage in order to prevail.

It should be kept in mind, though, that the black bourgeois line of the Lavas is mainly Right opportunism and secondarily "Left" opportunism. Today, some Party members overestimate the value of legal urban-based "nationalist" mass organizations like the Movement for the Advancement of Nationalism and such government measures as the Magna Carta of Labor, the Agricultural Land Reform Code and others. On the other hand, there is a minor undercurrent of infantile "Left" opportunism of excessively underestimating the value of legal mass organizations and of resorting to "Left" phrasemongering without actually engaging in thoroughgoing mass work and struggle against the exploiters of the people.

Modern revisionism has gained a small foothold in Philippine society through the Lava revisionist renegades and other Right opportunists. It is necessary to combat modern revisionism with the revolutionary theory and practice of Marxism-Leninism-Mao Tsetung Thought. Otherwise, the Communist Party of the Philippines will continue to suffer stagnation and reverses in the struggle for people's democratic power.

C. Military Errors

Errors in ideology and politics always lead to errors in the armed struggle. A party that does not seriously pay attention to this relationship is bound to fail in performing its central revolutionary task of seizing political power and consolidating it.

Armed struggle is the main weapon of the Communist Party of the Philippines in carrying out the people's democratic revolution. Without a people's army under the command of the Party, the people have nothing as Comrade Mao Tsetung has taught us in his theory and practice of the Chinese revolution. Being in a semi-colonial and semi-feudal country, our Party must integrate three necessary and inseparable components in waging a people's war in the countryside; namely, armed struggle, agrarian revolution and rural base building.

During the first 12 years of the existence of the Party, 1930 to 1942, the Party did not immediately develop these three components. In 1931, it met its first concrete experience of suppression by US imperialism and its running dogs. The reactionary state with all the weapons of coercion at its command succeeded in creating grave difficulties for the Party for so many years.

When the Party finally organized the guerrilla forces of the Hukbalahap on the basis of the popular anti-Japanese resistance, the Party leadership did not have a clear understanding of what it took to wage a people's war. When the Party and the army had their first serious setback at the hands of the Japanese fascists, the Party leadership adopted the "retreat for defense" policy. This policy involved the dissolution of the Hukbalahap "squadrons" and the formation of minuscule units composed of only three to five men at a time that the people's army needed to concentrate larger forces to deal punishing blows on isolated parts of the Japanese invasionary forces and their mercenaries. The dissolution of the Hukbalahap "squadrons" had far-reaching debilitating effects on the people's army.

The Party leadership had to abandon the "retreat for defense" policy and remuster the Huk "squadrons" in the face of persistent popular demand to annihilate the enemy. However, when US imperialism returned to reoccupy the Philippines, the Party and the Hukbahalap leadership again surrendered the military initiative to the USAFFE forces. Hukbalahap "squadrons" were too ready in welcoming and in merely assisting the US reoccupation forces when what was needed was for them to keep their forces distinct in fighting the retreating Japanese fascists. The Party leadership was too ready to abandon the military initiative to US imperialism for it was bent on returning to the city and conducting peaceful parliamentary struggle.

Even when US imperialism attacked the people and the people's army in a campaign to restore landlord power in areas that the Party and army controlled, the Party leadership ordered the disbandment of armed units of the people's army under the erroneous banner of "democratic peace" unlike in China where the vanguard Party held on to its arms and fought.

Under the Jose Lava leadership, the error of military adventurism and purely military viewpoint was perpetuated as an extreme counter-development of Right opportunism. The petty bourgeois world outlook was at the root of the "Left" subjectivist error of military adventurism. This outlook prevented the Party leadership from understanding the laws of development of a people's war in Philippine society and thus from adopting the correct strategy and tactics.

The Jose Lava leadership was marked by military impetuosity and petty-bourgeois vindictiveness manifested inside and outside of the Party. What was, however, in common between the "Left" opportunism and the Right opportunism it opposed was the petty-bourgeois illusion that the people's forces could be commanded from the city and that the city of Manila, the strongest base of the bourgeois state power, could be easily seized without building rural bases.

The selfish desire to seize power in the city in so short a time as two years without having laid down an extensive ground work among the people showed lack of understanding of protracted people's war. As "Left" opportunism emerged as the principal aspect of the Jose Lava leadership, Right opportunism persisted as a secondary aspect or as an undercurrent represented by Luis Taruc. As the power of the reactionary ruling classes was estimated to be weak because it was wracked by an internal split, the Jose Lava leadership gave orders to direct fire only against Filipino puppet troops and to strictly avoid attacks against US military personnel.

The underestimation of US military support for the local reactionaries was primarily "Left" opportunism. At the same time, there was the false belief that avoiding military engagement with US military personnel would make the fight for the Red army easier. This was Right opportunism lurking behind "Left" opportunism and was still a carryover of the counter-revolutionary rightist line during the anti-Japanese war that the United States would return to the Philippines in order to restore "democratic peace" after overcoming the Japanese fascists.

It was "Left" opportunism to hope for rapid military victory on uncertain grounds, such as the illusion that the bourgeois politicians, Laurel and Rodriguez, would lead revolts against the Quirino government from Batangas and Rizal in concert with the People's Liberation Army. And yet the element of Right opportunism is to be found in giving bourgeois politicians a decisive role in so central a question as the actual seizure of power. At this time the HMB had not yet gained enough strength to capture Manila: no more than 3,000 Red troops could be massed for the purpose, with the sure difficulties of over-straining the people's armed strength in all other places.

The predominating "Left" opportunist line of the Jose Lava leadership was evident in the issuance of military orders to the people's forces in the countryside from the city-based Secretariat or Politburo-In. Even in the countryside the Politburo-Out was distant from the main military forces and relied on camouflage rather than on developing a stable rural base on which it should have relied. There was still a great gap between the Party leadership and the masses consisting of unstable areas in Central Luzon and blatantly White areas in Southern Luzon.

While the Party headquarters in the city was distantly separated from the Politburo-Out and the latter was in turn distantly separated from the main forces of the people's army, orders were brought down making the people's armed forces leap over unstable and unreliable areas to simultaneously attack widely separated targets such as military camps, cities and provincial capitals. This kind of armed movement over-extended the strength of the people's army and further strained what had already been the over-stretched lines of communications and supplies. The raids of March 29 and August 26, 1950 conducted by the people's army in accordance with the "PB Resolutions" of January 1950 demonstrated fully the adventurist impetuosity of the Jose Lava leadership. In essence, it failed to recognize dialectically the ability of the enemy to make a counter-attack that could break the over-extended lines linking the Politburo-Out to the regional commands and so on and so forth. The enemy did counter-attack after the March and August raids by pitting 25,000 troops against the people's army of a lesser number dispersed all over Central Luzon, Manila, Rizal, Bicol and Panay.

A short while after the raids of August 26, the Party headquarters in the city was smashed systematically by the enemy in October 1950. Considering the extent of enemy success in this crackdown, the policy of rapid recruitment of Party members in the city was demonstrated to be a folly and a violation of the defensive and underground requirements of urban party work. No less than the highest organs of the Party were infiltrated by the enemy.

The failures of the military policy vis-a-vis the enemy were aggravated by the incorrect handling of Red cadres and fighters. Under the guise of "Bolshevization", the Jose Lava leadership adopted harsh methods on those who were found committing even minor errors. The death penalty was imposed on cadres and fighters even where a lighter punishment would have sufficed. In meting out punishments, the life history of erring cadres and fighters was not considered seriously and oftentimes the immediate error was isolated from the circumstances. What was mistaken for "Bolshevization" were the rules of war from bourgeois military books. This mishandling of cadres and fighters worsened as the peoples army suffered an increasing number of setbacks and a tendency towards disintegration occurred.

In its petty-bourgeois eagerness to seize power, the Jose Lava leadership instructed Party organs to put the military viewpoint in command, to make military-technical articles dominant in the HMB Bulletin and to study and adopt as a basic training guide the 90-week "Master Training Schedule"- a manual used by the US Army and the reactionary armed forces of the Philippines. These specific instances showed the utter lack of understanding of the nature of people's war.

As the armed struggle started to ebb during the latter part of 1951, the relationship between the people's army and the people was mishandled in a serious way. Distinctions were made between friendly and hostile barrios. The distinctions were made not for purposes of waging the correct propaganda campaign to win over the people from a hostile attitude to a friendly attitude but for purposes of making retaliatory and vindictive foraging attacks even against ordinary peasants some of whose work animals were confiscated to provide food for the beleaguered fighters of the people's army. It was not fully realized that aside from being a fighting force, the people's army was a propaganda and productive force.

It was as a result of the serious mistakes of the Jose Lava leadership and the effective counter-attacks of the enemy that a tendency towards roving rebel bands and a degeneration of these bands became more pronounced. The absence of genuine proletarian discipline, the wanton dispersal of the people's army and the concomitant loss of effective central command led the Party from one disaster to another.

After the Jesus Lava leadership assumed command, "Left" opportunism continued in the form of roving rebel tendencies on the basis of forced dispersal of armed units. With the central command lacking in a main armed force, the dispersed armed units now subject to massive "encirclement and suppression" operations of the reactionary army committed in the name of "struggle for survival" or "economic struggle" many abuses and excesses that the enemy used to its "psy-war" advantage. Taking advantage of real abuses and excesses of the "people's army", the reactionary army systematically used reactionary troops in civilian clothes to make their own abuses and excesses and blamed them on the people's army. A deep line of sectarianism within the Party leadership of Jose and Jesus Lava was taken advantage of by the enemy.

The Jesus Lava leadership could not correct the military adventurism of the Jose Lava leadership because it did not have any comprehensive understanding of the nature and requirements of a people's war. It was completely ignorant of how to conduct a people's war at its stage of strategic defensive and tactical offensive. As before, it was completely ignorant of how to smash an enemy campaign of encirclement and suppression. Because of its failure to grasp Marxism-Leninism, it was never able to regroup the dispersed armed units of the people's army which were attacked in a massive way by the reactionary army continuously from 1951 to 1955.

In 1955, under conditions of military defeat, the Jesus Lava leadership took a Rightist line and adopted parliamentary struggle as the main form of struggle. Jesus Lava became guilty of liquidationism when he actually disbanded armed units, including his own armed security, and chose to live the life of a city fugitive. The individual flights of the commander-in-chief of the people's army, Castro Alejandrino, and the general secretary of the Party, Jesus Lava, from the countryside to the city and their subsequent capture in the city proved conclusively the erroneous military line of the Party leadership.

It has only been in the area of Regional Command No. 2, particularly in the province of Pampanga and partially in Tarlac, Bataan and Nueva Ecija where remnants of the People's Liberation Army have persisted. It is not those who have slavishly followed the leadership of the Lavas who are now waging the armed struggle. Nevertheless, a thoroughgoing rectification of the black bourgeois line of the Lavas and the capitulationism of Luis Taruc must be waged particularly in this area. Roving rebel tendencies and practices must also be corrected here. What is to be generated is a genuine people's army that is under the effective command of a Marxist-Leninist party guided by Mao Tsetung Thought, that is a weapon for agrarian revolution and that builds up stable base areas.

It has been a disadvantage for the Party to have established its strength only in the areas of Greater Manila, Central Luzon and partially in Southern Tagalog although these areas have strategic value because it is here where bourgeois state power is most concentrated throughout the archipelago. However, new military strategy and tactics in line with Mao Tsetung Thought must be adopted taking into full account the weak links of the bourgeois state power on the basis of class analysis and turning the archipelago from a short-run disadvantage into a long-run advantage for the Party and the People's Liberation Army. The development of the people's main military forces and rural bases in Luzon other than in Central Luzon should be well-considered; and the other islands of Visayas and Mindanao should be utilized to disperse and dissipate the main forces of the enemy concentrated in Luzon.

D. Organizational Errors

Organizationally, the main disability of the Communist Party of the Philippines has been its failure to build up an organization that has a broad mass character and that is national in scale. Where the Party has been built, the principle of democratic centralism has not been applied correctly in the organizational life of the Party, resulting in errors of sectarianism and liberalism, and commandism and tailism, because of subjectivism and opportunism.

Building a party of a broad mass character requires a national system of party cadres who build up a great mass following. Under the difficult conditions existing in Philippine society, it is a wise policy to build the Party carefully. Recruitment and development of cadres must always conform to the standards of a proletarian revolutionary party.

A party with a broad mass character means that party cadres have a big mass following through the adoption of the correct ideology, political line, and principles and methods of organization. The Communist Party of the Philippines can have a broad mass character only if its cadres could truly lead masses of workers and peasants in revolutionary struggle. The Party guides the revolutionary struggle of the masses and in turn the struggle produces the best and most advanced fighters of the revolution who become party members.

Closed-doorism was a marked tendency of the Crisanto Evangelista leadership. Party work was concentrated in the trade union movement.

The Party gained strength during the anti-Japanese war only by waging revolutionary armed struggle and leading the peasant masses. In 1948, the Party regained revolutionary strength for some time until the errors of adventurism of the Jose Lava leadership undermined the revolutionary resurgence. In this instance, in was shown that the Party could gain real mass strength only to the extent that it merged with and led the peasant masses. In a semi-colonial and semi-feudal country like the Philippines, the Party can gain strength only by arousing and mobilizing the peasant masses in line with the agrarian revolution as the main content of the people's democratic struggle. In the final analysis, the proletarian revolutionary party in the Philippines can have a broad mass character only if it gains the mass support of the peasantry, particularly the poor peasants and farm workers.

Until now, Party members are relatively over-concentrated in Central Luzon and in the Manila-Rizal areas. Even in the previous high tides of the revolutionary movement in the Philippines, the Party did not succeed in broadcasting sufficiently on a national scale the people's democratic revolution through the systematic disposition of cadres.

In the course of his long period of being a trade union leader, Crisanto Evangelista developed a small amount of relations with other trade union leaders in the Visayas. But he himself, even as late as the later part of the thirties, had the illusion that if the Party could gain control over Central Luzon, then the whole of Luzon would easily follow; and if the Party could gain control over Luzon, then the whole archipelago would follow.

At the beginning of the anti-Japanese war, there was an attempt to send a team of cadres to the Visayas but it was called off. During the war, the Party and the Hukbalahap were built up mainly in the single region of Central Luzon. Even in the accessible region of Southern Tagalog, the Party was not able to seize leadership and initiative in the anti-Japanese war from pro-American guerrilla units. After the war, the question of sending cadres out to other islands was not immediately taken up seriously.

It was only at the height of the armed struggle under the Jose Lava leadership that Party cadres were sent out to Cagayan Valley, Bicol, Panay, Ilocos and Mindanao to build the Party and army. But these pioneering comrades were clearly not able to build the Party and army on strong foundations. They did not have sufficient time to do so because of the failure of the Party leadership to adopt a correct political line. The main policy of rapid military victory did not allow the cadres sufficient time to build the Party, the army and the united front on a more massive and nationwide scale and to develop all requisites for people's democratic power.

During the entire period of the Jesus Lava leadership, the failure to build a national organization persisted. This leadership merely presided over and hastened the destruction of old Party units as well as new ones established outside of Central Luzon. Even during the later part of the 1950s when legal mass organizations under the leadership of the Party could be established, there was no serious attempt made by the Party to build up legal mass organizations as the medium for Party expansion. It would only be after 1960 that, through the initiative mainly of new and reactivated old Party members, the Party would dare to push forward the resurgence of the revolutionary mass movement. Now the Party has started to make modest gains in building a Party that has a broad mass character and that is national in scale.

Through a national united front, the proletarian revolutionary party which is carrying out agrarian revolution, with the full support of the oppressed peasantry, can still broaden its support by allying itself with such supplementary revolutionary forces as the urban petty bourgeoisie and the national bourgeoisie.

In the Philippines, the Party first experienced a united front policy when it opposed fascism during the days of the Popular Front. But during this period, the powerful influence of the petty bourgeoisie within the Party started to corrode the revolutionary will of the Party in a subtle way.

After the war, the Democratic Alliance was put up as a formal unified front organization. But this alliance served only to support Right opportunism and allowed some bourgeois personalities to assume the leadership. The Party practically carried the sedan chair for them for some time until they scurried away when the armed struggle became intensified.

During the Jesus Lava leadership, no genuine united front could be built because of the failure to build a strong people's army and legal mass organizations under the leadership of the Party. At the time that the urban petty bourgeoisie and the national bourgeoisie were being agitated by Claro Mayo Recto to join the anti-imperialist movement, the Party failed to take advantage of the situation fully because of the liquidationist policy that gravely hampered and threatened the very organizational existence of the Party.

The Party failed in many instances to combine legal and illegal struggle in its organizational work. At the time that the Party was outlawed for the first time soon after its founding, there was no secret second line of leadership that could carry out Party tasks legally and illegally. At the beginning of the war, a second line of leadership replaced an incapacitated first line but the former had in the main been detached from mass work previously, having only engaged in limited political work among urban petty bourgeois elements.

As a result of erroneous political lines, grievous organizational errors were committed. Democratic centralism did not come into full play in order to arrive at the correct decisions.

The development of the black bourgeois line of the Lavas is the result of gross violations of democratic centralism. The astounding series of Lava leaderships has been the result of bourgeois maneuvers chronically causing falling-off and demoralization among Party cadres through a period of more than 30 years. Liberalism in the most vulgar forms like nepotism and favoritism was practised in the making of assignments and appointment or election to leading positions.

Liberalism marked the merger of the Communist Party of the Philippines and the Socialist Party. Members of the Socialist Party were taken wholesale into the Communist Party notwithstanding the ideological requirement of a Marxist-Leninist. The first and second lines of leadership adopted a liberal attitude to Party organization as they concentrated on urban and legal political work before the outbreak of the anti-Japanese war.

The big upsurge of liberalism and legalism represented by Vicente Lava, Jorge Frianeza and Pedro Castro after the anti-Japanese war had dialectical connections with an unrectified Right opportunist trend starting before the war. Jorge Frianeza advocated the complete dissolution of the people's army and a "united front" with the reactionary Roxas government; and Pedro Castro advocated the organization of a "mass party" for parliamentary struggle and the liquidation of illegal Party work. Within the Democratic Alliance, a liberal policy of allowing the predominance of bourgeois personalities occurred. It was itself an act of liberalism to allow the Democratic Alliance to play the central role in the political struggle of the masses.

Sectarianism was the principal organizational error of the Jose Lava leadership while liberalism was its secondary error. Isolated from the concrete conditions of the armed struggle in the countryside, this leadership was commandist in bringing down its orders. Among the fighting forces in the countryside, sectarian excesses occurred under the cover of the slogan of "Bolshevization". Contradictions among the people and minor infractions within the Party were considered as contradictions between the people and the enemy. Whereas a policy of persuasion and leniency was required in many cases, the harshest penalties were imposed on erring Party members and Red fighters. In the city, sectarianism was also practised in relation to the national united front. As a result of the failure of the Democratic Alliance, the importance of a consistent united front policy towards the middle forces was immediately discounted by the Jose Lava leadership.

Although the main organizational error of the Jose Lava leadership was sectarianism, it perpetuated liberalism in appointing to high Party positions and recruiting into the Party persons who happened to be relatives, personal friends and townspeople of the Lava family, without benefit of undergoing the tests of revolutionary mass struggle. Certainly, liberalism was essentially involved in the rapid recruitment policy in the city of Manila, a policy which allowed the penetration of the Party by enemy agents. The cornerstone of this policy was personal trust. The ludicrous example of liberalism was the appointment of Taciano Rizal to a decisively important position on the narrow consideration that he bore the name of the bourgeois national hero, Jose Rizal.

The Jesus Lava leadership carried substantially for some time the sectarianism of the Jose Lava leadership. For a number of years, the Party leadership represented by Jesus Lava resorted to the sectarian method of intimidation to put Party members into line and there were many cases of cadres executed for flimsy reasons. On the basis of mere suspicion, Party members suffered the death penalty.

When Right opportunism prevailed, the Jesus Lava leadership practised liberalism by coddling Party members whom it dissuaded from joining the revolutionary mass struggle. The main line of parliamentary struggle inevitably degenerated into liquidationism. The flight of the Party leaders from the countryside to the city resulted in the neglect of Party organizations in the countryside and in the disastrous liquidationist "single file" policy which destroyed in a big way the collective life of Party organizations, cut off lines of responsibility between higher organs and lower organs and isolated the Party from the people.

The Jesus Lava leadership became reduced to the general secretary alone, made one-man decisions, issued political transmissions from some secluded room and made appointments to high Party positions on the basis of blood and personal relations. During the late fifties, opportunities for regrouping Party and armed units in the countryside were completely disregarded and parliamentary struggle itself was not properly conducted. It would only be during the early sixties that party rebuilding and the establishment of mass organizations were effected by the Party members independent of the isolated Party leadership.

In the main, the black bourgeois line of the Lavas is organizationally the disease of liberalism, liquidationism and the consistent violation of democratic centralism. A thoroughgoing rectification movement to remove the ideological, political and organizational roots of the black bourgeois line of the Lavas must be conducted in order to rebuild the Party in accordance with Marxism-Leninism-Mao Tsetung Thought. The black bourgeois line of the Lavas can still persist if no serious efforts are taken to repudiate organizationally its ideological and political agents within the Party.

V. THREE MAIN TASKS

A. Party Building

Without a revolutionary theory, there can be no revolutionary movement. In this era when imperialism is heading for total collapse and socialism is advancing towards worldwide victory, there can be no revolutionary movement without being guided by today's highest development of Marxism-Leninism, Mao Tsetung Thought. In rebuilding the Communist Party of the Philippines, therefore, we must apply the universal truth of Marxism-Leninism-Mao Tsetung Thought on the concrete practice of the Philippine revolution; in party rebuilding, in developing the armed struggle and in utilizing the national united front to achieve the people's democratic revolution.

What we need to rebuild in the Philippines today is a proletarian revolutionary party that is armed with Mao

Tsetung Thought. The Philippine revolutionary movement cannot possibly advance without moving ahead with the theory and practice of the world proletarian revolution. The proletarian revolution has been continuously advancing, passing three major stages: the first stage was led by Marx and Engels by developing the theory of scientific socialism; the second stage was led by Lenin and Stalin by developing the theory and practice of proletarian dictatorship in the era of imperialism; and the third stage is now guided by Comrade Mao Tsetung. Even in the second stage, Comrade Mao Tsetung was already in the vanguard of the international communist movement by outstandingly developing the theory of people's war in a semi-colonial and semi-feudal country.

In this era of Mao Tsetung Thought, the Communist Party of the Philippines cannot achieve its immediate goal of people's democracy and its ultimate goal of socialism without applying Mao Tsetung Thought on the concrete conditions of the Philippines and without grasping the six components of today's Marxism-Leninism: philosophy, political economy, social science, people's war, party building and the proletarian cultural revolution. The Communist Party of the Philippines can be a proletarian revolutionary party only if it grasps the advances in philosophy, political economy and social science contributed by Comrade Mao Tsetung and his theory and practice of people's war, party building and the great proletarian cultural revolution.

As a proletarian revolutionary party, the Communist Party of the Philippines comprehensively differentiates itself from bogus and revisionist parties and groups by adopting Mao Tsetung Thought as its supreme guide and by applying it in revolutionary practice. The Party sets itself free from subjectivism, Right and "Left" opportunism and other manifestations of the black bourgeois line by adhering to Mao Tsetung Thought in theory and in practice. Only with the guidance of Mao Tsetung Thought can the Party cleanse itself of the black bourgeois line of the Lavas and all other ideological, political and organizational errors that have hampered and hindered the victorious advance of the people's democratic revolution in the Philippines.

Mao Tsetung Thought draws the demarcation line between the true proletarian revolutionaries on the one side and the bourgeois pseudo-revolutionaries and revisionists on the other. In an international revolutionary movement that is beset with modern revisionism directed and led by the revisionist renegade clique in Moscow, Mao Tsetung Thought stands out to illumine the whole world including the Philippines and to push to the darkest corners the treasonous modern revisionist concoctions of the three "peacefuls" and two "wholes". Adhering to Mao Tsetung Thought and holding firmly that the central task of a revolutionary movement is the seizure and consolidation of political power, the Communist Party of the Philippines cannot be confused by the false revisionist theory of peaceful coexistence, peaceful transition, peaceful competition, party of the whole people and state of the whole people being peddled by the Soviet revisionist ruling clique internationally and by the Lava revisionist renegades locally. Modern revisionism is the main danger today in the international communist movement and likewise in the Philippine revolutionary movement.

The Great Proletarian Cultural Revolution in the People's Republic of China, however, has consolidated a great base area, an iron bastion, of the world proletarian revolution under the leadership of Comrade Mao Tsetung and has arisen as the epoch-making weapon against modern revisionism in the whole world and against the restoration of capitalism within socialist society. The People's Republic of China serves today as a stable base area of all revolutionary peoples now surrounding the cities of the world from the world's countryside of Asia, Africa and Latin America. Mao Tsetung Thought has taken deep roots among 700 million Chinese people and in the whole world through genuine Marxist-Leninist parties that uphold Mao Tsetung Thought as the Marxism-Leninism of this era.

In the Philippines today, Mao Tsetung Thought is guiding a rectification movement within the nucleus of the proletarian dictatorship, the Communist Party of the Philippines. A thoroughgoing rectification movement, which is a widespread movement of education in Marxism-Leninism-Mao Tsetung Thought, is being waged to rid the Party and its mass organizations of the failures and errors of the Lavas that are persisting ideologically, politically and organizationally. The black bourgeois line of the Lavas is in the main Right opportunism which is the bourgeois soil for modern revisionism in the Philippines. The treasonous current of modern revisionism has taken roots in the subjectivist and Right opportunist line that the Lavas have perpetuated for the last more than three decades and that the semi-colonial and semi feudal condition of Philippine society has encouraged. Under the banner of modern revisionism, the political agents of the Lavas are striving hard to cut off the armed struggle from the legal struggle by spreading slanders and lies against those engaged in developing armed struggle and against the most militant cadres of the Party.

A thoroughgoing rectification movement chiefly directed against the black bourgeois line of the Lavas and modern revisionism should be carried out through to the end among cadres, following the pattern of unity-criticism-repudiation-unity. This rectification movement is a test of the ability of the Communist Party of the Philippines to make self-criticism and to rid itself of long-standing and major errors and shortcomings that have too long undermined the Philippine revolutionary movement and deprived the people of revolutionary triumph. Without this rectification movement, party rebuilding cannot be achieved.

Ideological building with Marxism-Leninism-Mao Tsetung Thought is the first requisite in rebuilding the Communist Party of the Philippines. The Revolutionary School of Mao Tsetung Thought within the Communist Party of the Philippines is doing great service to the cause of the Philippine revolution by propagating Mao Tsetung Thought and by playing a decisive role in the present rectification movement. This rectification movement has to be done, especially at a time that we need to rebuild the Party on the solid foundation of Marxism-Leninism-Mao Tsetung Thought and the activities of the local revisionist renegades are being intensified with the aid of the Soviet revisionist ruling clique and US imperialism to spread modern revisionism, develop a city-based and city-oriented Party that is afraid of armed struggle, foster relations between the reactionary Philippine government and the revisionist renegade ruling cliques and disarm the peasants politically by relying mainly on the reactionary government's "land reform" programme.

Comrade Mao Tsetung has said: "A well-disciplined Party armed with the theory of Marxism-Leninism, using the method of self-criticism and linked with the masses of the people; an army under the leadership of such a Party; a united front of all revolutionary classes and all revolutionary groups under the leadership of such a Party - these are the three main weapons with which we have defeated the enemy." These are the three main weapons that the Party and all its cadres and members must a strive to develop in order to achieve the present main task of seizing political power.

The Communist Party of the Philippines must be rebuilt as the highest form of organization of the leading class, the proletariat. To be such, it must be armed with Mao Tsetung Thought, the acme of Marxism-Leninism in this era. By grasping the proletarian revolutionary ideology, our Party affirms its class nature in a clear-cut way; but the ultimate test lies in revolutionary practice and further revolutionary practice. It is not enough to lay down a nicely drafted programme. It is necessary to sustain it with consistent and arduous mass struggle, transforming Mao Tsetung Thought into a powerful material force by arousing and mobilizing the broad masses of the people to take revolutionary action. In other words, our Party as a proletarian revolutionary party must integrate theory and practice. Our cadres must go deep among the masses of workers and peasants. They must be well-distributed on a national scale in order to build up a nationwide party. The Party must concentrate on arousing and mobilizing the peasant masses, including the farm workers, as the main ally of the proletariat and as the main force of the people's democratic revolution.

The Party must implement the great strategic principle of making the countryside surround the cities and put principal stress on party work in the countryside instead of in the city, but without neglecting party work in the latter. Our cadres must conduct their political work with the style of hard work and frugality and in the creative spirit of self-reliance and must always be ready to make self-criticism in order to improve their political work constantly. They must trust and rely on the masses, arousing and mobilizing them against the exploiters.

In the countryside, the people's army should be constantly built up from among the exploited peasantry under the leadership of the proletariat and the Party. A programme of agrarian revolution should be implemented in order to fulfill the main content of the people's democratic revolution. To make possible and protect the gains of the agrarian revolution, the Party should develop rural bases and direct a wide range of fighting areas, from stable base areas to guerrilla zones.

The Communist Party of the Philippines makes class analysis and distinguishes its friends from its enemies. The Party recognizes the poor peasants and farm workers as the most reliable allies of the working class. To succeed in the people's democratic revolution, an alliance of the working class and the peasantry must be developed as the basis for a national united front which includes the urban petty bourgeoisie and the patriotic sections of the national bourgeoisie as supplementary allies. At the same time, the Party is ever alert to the dual vacillating class character of the national bourgeoisie as an ally in the people's democratic revolution. The Party, in keeping and utilizing the national united front, realizes that it should maintain its class leadership, independence and initiative. Proletarian class leadership, independence and initiative are best maintained as our cadres constantly build Party and our people's army. The national united front should be lined up primarily against the class forces of counter-revolution, the US imperialists, the compradors, landlords and bureaucrat capitalists and serve the establishment and advance of Red political power. In the concrete conditions of the Philippines today, the Party should employ armed struggle and the national united front skillfully and likewise, legal and illegal methods and secret and open work.

Imbued with proletarian internationalism, the Communist Party of the Philippines is determined to fulfill its international obligation to fight US imperialism and all its local reactionary agents, the compradors, the landlords and bureaucrat capitalists through to the end. The Party assumes it as an international obligation to combat modern revisionism and a resurgent Japanese militarism now increasingly in alliance with US imperialism to keep the Philippines in colonial bondage. The struggle of the Filipino people against these enemies of national independence, social liberation and progress is a contribution to the worldwide struggle now being waged by all oppressed nations and peoples. In Asia, especially in Southeast Asia, the Philippines has too long served as the bastion of US imperialism, feudalism and bureaucrat capitalism. If the Filipino people are to deal powerful blows against these, then they shall have assisted other oppressed nations and peoples through common struggle. The Communist Party of the Philippines is aware that all other nations and people fighting US imperialism and its reactionary allies are reciprocally assisting the Filipino nation and people through common struggle. The Filipino proletariat is bound by the spirit of proletarian internationalism with all workers and peoples of the world.

B. Armed Struggle

It is a fundamental task of the Communist Party of the Philippines to give proletarian revolutionary leadership to the peasantry. The people's democratic revolution which our Party is waging is essentially a peasant war. The struggle for land among the vast majority of our people is the main content of the people's democratic revolution that we are trying to achieve in our semi-colonial and semi-feudal country. The liberation of the peasantry from feudal exploitation and its mobilization as the main force of the people's democratic revolution are of decisive significance to the revolutionary triumph of the proletariat as the leading class.

Since industry is not well developed in our semi-colonial and semi-feudal country, the number of industrial workers is small. The proletariat through its party must therefore develop its alliance with the peasantry and lead the peasantry as the main force of the people's democratic revolution. Because of its exploited condition, the peasantry is the most reliable ally of the proletariat. Its massive strength provides the overwhelming popular support for the proletarian revolutionary party. By giving this support, the peasantry ensures the victory of the proletarian class leadership. As a proletarian revolutionary party, the Communist Party of the Philippines must rely mainly on the peasantry to conduct armed struggle and seize power. The people's democratic revolution is basically a peasant war under the leadership of the proletariat and its party guided by Mao Tsetung Thought.

In going to the countryside, the Party must make the correct class analysis and take the correct class line. In our semi-colonial and semi-feudal society, the peasant problem constitutes the main problem both politically and economically. It is therefore necessary for the Communist Party of the Philippines to conduct thoroughgoing class analysis to be able to understand the problem in the countryside so that in giving leadership to the class struggle in the countryside it will be able to distinguish between its real friends and its real class enemies; so that it can mobilize the correct class forces to train their guns against their class enemies.

The basis for class analysis is the relationship between the exploited and the exploiter and the ownership of the means of production. By knowing the relations of exploitation we determine the economic position of each class or stratum and their corresponding political attitudes. Through their ownership of the means of production, the exploiting classes maintain a system of exploitation. In the countryside, they maintain a feudal and semi-feudal system of exploitation. In waging the people's democratic revolution, the Party aims at overthrowing this system of exploitation by launching a peasant war against the feudal and semi-feudal exploiters. In the countryside, the main exploiter is the landlord class. This class relies mainly on feudal exploitation. The landlord owns lands tilled by poor peasants who pay rent to him and who are further exploited in several other ways, such as usury, menial service and tributes.

The rich peasant stratum also engages in exploitation; a considerable part of its living depends on exploitation but the rich peasant is distinguished from the landlord in that although he owns lands more than sufficient for his household, he still tills the soil. The rich peasant participates in exploitation by hiring farm workers, renting out surplus land, surplus work animals and implements, by practising usury and other forms of exploitation. The middle peasant owns a piece of land sufficient for his family; but his status ranges from being on the edge of bankruptcy to having a piece of land a little more than sufficient for his household needs and having other sources of income. The poor peasants and farm workers are those who have to work mainly for the landlords and be exploited by them. They are the most oppressed stratum of the peasantry and they are, therefore, the most interested in the people's democratic revolution and the most reliable allies of the proletariat. They compose the majority of the rural population in the Philippines.

The correct line in the countryside can be implemented by arousing and mobilizing the poor peasants and farm workers mainly and by winning over and uniting with the middle peasants, especially the lower middle and middle middle peasants, into an anti-feudal revolutionary united front. The rich peasants, including those who have traditionally taken leading positions in the barrios, can be neutralized with the growing might of the poor peasants and farm workers. The Party must do painstaking work to arouse and mobilize the poor peasants and farm workers and raise their prestige so that they can assume responsibility for the revolution. The Party must see to it that a revolutionary anti-feudal barrio committee, controlled by the poor peasants and farm workers must ultimately replace or take over the "barrio councils" controlled by the landlords, corrupt government official and rich peasants.

The implementation of the class line in the countryside would depend on painstaking remoulding of the attitudes of Party cadres towards the poor peasants, lower middle peasants and farm workers. The Party must educate its cadres through revolutionary practice to make them understand that once the poor peasants, lower middle peasants and farm workers have been aroused and mobilized they are the staunchest supporters of the revolution. We cannot rely mainly on the middle peasants. The social base of the revolution in the countryside are the poor peasants, lower middle peasants and farm workers. The middle peasants may accept the leadership of the Party when it suits their interest but when it will suit their interest to accept the class leadership of the bourgeoisie, they will do so. In times when reaction becomes ruthless, the middle peasants may vacillate and may even betray the movement. It is important to keep this in mind in our mass work in the countryside among the peasantry. It is not only in the national democratic revolution that we must rely mainly on the poor peasants, lower middle peasants and farm workers; after the seizure of state power by the proletariat and during the period of transition to communism, these strata will continue to be the social base for the consolidation of the dictatorship of the proletariat.

The Communist Party of the Philippines must rely on peasant revolutionary bases to defeat the reactionary state power in the countryside before capturing the cities. Comrade Mao Tsetung has extensively shown with genius in theory and in practice how the countryside can encircle the cities in the course of armed struggle in a semi-colonial and semi-feudal country. The universal truth of the theory of using the countryside to encircle the city has been proven invincible. There are, however, the local revisionists who reject the universal truth of this revolutionary theory and who overstress the fact that the Philippines is an archipelago, unlike China with a vast contiguous land area and population, with the view of obscuring and denying the basic class analysis and dialectics involved in the theory of using the countryside to encircle the city.

The theory of people's war is universal and applies to Philippine conditions. Because of the uneven development of politics and economy in the era of imperialism, the weak links of bourgeois state power are to be found in the countryside. The counter-revolutionary army is spread thinly over the country in maintaining control over main communication and transportation lines. This disposition of counter-revolutionary forces would leave the widest areas of the countryside for the development of the peasant war under the leadership of the proletariat. In the countryside, the Party must go deep among the peasant masses in order to develop the main force of the people's democratic revolution. The people's democratic forces should develop and accumulate their armed strength in the backward areas in the countryside and turn them into the most advanced political, economic, military and cultural bastions from which a protracted struggle can be waged by the people's army in order to win over-all victory over the counter-revolutionary army. The countryside certainly provides so many times vaster an area for maneuver than the cities. In the Philippines, the area for maneuver in the city is extremely limited for armed struggle. The cities are actually the bastions of bourgeois state power before the people's democratic forces develop the capability of capturing them. The counter-revolutionary army must first be defeated in the countryside. What also makes bourgeois state power weak in the countryside is that contradictions within the counter-revolutionary front keep on arising. By its own laws of motion, whichever group in the counter-revolutionary front is ascendant would keep a big armed force in the city to maintain its city-based political power.

In line with Mao Tsetung Thought, the Communist Party of the Philippines must consciously shift its center of gravity to the countryside. All previous Party leaderships in the Philippines have suffered failures that were singularly characterized by political activity that had its center of gravity in the city of Manila. The shift from the city to the countryside means that the headquarters of the people's democratic revolution should be shifted from the city to the countryside where the main forces of the revolution are to be found. This shift does not mean the neglect of the urban struggle but it is a matter of determining which is the principal and which is secondary. The principal form of struggle is waged in the countryside; the secondary one, in the city. It is in the countryside that the people's armed forces can take the offensive against the enemy, while in the city the revolutionary forces must take the defensive until such time that the people's armed forces in the countryside can seize the city.

Developing the people's war in the country entails three inseparable components, namely, armed struggle, agrarian revolution and rural bases. By engaging in armed struggle and winning more battles, conditions are created for enlarging base areas. The base areas are utilized by the people's armed forces to entrap the enemy forces, whether they are in the form of "special forces", big operations or what else the enemy can launch. By having more base areas, there are more areas where to wage the agrarian revolution. By waging the agrarian revolution, the base areas become more consolidated because the feudal forces and their political power are wiped out. The political power of the revolutionary forces is developed as the peasants become enthusiastic and join the advancing Red army. Armed struggle, agrarian revolution and rural bases promote each other. The people's democratic power is developed in the countryside through warfare. As rural bases become consolidated politically and economically, a state within a state is created. An armed independent regime, a base government of the people is created in the countryside.

The agrarian revolution that the Party should strive for in waging people's war should entail essentially the confiscation of lands from the landlords and distribution of these lands to the peasants without cost. Feudal land ownership is to be eliminated within the base area. Pursuing the correct class line in the countryside, the Party and the people's armed forces should rely on the poor peasants and farm workers, unite with the middle peasants, neutralize the rich peasants and wipe out landlordism and promote production.

In waging the agrarian revolution, the Party and the people's armed forces should be aware of two basic stages of development. At a stage when an area is unstable, they should make constant preparations for converting it into a base area by exercising armed power in wiping out the local tyrants, enemy detachments and spies, bandits and cattle rustlers and in compelling lower rent and lower interest rates in order to weaken the enemy and mobilize the masses. As the masses are fully mobilized organizationally, politically and ideologically and a well-consolidated base area has emerged from the struggles of the masses themselves, confiscation of lands from the landlords and equal distribution of these lands to the peasants can take place.

The Party and the people's armed forces should trust and rely on the masses in raising their political consciousness. They should let the masses educate themselves. Initially, they should recognize the roots of suffering among the masses; and subsequently, through reason and struggle meetings, grievances against the exploiting classes can be poured out by the peasants to educate themselves. As the Party and the people's armed forces direct the peasant war against the three pillars of feudal power, the big landlords, the despotic landlords and the landlords in authority, the peasants gain experience in class dictatorship over the exploiting classes. Through reason and struggle meetings and through the people's courts and the rendering of sentences commensurate to the crimes of the feudal exploiters and other criminals, the peasant masses become more deeply committed to the people's democratic revolution and they willingly let their best sons and daughters join the Communist Party of the Philippines and the people's army.

Comrade Mao Tsetung has said: "The seizure of power by armed force, the settlement of the issue by war, is the central task and the highest form of revolution. This Marxist-Leninist principle of revolution holds good universally for China and for all other countries. But while the principle remains the same, its application by the party of the proletariat finds expression in various ways according to varying conditions"

The central task of the Communist Party of the Philippines is to seize political power. In waging armed struggle to achieve the people's democratic revolution, the Party must grasp Comrade Mao Tsetung's theory of using the countryside to encircle and capture the cities and likewise his analysis of a semi-colonial and semi-feudal country. In the Philippines, however, there is the special condition of being an archipelago that requires particular attention. While it is necessary to build the people's military forces in the main island of Luzon to overthrow the bourgeois state power that is centrally seated in the city of Manila, the other islands of Visayas and Mindanao can be converted from an initial disadvantage to a long-run advantage by establishing there armed fronts and rural bases that can disperse and dissipate the counter-revolutionary armed power now concentrated in Luzon, particularly in Central Luzon and Greater Manila. At any rate, taking into consideration all special conditions, Comrade Mao Tsetung's theory of using the countryside to encircle the city and his class analysis hold true universally, for the Philippines and for every significant island of the Philippines. In the stage of strategic defensive, the development of guerrilla warfare on a national scale will surely dissipate and prepare the total destruction of the strength of the enemy.

Comrade Lin Piao has brilliantly systematized and extended on a world scale Comrade Mao Tsetung's theory of people's war by developing the thesis that the world's countryside, that is, Asia, Africa and Latin America, encircle the cities of the world. US imperialism, the main enemy of the peoples of the world and principal guardian of reaction, is over-extended throughout the countryside of the world. It is in this countryside of the world that the oppressed peoples, like the Filipino people, can have plenty of area for maneuver and deal deadly blows on every weakened link of the over-extended imperialist chain. US imperialism is in no position to maintain even an effective strength throughout the world's countryside while it has to impose its class interests against the national liberation movements, the socialist states, the Afro-American people, the American working class, and even against its own capitalist rivals in so many parts of the world all at the same time. While the manpower and resources of US imperialism are limited, what is most essential is that its aggressive class character is hated by all peoples of the world and is met by just and progressive revolutionary people's wars. In Vietnam alone, US imperialism and its allied troops cannot win over the valiant and patriotic Vietnamese people. In many more places, it will continue to be defeated resoundingly by revolutionary armed struggles. Armed with invincible Mao Tsetung Thought, the peoples of the world are waging people's wars and thus, are proving the historical truth that this is the era when imperialism is heading for total collapse and socialism is marching towards worldwide victory.

C. The National United Front

The national united front is a component part of the political line of the Communist Party of the Philippines. The Philippine revolution is a revolution of the toiling masses against US imperialism, feudalism and bureaucrat capitalism. The national united front must serve this political line.

The highest task of the people's democratic revolution is the seizure of state power by armed force and the consolidation of people's democratic power as the transitional stage toward socialism. The national united front must serve this central task. The Communist Party of the Philippines stands firmly wielding and utilizing both weapons of armed struggle and the national united front against the enemy. Through the national united front, the Party extends widely its political influence and gains the widest support of the masses and other progressive classes and strata as it establishes the independent strength of the leading class, the proletariat, through a national war or an agrarian revolution supported mainly by the peasantry.

For failure to clarify and use correctly the national united front as a weapon of the people's democratic revolution, previous Party leaderships have been responsible for several revisionist misconceptions regarding it. There are those who regard the national united front as the opposite of armed struggle. Violating the Marxist-Leninist theory of state and revolution, they also consider the national united front as the main weapon and parliamentary struggle as the main form of struggle. The Lavas are mainly responsible for this revisionism, this treason to Marxism-Leninism-Mao Tsetung Thought.

Before the outbreak of the anti-Japanese war, the Popular Front was considered by the Party leadership as merely the license for engaging mainly in parliamentary struggle; no preparations for anti-fascist armed struggle were seriously made. During the war, the Right opportunists ludicrously maintained the anti-fascist united front against Japan as a "united front" mainly with US imperialism and the commonwealth government so that the line of opposing the return of US imperialism and its puppet commonwealth government was obscured. After the anti-Japanese war, the Democratic Alliance, as a formal united front organization, assumed leadership over all progressive forces; and bourgeois personalities close to the Lava brothers assumed the leadership and initiative therein. The Party lost strength, initiative and independence when its leadership decided to lay down its arms and to engage mainly in parliamentary struggle through the Democratic Alliance.

Until now, there is the false notion fostered by Right opportunists and revisionists that a national united front must always have a definite organizational form like the Democratic Alliance or the Movement for the Advancement of Nationalism whose unity, for the purpose of parliamentary struggle, must be preserved by all means and above all. In the broad experience of successful revolutionary movements, the national united front does not necessarily have a formal organization. Neither is its function limited to parliamentary struggle. As a matter of fact, the best form of united front is wherein the Party has an independent and strong people's army to command. If the Party is involved in any formal united front organization in the course of either armed struggle or legal struggle, it must always be prepared by having its own independent strength and initiative to meet any betrayal or compromise with the enemy that the national bourgeoisie might make due to its dual class character.

The key question in the national united front is whether a proletarian revolutionary class leadership is at the helm of all other progressive forces fighting in common against the enemy in the armed and legal fronts. Whether there is a formal united front organization or not, the Communist Party of the Philippines must maintain its revolutionary vanguard role, its independence and initiative.

The Communist Party of the Philippines must engage in the national united front in order to tap all positive forces in the armed and legal fronts against the enemy. The national united front policy is pursued in order to expand the influence of the revolutionary armed forces, isolate the enemy and its die-hard elements and recruit the broad masses of the people to the side of the people's democratic revolution.

The special task of the national united front is to win over the middle forces and elements in order to isolate enemy die-hards. To be able to do this, the Party must make clear and repeated class analysis which can distinguish the middle forces and elements from the die-hard reactionaries, the principal enemies from the secondary enemies, the enemies of today from the enemies of tomorrow; and among friends, the reliable from the unreliable.

The Party's policy of the national united front is a proletarian policy concerning classes in Philippine society. In developing the national united front, we must distinguish our enemies from our friends and vice versa.

Chairman Mao has said: "Who are our enemies? Who are our friends? This is a question of first importance for the revolution .... A revolutionary party is the guide of the masses, and no revolution ever succeeds when the revolutionary party leads them astray. To ensure that we will definitely achieve success in our revolution and will not lead the masses astray, we must pay attention to uniting with our real friends in order to attack our real enemies. To distinguish real friends from real enemies, we must make a general analysis of the economic status of the various classes in Chinese society and of their respective attitude towards the revolution."

The national united front should be based on the alliance of the working class and the peasantry under the leadership of the working class and the Communist Party of the Philippines. The national united front should include other progressive classes and strata in Philippine society which unite with the masses on the basis of a common political programme. This political programme, accepted in common by the working class, the peasantry, the petty bourgeoisie and the national bourgeoisie, should correspond to the general line and programme of the Communist Party of the Philippines. This political programme must serve to weld together the broadest unity of progressive forces and groups to isolate US imperialism and the die-hard reactionaries, composed of the comprador bourgeoisie, the landlord class and the bureaucrat capitalists.

The programme of the Party and the national united front should include mainly the liquidation of feudalism and the free distribution of land to poor peasants, lower middle peasants and farm workers, and the nationalization of industries and enterprises owned and controlled by the foreign monopoly capitalists and the compradors bourgeoisie. This programme can be achieved fully only with the seizure of state power through armed force by the people under the leadership of the proletariat. The state sector in the present economy and "land reform" under the reactionary state should not be confused with the real nationalization of the economy and agrarian revolution in the liberated areas or in the people's democratic state.

In adhering to the national united front, the Communist Party of the Philippines must maintain its independence, ideologically, politically and organizationally. It must unite with the progressive forces within the national united front but it should not surrender its fundamental class interests and those of the proletariat and the peasantry to the bourgeoisie. It must always conduct independent mass work, mainly among the peasants, so that it has its own political strength to rely on in any event. The national united front is essentially an instrument to win over the middle forces and elements and to isolate enemy die-hards.

It is the relationship of the Party with the national bourgeoisie within the national united front that requires special attention. This is primarily because the national bourgeoisie has a dual class character, one aspect of which is progressive and the other reactionary. In dealing with the national bourgeoisie, we must avoid two dangerous pitfalls; namely, "Left" opportunism and Right opportunism. To dismiss the national bourgeoisie as completely reactionary is "Left" opportunist and sectarian; and to regard the national bourgeoisie as completely revolutionary is to be Right opportunist and capitulationist. It is necessary at all times for the Party to adopt a revolutionary dual tactic towards the national bourgeoisie, combining unity and struggle. If the Party loses sight of the reactionary aspect of the national bourgeoisie, it would be unprepared for any betrayal of the revolution by this class. Revolutionary vigilance is required in our relations with the national bourgeoisie. If the Party loses sight of the progressive character of this class and does not recognize it as an ally within a certain period of time and to a certain limited extent, it would fail to take advantage of actual contradictions between this class on the one hand and foreign monopoly capitalism and feudalism on the other.

In order to develop the cooperation of the national bourgeoisie, the Party must have its own strength; otherwise, this class and its representatives would be reluctant to cooperate. The Party must respect the legitimate interests of all middle forces, with concessions actually granted to them without undermining the interests of the people and the leadership of the proletariat. At all times, resolute struggle must be waged against the enemies of the national united front so that trust in the Party would grow among the people and all middle forces.

In its relations with revolutionary forces throughout the world, the Party pursues the policy of the international united front. All revolutionary and progressive forces that can be united against the main enemy of the peoples of the world, US imperialism, should be united. Modern revisionism with its slogan of "united action" should be rejected as the ideology of the international scabs who are serving and seeking peace and d,tente with US imperialism.

In the international communist movement, the biggest danger today is modern revisionism. Likewise in the Philippines the main danger is modern revisionism in the form of the Lava revisionist renegade line and all other forms of Right opportunism. The collaboration between US imperialism, modern revisionism and all forms of reaction should be continuously exposed and attacked by the international united front and the national united front.

US imperialism and all other reactionaries are paper tigers. All the nuclear weapons and all the military technology of US imperialism cannot frighten us. Although our fraternal people, the Chinese people, have the atom bomb for the defense of the revolutionary peoples, what is more important for all fighting peoples is the human factor, the surging forces of the masses under the inspiration of Mao Tsetung Thought and under the leadership of the proletariat and the Communist Party. Mao Tsetung Thought is their spiritual atom bomb. They are bound by the spirit of proletarian internationalism in the world proletarian revolution and in the international united front against US imperialism, modern revisionism and all reaction.

Although our Party and people welcome political and material support from fraternal parties and peoples, under the spirit of proletarian internationalism and within the framework of the international united front, we must rely mainly on ourselves first of all and wage the people's democratic revolution as part of the world proletarian revolution.

Armed with invincible Mao Tsetung Thought, the Communist Party of the Philippines will surely triumph and the Filipino people under the leadership of the revolutionary proletariat will achieve people's democracy first and socialism next.

Ratified by the Congress of Re-Establishment of the Communist Party of the Philippines

26 December 1968

Program for a People's Democratic Revolution

Ratified by the Congress of Re-Establishment of the Communist Party of the Philippines

1968

I. THE BASIC CONDITION OF THE PHILIPPINES TODAY

The basic condition of the Philippines today is that of a semi-colonial and semi-feudal country dominated by the U.S. imperialists, the comprador bourgeoisie, the landlords and the bureaucrat capitalists. These vested interests mercilessly exploit the broad masses of the people.

US imperialism and domestic feudalism are the main problems afflicting the whole nation and from which the masses of the people aspire to be liberated.

The Philippine revolution against Spanish colonialism failed to achieve the goals of national liberation and the elimination of feudalism. The flabby leadership of the ilustrados (liberal bourgeoisie) failed to win the revolution by playing into the hands of U.S. imperialism which brutally massacred the Filipino people and deprived them of their national independence and democratic rights in the course of the Filipino-American war and thereafter.

Since the beginning of this century, U.S. imperialism has made use of feudalism as its social base in the Philippines. With the defeat of the old type of national democratic revolution, which was imbued mainly with the ideas of liberalism, U.S. imperialism has succeeded in employing domestic puppet forces to frustrate the revolutionary aspirations of the Filipino people and deprive them of their national freedom, class freedom and individual rights.

U.S. imperialism has bred and made use of the comprador bourgeoisie as its principal agency in perpetuating a semi-colonial and semi-feudal type of economy, culture and political system. The landlord class has persisted as the most important ally of U.S. imperialism and the comprador bourgeoisie in the perpetuation of feudal and semi-feudal relations in the vast countryside. The bureaucrat capitalists have also emerged under the imperialist tutelage for "self-government and democracy" to perpetuate the dominance of U.S. imperialism, the local comprador bourgeoisie and the landlord class in the present reactionary puppet state.

The combined oppression of US imperialism and feudalism involves the inequitable colonial exchange of cheap local raw materials (sugar, coconut, abaca, logs and mineral ore) and finished products imported chiefly from the United States and the investment of US surplus capital in the Philippines chiefly to foster the semicolonial and semifeudal type of economy that exploits the toiling masses of workers and peasants.

During the direct and indirect rule of U.S. imperialism in the Philippines, the Filipino toiling masses have been exploited to serve the excessive hunger for profits of the U.S. monopoly capitalists and the local reactionaries. The acute exploitation of the masses of workers and peasants, a general state of backwardness in society and the corruption and brutality of the bourgeois reactionary state characterize the Philippines today.

The Filipino working class has significantly grown in number and experience since the later period of Spanish colonial rule. But its further growth has been stunted because of the limitations on local industrialization and emphasis on raw-material production and, lately, on mere re-assembly plants, new plantations, mines and businesses in the grip of foreign monopoly capitalism. The Filipino working class has suffered extremely low wages and the whole nation has suffered lack of opportunity and the remittance of super-profits from the Philippines by foreign monopolies and heavy indebtedness to imperialist banks.

Despite the emphasis on raw-material production, there is the stagnation of Philippine agriculture and the exploitation of poor peasants and farm workers in areas where feudalism persists; and in areas where modern plantations are in operation both regular and seasonal agricultural workers also suffer low wages and sub-human levels of working and living conditions.

The rural poor, composed mainly of poor peasants, farm workers and poor fishermen; and the urban poor, composed mainly of workers, peddlers, poor handicraftsmen and the unemployed living in city slums, comprise together more than 90 per cent of the population. Though they are the overwhelming majority in the Philippines, they are now the most deprived and oppressed politically, economically, socially and culturally. They are the vast source of revolutionary power against foreign and feudal exploitation.

The urban petty bourgeoisie also suffers from the state of foreign and feudal exploitation. Though it lives in relatively better comfort than the urban and rural poor, its very limited and usually fixed income is subject to the pressure of foreign and feudal exploitation. It can easily be won over to the side of the revolution because it is not free from the abuses of the state on its livelihood and democratic rights.

The national bourgeoisie is the most wealthy of the forces that may be won over to the side of the revolution. It is restricted by foreign and feudal domination in its goal of nationalist industrialization. Though it wishes to lead the patriotic and progressive classes through its entrepreneurship and its political actions, its kind of class leadership has already been surpassed historically by the revolutionary class leadership of the working class. The vacillating dual character of the national bourgeoisie should be recognized by the working class while working for a national united front of all patriotic and progressive classes, groups and individuals under the leadership of the working class.

At this stage of Philippine history and world history, it no longer suffices to have the old type of national democratic revolution. The era of imperialism has long invalidated the leadership of the bourgeoisie. An exceedingly high stage of the world proletarian revolution has been achieved with the ascendance of Mao Tsetung Thought, the acme of Marxism-Leninism in this era. The Communist Party of the Philippines itself can never hope to lead the Filipino people if it does not rid itself of modern revisionism or the black bourgeois line, particularly of the Lavas and the Tarucs, that has marked its history.

The national bourgeoisie and the urban petty bourgeoisie, the latter especially, are allies of the working class within the national united front but they have long become inadequate at leading the Philippine revolution in the era of imperialism as demonstrated as early as the start of the armed conquest of the Philippines by U.S. imperialism when the liberal bourgeois leadership capitulated.

The class leadership in the Philippine revolution is now in the hands of the working class. A proletarian revolutionary leadership, guided by Marxism-Leninism-Mao Tsetung Thought, is what makes the people's democratic revolution a new type of national democratic revolution. We are now in the world era in which U.S. imperialism is heading for total collapse and socialism is advancing to worldwide victory. By adopting Mao Tsetung Thought as the supreme guide for our revolutionary actions, we cleanse the vanguard Party of its weaknesses (as presented by the document of the rectification, Rectify Errors and Rebuild the Party") and strengthen it to become the invincible force at the core of the revolutionary mass movement.

The Communist Party of the Philippines is now re-established and rebuilt as a Party of Marxism-Leninism-Mao Tsetung Thought. It is the most advanced detachment of the Filipino working class leading the Philippine revolution forward. It strives to be a well-disciplined Party armed with the theory of Marxism-Leninism-Mao Tsetung Thought, using the method of criticism and self-criticism and closely linked with the masses of the people. It wields the two weapons of armed struggle and the national united front to deal death blows at U.S. imperialism and feudalism.

There is only one road which the working class under the leadership of the Communist Party of the Philippines must take. It is the road of armed revolution to smash the armed counter-revolution that preserves foreign and feudal oppression in the Philippines. In waging armed revolution, the working class must rely mainly on the mass support of its closest ally, the peasantry. The peasantry is the main force of the people's democratic revolution. Without the peasantry's support, without waging an agrarian revolution that responds to the peasantry's struggle for land, no genuine and formidable people's army can be built and no revolutionary base area can be established. The peasant struggle for land is the main democratic content of the present stage of the Philippine revolution.

From the countryside, the people's democratic forces encircle the cities. It is in the countryside that the enemy forces are first lured in and defeated before the capture of the cities from the hands of the exploiting classes. It is in the countryside that the weakest links of the reactionary state are to be found and the people's democratic forces can surround them tactically before defeating them strategically. It is in the countryside that the people's army can accumulate strength among the peasants by combining armed struggle, agrarian revolution and the building of revolutionary base areas. The Party and the people's army must turn the backward villages into advanced military, political and economic and cultural bastions of the people's democratic revolution.

A true national united front exists only when it is founded on the alliance of the working class and the peasantry and such alliance has been strongly welded by armed struggle, by the creation of a people's army mainly among the peasants by the working class party, the Communist Party of the Philippines. A true united front is one for carrying out armed struggle. The urban petty bourgeoisie can join such a united front. The national bourgeoisie can also lend direct and indirect support to it although it always carries its dual character, its contradicting progressive and reactionary aspects. In a national united front of workers, peasants, urban petty bourgeoisie and the national bourgeoisie, the proletarian revolutionary party can best guarantee its leadership, independence and initiative only by having the people's army firmly at its command.

In the countryside, a revolutionary anti-feudal united front must also be created. The working class must rely mainly on the poor peasants and farm workers, then win over and unite with the middle peasants and neutralize the rich peasants. In its close alliance with the masses of poor peasants and farm workers, the working class undertakes armed struggle, agrarian revolution and the building of revolutionary base areas to build the strong foundations of people's democracy.

While the old democratic leadership of the bourgeoisie no longer applies to the Philippine revolution at this historical stage, the working class and the Communist Party of the Philippines cannot accomplish both democracy and socialism at one blow. While on a world scale socialism has already taken firm roots with the People's Republic of China as its main bulwark, the Party must first achieve a new type of national democratic revolution, a people's democratic revolution in the concrete semi-colonial and semi-feudal conditions of the Philippines, before reaching the stage of socialist revolution. Socialism cannot be immediately achieved when the Filipino people under the leadership of the working class still have to liberate themselves the foreign and feudal oppression.

However, the people's democratic revolution rejects the old liberal leadership of the bourgeoisie. U.S. imperialism has long made use of the jargon of liberal democracy to deceive the people. In upholding proletarian revolutionary leadership, the Party does not mean that socialism shall be achieved without passing through the stage of national democracy. Neither does it mean that such progressive strata of local bourgeoisie as the petty bourgeoisie and the national bourgeoisie have no more place in the revolution. They do have a role to play as national-democratic allies of the working class. Indeed, people's democracy is a new type of democracy because of its proletarian, instead of bourgeois, leadership. But this proletarian revolutionary leadership assumes the present democratic task of waging protracted peasant war, an agrarian revolution, and organizing a national united front of workers in alliance with the peasantry, the urban petty bourgeoisie, the intelligentsia and the national bourgeoisie. The proletarian revolutionary leadership and the worker-peasant alliance are the most important links between the stage of the people's democratic revolution and the stage of socialist revolution.

The immediate and general programme of the Filipino people and the Communist Party of the Philippines is a people's democratic revolution and the long-term maximum programme is socialism. It is dishonest, demagogic and utopian to insist that socialism is the immediate goal under conditions that the people are still dominated and exploited by U.S. imperialism and domestic feudalism.

In the political field, the Communist Party of the Philippines advances the revolutionary leadership of the working class, fights to overthrow the reactionary bourgeois regime and all reactionary classes supporting it and, in its stead, establishes a people's democratic state system, a coalition or united front government of the working class, peasantry, the urban petty bourgeoisie and national bourgeoisie. In the economic field, the Party fights for a self-reliant economy, a just and prosperous people's livelihood and a national industry and trade emancipated from foreign monopoly capitalism and feudalism which have restricted and exploited the productive efforts of the people including patriotic businessmen, industrialists and petty producers. In the field of culture and education, the Party fights for the development of a national, scientific and mass culture and education. In the military field, the Party commands and builds up a people's army that serves as the mainstay of the national and social liberation movement and, consequently, of the people's democratic state system.

II. PROGRAMME FOR A PEOPLE'S DEMOCRATIC REVOLUTION

The Communist Party of the Philippine is determined to implement its general programme for a people's democratic revolution. All Filipino Communists are ready to sacrifice their lives for the worthy cause of achieving the new type of democracy, of building a new Philippines that is genuinely and completely independent, democratic, united, just and prosperous. We are all keenly aware that the present bourgeois state and the reactionary classes that it serves will never surrender their political and economic power without a fight.

The Party is highly conscious that in rebuilding itself as the principal instrument of the leading class and in building a united front of all patriotic and progressive forces, it must build a strong people's army that can weld together the workers and peasants and destroy the local reactionary state and the interventionist forces of U.S. imperialism.

The Communist Party of the Philippines is the core of the revolutionary mass movement against foreign and feudal oppression and for the establishment and consolidation of a people's democratic state. In the exercise of its leadership, the Party hereunder states ten guidelines for its general programme:

1. Destroy the Forces of US Imperialist and Feudal Oppression in the Philippines

National sovereignty and democracy can never be obtained without the destruction of the forces of U.S. imperialism and domestic feudalism whose basic interests lie in the continued national and class enslavement and exploitation of the Filipino people. The overriding interest of the Filipino people now is to fight for national liberation and people's democracy. They must take the road of armed revolution to defeat the armed counterrevolution; and all patriotic and progressive classes, parties, groups and individuals must be aroused and mobilized to isolate and then destroy the power and influence of the U.S. imperialists, the comprador bourgeoisie, the evil gentry, the bureaucrat capitalists and all their political and armed agents. The political power and influence of these exploiters can be isolated, destroyed and replaced by both waging the armed struggle and building the national united front. As a proletarian revolutionary party, the Communist Party of the Philippines should not be tied down by legalist and parliamentary struggle. The Party should concentrate on building up the people's democratic power in the countryside before seizing the cities and, simultaneously, on discrediting the monopolization of political power by the bourgeois political parties, like the Nacionalista Party, the Liberal Party and others, which actually perpetuate the same single party of class interests.

2. Establish a People's Democratic State and a Coalition or United Front Government

The ultimate goal of the people's democratic revolution is the establishment of a people's democratic state and a coalition or united front government. The people's democratic state is under the leadership of the working class and it includes the participation of all democratic classes, i.e., the workers, peasants, petty bourgeoisie and the national bourgeoisie. Its government is a coalition or united front of all democratic classes. In the course of the protracted people's war, a national liberation front may be created to combine all available forces and elements to isolate and destroy the enemy and prepare for a democratic coalition government. In the meantime, while a nationwide coalition government cannot yet be established, the masses of workers and peasants under the proletarian revolutionary leadership can establish an armed independent regime in the countryside where they shall learn to govern themselves, defend and advance their independence and democratic gains and manage well their relations with all friends and sympathizers. The armed independent regime is the nucleus of the People's Democratic Republic of the Philippines.

3. Fight for National Unity and Democratic Rights

The firmest national unity founded mainly on the basis of the class interest of the workers and peasants must be created. On this popular basis, all patriotic and progressive classes, groups and individuals shall enjoy political and economic rights that U.S. imperialism and feudalism have deprived them of. Individual initiative and enterprise on the part of fishermen, handicraftsmen, intellectuals, the urban petty bourgeoisie and the national bourgeoisie shall be respected, encouraged and assisted. All efforts shall be exerted by the state, cooperative and private sectors to provide every citizen a decent livelihood. All democratic classes, groups and their members shall enjoy all such democratic rights as freedom of domicile, person, thought, belief, religion, speech and assembly in a democratic bill of rights. The interests and rights of overseas Filipinos shall be protected; they shall be allowed to have the amplest contact with their kith and kin in the Philippines or to return from the United States or elsewhere.

4. Follow the Principle of Democratic Centralism

The national government shall have central authority over the local government at various levels. The government, however, shall base its decisions on the needs and aspirations of the broad masses of the people and the lower levels of government. This is centralized leadership based on democracy guided by centralized leadership. At every level of the government (barrio, municipality, city or district, provincial, regional), there shall be elected representative bodies where decisions are taken democratically for every corresponding area. A lower representative body shall be subordinate to a higher representative body. Any part of the government shall be subordinate to the people's revolutionary congress which represents nationally the sovereign Filipino people. In all elections or voting on any question, the rule of the majority shall be followed.

5. The People's Liberation Army

There can be no people's democratic state without a people's army whose principal and most essential function is to defend and secure it. The people's army, composed mainly of fighters from the peasantry, must be under the leadership of the working class and the Communist Party of the Philippines. The most pressing task of the people's army now is to defeat and destroy the reactionary imperialist-created and imperialist-supported Armed Forces of the Philippines and all other kinds of armed power in the hands of the exploiting classes and the reactionary state at all levels. The people's democratic government can be established only with the triumphant advance of the people's army. The people's army shall be a fighting force, a propaganda force and a productive force closely linked with the masses of the people. It constantly strengthens itself ideologically, politically and organizationally with Mao Tsetung Thought. The armed strength of the people's army includes its regular mobile troops, the guerrilla units, and the militia and self-defense corps and armed city partisans. The Party should see to it that troops are well-provisioned and the welfare of the families of fighters are well taken care of.

6. The Land Problem

The main content of the people's democratic revolution is the struggle of the peasants for land. The people's democratic revolution must satisfy the basic demands of the poor peasants and farm workers for land. The agrarian revolution is the necessary requirement for the vigorous conduct of the armed struggle and the creation and consolidation of revolutionary base areas. Land shall be distributed free to the landless. Usury and all other feudal evils shall be wiped out. Plantations and estates already efficiently operated on a mechanized basis shall be converted into state farms where agricultural workers shall establish proletarian power and provide themselves with better working and living conditions. In the whole countryside, mutual aid teams and mutual labor exchange systems shall be created as the initial steps towards higher forms of agricultural cooperation. Through agricultural cooperation, production shall be raised and be well-planned, the sale of produce shall be assured at the best price possible and welfare services guaranteed. The higher purchasing power of the peasantry shall allow the ceaselss expansion of industrial production. The basis of the national economy shall be agriculture because it fulfills the food and raw material requirement of expanding industrialization and because it is mainly the peasantry that absorbs the products of industrialization.

7. The Problem of Industry

Foreign monopoly capitalism and feudalism which have hindered the growth of national industry are firmly opposed by the people's democratic revolution. All efforts towards the growth of national industry as the leading factor of the economy shall be mustered by the people's democratic government. There shall be three sectors in the national economy: the state sector, the cooperative sector and the private sector. All major sources of raw materials and energy, all heavy and basic industries and all nationalized enterprises shall be run by the state sector. The private sector run by patriotic entrepreneurs and merchants shall be given assistance and support by the people's democratic government. All peasants, fishermen and handicraftsmen shall be encouraged to organize themselves into cooperatives so as to increase their productivity and assure themselves of a ready market. While building up the state and cooperative sectors of the economy as factors of proletarian leadership and socialism, the people's democratic government shall encourage and support all private initiative in industry so long as this does not monopolize or adversely affect the people's livelihood. The people's democratic government shall exercise regulation of capital only to protect the people's livelihood and guarantee a people's democracy.

8. The Problem of Culture, Education and the Intellectuals

A people's democratic cultural revolution is necessary to rid the nation of the stultifying dominance of imperialist and feudal culture and education. It must advance instead a national, scientific and mass culture truly serving the interests of the people. It shall see to it that the educational system and the mass media are securely in the hands of the people's democratic forces. Education at all levels shall be free, irrespective of class, religion, creed, sex or color. It shall promote the national language as the principal medium of communication in Philippine society. It shall give full encouragement and support to scientific experiment and technological progress. It shall see to it that the national language, art and literature shall be given revolutionary content and relate the revolutionary struggles of workers, peasants, soldiers and other participants of the revolution. Old forms as well as foreign forms of art and literature may be adopted so long as these can be given revolutionary content and suit the national aspirations of the people. The working class assumes leadership in the field of culture and education in line with its leading revolutionary role. But it welcomes wholehearted support of intellectuals for the revolution. All democratic intellectuals are given all the opportunity to serve the people and remould their own thinking. While freedom of thought and religion shall be accorded respect, proper safeguards shall be taken to keep this freedom from being systematically employed to resist the people's democratic revolution or hurt the people's interests. In the course of the protracted people's war, the Party shall transform backward villages into cultural bastions of the Philippine revolution. Illiteracy and superstition among the masses shall be wiped out and the scientific spirit of Marxism-Leninism-Mao Tsetung Thought shall prevail.

9. The Problem of National Minorities

National minorities in the Philippines have been abused and grossly neglected. U.S. imperialism, the local reactionary government and the Christian churches have too long regarded the national minorities as mere objects of bourgeois charity and Christian proselytization. The four-million people belonging to the national minorities, especially those of Mindanao and the mountain provinces, can be powerful participants in the revolutionary overthrow of U.S. imperialism and feudalism. The bourgeois government, reactionary scholars and Christian chauvinists talk loud about national integration but they stand in reality for the exploiting classes that are the main sources of abuse and oppression. The main concern of the national minorities is land; the abuses of landlords, loggers and landgrabbers; and exploitation in mines and plantations. A new type of leadership, a revolutionary one must be encouraged to rise among them so as to supplant the traditional leadership that has failed to protect them and has merely contributed to and participated in their exploitation. With regard to naturalized Filipinos and foreign nationals, the class approach must be firmly taken so as to do away with "Malay" racism and chauvinism. Residents or citizens of Chinese ancestry are very often the target of racist and chauvinist attacks launched by the U.S. imperialists, modern revisionists and other local reactionaries in line with their anti-China, anti-communist and anti-people policy. The Kuomintang comprador big bourgeoisie should be thoroughly exposed and attacked for its class position and for the fact that it is an accomplice of U.S. imperialism, modern revisionism and all reaction.

10. The Problem of Foreign Policy

The foreign policy of the Philippine bourgeois government is dictated by U.S. imperialism and the internal reactionary classes. The diplomatic relations and foreign trade of the Philippines is dictated upon by the United States, together with its reactionary allies like resurgent militarist Japan. Relations with the revisionist states have been initiated only because of the permission granted by the United States which recognizes modern revisionism as its chief accomplice in maintaining neo-colonialism throughout the world, including the Philippines. The imperialists and the modern revisionists are maintaining all-round cooperation to save puppet states like the reactionary puppet state in the Philippines. The only true basis for an independent and active foreign policy is the overthrow of the internal power of U.S. imperialism and its local lackeys in the Philippines, and the abrogation of all treaties, executive agreements and statutes that define "special relations" with the U.S. government and its imperialist allies. The people's democratic government shall truly broaden its foreign policy by opening diplomatic and trade relations with its powerful neighbor and friend, the People's Republic of China, and all other countries willing to have relations in the spirit of mutual respect for national sovereignty and on the basis of equality and mutual benefit. The people's democratic government shall give moral and material support to the revolutionary movements of oppressed peoples abroad and shall maintain the firmest alliance with genuine socialist states like the People's Republic of China and the People's Republic of Albania. It shall be inspired by the principle of proletarian internationalism and guided by the policy of the international united front. It regards the People's Republic of China as an iron bastion of the world proletarian revolution and as a reliable friend of all oppressed peoples, including the Filipino people.

III. OUR SPECIFIC PROGRAMME

Our general programme will fundamentally remain unchanged during the entire stage of the people's democratic revolution. But from phase to phase during this general stage, our specific and immediate demands shall change.

Hereunder are our specific and immediate demands:

In the Political Field

1. Attack, isolate and destroy the bourgeois reactionary state, the U.S. imperialists, the landlords and all local tyrants in our country until their doom;
2. Establish the armed independent regime and develop the people's ability in the conduct of the government
3. Purge our ranks of modern revisionists and all other opportunists who sabotage our revolutionary efforts and expose the bankruptcy of bourgeois legalism and parliamentarism;
4. Campaign for a people's democratic constitution and demand the revocation of the bourgeois constitution and all counterrevolutionary laws, executive agreements and treaties;
5. Expose the curtailment of the political rights of workers, peasants, intellectuals and patriotic citizens who fight against foreign and feudal oppression, and allow the free operation of or

support every democratic party or mass organization;
6. Fight the rise of fascism and use of murder and all other forms of intimidation against the people and their revolutionary and democratic leaders and organizations;
7. Punish the evil gentry and corrupt government officials and subject them to public trial by the people's court whenever possible;
8. Replace or re-organize the barrio councils and promote the leadership of the poor peasants and farm workers through revolutionary barrio committees;
9. Cooperate with all organizations and groups that can help build the national united front and isolate the die-hard enemies of the people's democratic revolution; and
10. Assure low-ranking officials and rank-and-file employees in the reactionary government that they shall be reintegrated into the people's democratic government so long as they do not participate directly in the commission of public crimes and so long as they secretly cooperate with the revolutionary movement.

In the Economic Field

1. Render ineffective the Parity Amendment, the Laurel-Langley Agreement, the Economic and Technical Cooperation Agreement, the Agreement Relating to Entry Rights of American Traders and Investors, Agricultural Commodities Agreement and the Investment Incentives Law and all other such legal instruments that bind our country economically to U.S. imperialism and all its local lackeys, and reject the old and new loan

agreements made by the bourgeois reactionary government, including the "aid" agreements;

2. Encourage the people and the national bourgeoisie to build a self-reliant economy and at the same time confiscate foreign goods that depress or eliminate the local production of goods by patriotic Filipino citizens while urging the broad masses of the people to boycott imperialist businesses and consumer goods;
3. Outlaw bureaucrat capital and all property gained through corrupt and criminal means;
4. Help improve the livelihood of workers, peasants, farm workers, fishermen and handicraftsmen by exercising price control in base areas and providing work for the unemployed; and organize the peasants, fishermen and handicraftsmen into elementary cooperative units (mutual aid teams and labor exchange systems) and support every movement for the economic emancipation of the people;
5. Compel the reduction of rent and interest rates in guerrilla zones and abolish rent in the liberated areas, abolish exorbitant taxes and miscellaneous levies and establish a consolidated progressive tax, collecting a fair agricultural tax and also a fair business tax from the petty and the national bourgeoisie;
6. Help the workers in the factories, mines, plantations, transportation lines and offices to conduct strikes successfully;
7. Expose the deceptive and reactionary character of the Magna Carta of Labor, the Agricultural Land Reform Code and such other bourgeois measures pretending to support the economic and social struggle of the exploited masses;

8. Protect and encourage Filipino-owned commerce and industry by providing market guarantees, protection, credit and tax relief;
9. Support the national minorities in their fight against landlords, landlords, landgrabbers, mining companies, logging concessionaires and plantations; and
10. Safeguard the people's health and expand medical services.

In the Military Field

1. Organize and train units of the people's army; armed propaganda teams, guerrilla units, regular mobile troops, militia and armed city partisans;
2. Campaign against the U.S. military bases and U.S. military assistance and all treaties (U.S.-R.P. Military Bases Treaty, Military Assistance Pact and Mutual Defense Treaty, the SEATO, etc.) that bind the reactionary government and army to the U.S. imperialists, and also against the anti-democratic intent of "civic action," the "Peace Corps" and other counter-insurgency projects of the U.S. imperialists;
3. Destroy the military units of the reactionary government and of the US imperialists and capture useful military equipment;
4. Punish the spies and all subversive agents (especially members of the CIA and DIA) of U.S. imperialism and their local reactionary cohorts;
5. Campaign against the drafting of youth, workers and peasants by the reactionaries for military camp training and service and also against the P.M.T., R.O.T.C. and Philippine

Military Academy because of their reactionary orientation;
6. Eliminate cattlerustling and piracy, banditry and all other activities that prey on the poor;
7. Destroy the terror squads like the Home Defense Corps and the "Monkees", and disarm and disband the bodyguards of bureaucrat capitalists, civilian guards of landlords and strike-breakers;
8. Organize the oppressed national minorities to take up arms against imperialist and feudal oppression;
9. Wage a war of annihilation but exercise leniency on captured combatants so as to demoralize the enemy; and
10. Cooperate with all other armed movements or groups fighting against imperialist and feudal oppression.

In the Cultural Field

1. Develop a national, scientific and mass culture responsive to the needs and aspirations of the Filipino people;
2. Campaign against imperialist and feudalist or Church control and influence over the educational system and mass media;
3. Propagate the national language as the principal medium of instruction and communication;
4. Develop a people's democratic culture and put revolutionary content in art and literature while combatting the decadent literature of "universal humanism," pessimism, escapism, class reconciliation and all other pernicious bourgeois trends;

5. Combat Christian chauvinism against the national minorities;
6. Support the progressive movements and actions among students, teachers and all intellectuals;
7. Guarantee the better livelihood of teachers and other staff members of educational institutions and guarantee academic freedom;
8. Respect the freedom of thought and religious belief and use patient persuasion in gathering support for the people's democratic revolution;
9. Denounce imperialist study and travel grants; and
10. Fight for free education at all levels and wipe out illiteracy and superstition among the masses and rouse them to a revolutionary and scientific spirit.

In the Field of Foreign Policy

1. Base Philippine foreign policy on the Filipino people's sovereignty and self-reliance, and cooperate with all friendly revolutionary people's governments and movements on the basis of mutual respect and mutual benefit;
2. Fight against all unjust treaties and agreements imposed by U.S. Imperialism;
3. Develop the firmest relations with the People's Republic of China, People's Republic of Albania and all revolutionary governments and peoples;
4. Support the revolutionary struggles of all oppressed peoples in Asia, Africa and Latin America; and all neighboring oppressed peoples of Vietnam, Laos, Indonesia, Thailand, Kalimantan Utara, Malaya, Burma, Korea and others;

5. Expose the United Nations as a tool of U.S. imperialism and its revisionist renegade accomplices in the crime of neo-colonialism;
6. Oppose every treacherous maneuver of all revisionist states and parties in their collaboration with U.S. imperialism;
7. Resist the attempt of US imperialism to make use of Japan and the revisionist renegade clique led by the Soviet Union as tools in the exploitation of the Philippines;
8. Oppose such "regional" arrangements as the Asian Development Bank, Association of Southeast Asian Nations (ASEAN), the Asian Pacific Council (ASPAC), and the like that reinforce the SEATO and other longstanding instruments of US imperialism in the region;
9. Campaign against the imperialist advisers and survey missions in the bourgeois reactionary government; and
10. Uphold the spirit of proletarian internationalism and the policy of the international united front.

IV. CONDITIONS FOR REVOLUTION ARE EXCELLENT

The objective conditions for the implementation of our general and specific programmes are excellent. U.S. imperialism, modern revisionism and all reactionary forces are receiving crushing blows from the oppressed peoples of the world and are in a state of disintegration. This is indeed the era when imperialism is heading for total collapse and socialism is advancing to worldwide victory.

Increasingly, armed struggles in the countryside of the world, Asia, Africa and Latin America, are ever intensifying and expanding to tear apart and destroy the overextended power of U.S. imperialism and all its reactionary allies. In the close vicinity of the Philippines, the tide of people's war is ever rising under the powerful inspiration of Mao Tsetung Thought. The heroic peoples of Vietnam, Laos, Thailand, Indonesia, Burma, Malaya and others are fighting U.S. imperialism and feudalism. The Filipino people and the Communist Party of the Philippines are fortunate to be within the storm center of the world proletarian revolution.

Because of its losses in the Vietnam war, because of its expensive but futile aid to its puppet governments and because of its failure to further expand its foreign trade, U.S. imperialism is rocked in its very heartland by a serious crisis that is now agitating the American workers and youth, both Afro-American and White, who refuse to be carried away into imperialist wars of expansion and to be abused economically and politically at home. The deepening internal and external crisis of U.S. imperialism is clearly depriving the Filipino reactionaries of a significantly great amount of imperialist protection and support.

The crisis of over-production severely afflicts the entire world capitalist system today and is profoundly agitating its own working class and youth that it viciously exploits. All capitalist countries are now engaged in cut-throat competition because each is trying to save itself from economic and political crises at the expense of the other. Although all capitalist countries are united in manipulating the revisionist renegade states and parties and shifting the burden of their financial crisis on the backs of their colonies and semi-colonies, they only aggravate the hopeless situation of their puppets and intensify the aspirations of the oppressed peoples to be freed of their imperialist yoke.

Modern revisionism spearheaded by the Soviet revisionist clique is failing to be an effective accomplice of U.S. imperialism in their mutual crime of neo-colonialism. The Soviet revisionist renegade bloc is fast disintegrating. The Soviet aggression against the Czechoslovak people has demonstrated the treacherous character of modern revisionism. While U.S. imperialism and Soviet social-imperialism collude in claiming their respective spheres of influence, they also struggle to redivide the same.

While U.S. imperialism and modern revisionism are in deep crisis, the People's Republic of China has consolidated itself as an iron bastion of socialism and the world proletarian revolution by carrying out the epochal Great Proletarian Cultural Revolution and by holding aloft Mao Tsetung Thought to illumine the road of armed revolution throughout the world. Also, in the Eastern European heartland of modern revisionism, the People's Republic of Albania stands forth as an advance post of the world proletarian revolution and Mao Tsetung Thought and is encouraging all the oppressed peoples and Marxist-

Leninists there to rebel against the ruling revisionist renegade cliques.

The most significant development in the entire history of the Filipino people so far is the re-establishment and rebuilding of the Communist Party of the Philippines as a party of Mao Tsetung Thought. This occurs at a time when world and national conditions are extremely favorable for revolution under the leadership of the proletariat.

The Philippine reactionary state can no longer rely on the "unlimited" support of the crisis-stricken U.S. imperialism and the world capitalist system. What the United States and other capitalist powers are vainly trying to do is to shift the burden of their economic and financial crisis on the backs of colonies and semi-colonies like the Philippines. This will only aggravate the foreign and feudal oppression of the Filipino people and will only goad them to take up arms.

The Philippine reactionary state is increasingly unable to rule in the old way. Armed opposition to it by the Filipino people under the leadership of the Communist Party of the Philippines is sure to doom foreign and feudal oppression. It is both a patriotic and internationalist duty to fight U.S. imperialism and all its reactionary allies. Defeat of U.S. imperialism and modern revisionism and all domestic reactionaries in the Philippines is bound to have far-reaching world significance because our country has long served as a bastion of all these evils in this part of the world.

Ratified by the Congress of Re-Establishment of the Communist Party of the Philippines

26 December 1968

Our Urgent Tasks

Amado Guerrero

Introduction

This is a statement of the urgent tasks of the Communist Party of the Philippines in the light of the Third Plenum of the Central Committee and the most recent circumstances. Here included are the conditions, forces, methods, trends and reasons involved in carrying out such tasks.

We must unite wholeheartedly and firmly to carry out these tasks for the single purpose of winning the life-and-death struggle against the fascist dictatorial regime of the U.S.-Marcos clique and in the process carry forward the people's democratic revolution in a comprehensive way.

Each one of us in the Party must take as much assignment and responsibility as possible, fearing neither hardship nor sacrifice and always devoting ourselves to serving the people. All of us must exert the utmost effort to lead our people towards national liberation and social emancipation.

1. Carry Forward the Antifascist, Antifeudal and Anti-Imperialist Movement!

We must resolutely carry forward the antifascist, antifeudal and anti-imperialist movement. This is the current combative expression of our general line of people's democratic revolution against U.S. imperialism, feudalism and bureaucrat capitalism.

The Marcos fascist dictatorship is the main force of armed counter-revolution and is ruthlessly conducting a civil war.

Thus, we must give first place to the antifascist movement. We must do everything we can to push forward the democratic armed revolution against the fascist armed counterrevolution.

Everywhere in the country we must focus on the abuses of the Marcos fascist dictatorship. In the entire semicolonial and semifeudal history of the Philippines, there is no regime more infamous than this for the political tyranny and economic crisis it has unleashed against the broad masses of the people.

The "new society" (variably calling itself "constitutional authoritarianism", "crisis government" and now lately "new democracy") is but the old society gone far worse and far more intolerable. The reactionary state has shorn itself of all its bourgeois democratic embellishments and is nakedly acting as the coercive instrument of the big comprador-landlord-bureaucrat clique of Marcos and U.S. imperialism.

We have the Marcos fascist dictatorship as the narrowest and weakest target on which to concentrate the broadest and strongest possible attack by the people. But to achieve the most profound, most wide-ranging and most forward results in the antifascist movement, we must deliberately and clearly link it to the antifeudal and anti-imperialist movements. It is only thus that we can effectively strike at the very essence and main body of the reactionary state.

Otherwise, we would be merely calling for the restoration of formal democratic rights and worn-out processes of the ruling system. Like bourgeois democrats, and not proletarian revolutionaries, we would be going after forms and we would be missing the content of a people's democratic revolution.

To deepen the antifascist movement, we must vigorously wage the antifeudal movement. By doing so, we develop the main force for overthrowing or causing the overthrow of the fascist dictatorship. We respond no less to the main demand of the people's democratic revolution and win the abiding interest of the most numerous class, the peasantry, in the armed revolution.

To raise the level of the antifascist movement, we must vigorously undertake the anti-imperialist movement. We must make U.S. imperialism pay the ultimate price for having masterminded the Marcos fascist dictatorship and having been the most aggrandized by it. The longer Marcos stays in power, the stronger the anti-imperialist movement should become.

So long as we pay comprehensive attention to the antifascist, antifeudal, and anti-imperialist movement, there is no chance for U.S. imperialism and the local reactionaries to confuse the people and derail the revolution one day by simply replacing the current fascist dictatorship with another.

The Marcos fascist dictatorship is a measure of the weakening and desperation of the entire ruling system, rather than of strengthening and stability. This open terrorist rule is the absolute proof that the ruling classes can no longer rule in the old way.

The political crisis continues to worsen. The split among the reactionaries has continued to widen and become more virulent. The revolutionary mass movement, under the leadership of the revolutionary proletariat, has proven to be resilient and has expanded and intensified, instead of being crushed by the fascist counterrevolution.

Though at first taken by surprise by the ultra-rightist coup, Marcos' political rivals have gone on to disseminate anti-Marcos propaganda in their so-called bailiwicks and maneuver for influence in the very same reactionary armed forces manipulated and used by Marcos for his fascist autocratic purposes. In the years to come, the gun will become more important than ever in the conflicts of the reactionaries.

The alliance of the Macapagal, Aquino, Lopez and Manglapus groups is not idle. Though U.S. imperialism continues to get what it wants from the Marcos fascist dictatorship, it has already assured this alliance that it should do what it can to stand in reserve in the face of Marcos' gross unpopularity. U.S. public opinion and certain U.S. business interests recognize the fact that even as the Marcos fascist dictatorship is a short-term asset for U.S. imperialism, it is a long-term liability.

The Marcos fascist dictatorship has given no quarters to its political rivals. The ultra-rightist coup of the executive against co-equal branches of the reactionary government, against the constitutional convention and against all kinds of opposition carried extremely vindictive measures. Properties have been extorted for the personal gain of Marcos and his henchmen. The Marcos press monopoly and other Marcos assets in far larger enterprises consist mainly of robbed property.

The series of fake referendums have in progression served to merely endorse the arbitrary martial law proclamation and the autocratic rule of Marcos. The "new" constitution, the indefinite nonconvening of the interim national assembly, the supplantation of national and local elections by presidential appointment and the projection of Imelda as second-in-command and successor of the fascist dictator close every peaceful avenue to political power for Marcos' political rivals.

The broad masses of the people have suffered most from the fascist counterrevolution. More than 95 percent of victims of illegal mass arrests and mass detention, massacres, assassination, torture, forced mass evacuation, illegal searches and looting, sexual molestation, bombardment, extortion and the like come from the ranks of ordinary people. Hundreds of thousands have become victims of direct physical abuse by the fascists.

At least three million people have been displaced, especially in the countryside, through fascist intimidation. People have been forced to abandon their homes, crops and small landholdings due to enemy "counterinsurgency" campaigns, expansion of corporate farming, "infrastructure" projects and real estate speculation.

The elimination or drastic diminution of political and economic rights and opportunities is causing incalculable suffering to the broad masses of the people. In such a situation, more people are liable to suffer oppression of the most direct and brutal kind.

The mass organizations of national-democratic character and the critical press are banned. The workers are deprived of their right to strike and the effective exercise of their trade union rights. The right of the peasants to self-organization is sabotaged by military operations and by the imposition of the "samahang nayon". The students, together with their teachers, are under close guard and even student governments and publications are prohibited.

Every means of democratic expression is shut off. All forms of mass action opposing fascist, feudal and imperialist abuses are expressly prohibited. Even private conversations are liable to be considered "rumor-mongering". Ownership and operation of even mimeographing machines and other minor printing equipment are also severely restricted. There are not only the written penalties but also the far more severe penalties imposed by the fascist torturers, murderers and extortionists.

Under the suffocating fascist martial rule, the broad masses of the people have no course but to fight back. They learn daily to resist their enemy. The Marcos fascist dictatorship has stood out as the best teacher by negative example. The learning process is so deep-going that the people increasingly detest not only the Marcos fascist dictatorship but also the entire ruling system.

The Marcos fascist dictatorship has, instead of effecting "peace and order", fanned the flames of armed resistance. The New People's Army, led by the Party, has only strengthened itself and expanded in the face of fascist abuses and barbarities. There are now tested guerrilla forces of the people's army in all regions outside Manila-Rizal.

The armed resistance for self-determination among the people of southwestern Mindanao has been ignited and fueled by the abuses of the Marcos fascist dictatorship. This has constituted a great though indirect support to the revolutionary armed struggle of the New People's Army.

A revolutionary underground is thriving all over the country. This is composed mainly of basic revolutionary forces led by the Party. Allied forces and other antifascist forces also have their own underground activities. In time to come, a powerful groundswell will overthrow the Marcos fascist dictatorship.

The Marcos fascist dictatorship is extremely isolated and is under fire from all directions. Contrary to its wishes it cannot be at the center of a "balancing act" between left and right. It is the ultra-right. It has made itself the target of a broad antifascist movement.

The economic crisis has rapidly worsened, making the core of the political tyranny more rotten everyday. This crisis is generated by the Marcos fascist dictatorship through its own profligacy and corruption and its subservience to U.S. imperialism which is shifting the burden of its crisis to a semicolonial dependent like the Philippines.

All our Party cadres and members must be well acquainted with the fast changing economic data in the country as a whole and in the local areas where they are so that they can give clear substance to their propaganda and agitation.

Prices have been soaring since 1970 but these have been soaring even more rapidly since the imposition of fascist martial rule. Price increases have been by several hundreds of percent since 1972. Imported commodities lead the way. The repeated oil price increases obtained by the U.S. oil companies alone have been a major factor in pushing up prices in the country.

Severe scarcities of locally produced commodities have been occurring and have been pushing up price because the main focus of the fascist regime is to encourage production of raw material for export and build up the "infrastructure" for it. Domestic prices of exportable commodities have risen so fast because exports are being made without prior attention to local needs. Food production is also grossly inadequate and food requirements are dependent on imports.

The income of the toiling masses are forced down to yield high profits to the U.S. and other foreign monopolies and the local exploiting classes. Wage levels have sunk too far below the price of basic commodities. The wage increases recently announced by the fascist regime do not correspond to the inflation since 1970 and can be completely circumvented due to the loopholes provided by the antilabor fascist regime.

It is openly admitted in watered-down statistics of the reactionary government that the purchasing power of the peso has gone down from 1965 to 1970 to 74 centavos and more rapidly from 1970 to 1975 to 33 centavos. This is bad enough. But the fact is that the purchasing power of the peso has certainly gone down to far less than 20 centavos.

According to no less than the National Economic Development Authority, the top economic agency of the fascist regime, a worker must earn P45.00 daily for his family to subsist. Another agency, the Private Development Corporation of the Philippines, has also arrived at the slightly higher figure of P46.00. Even when applied faithfully, the new minimum wage of P10.00, P9.00 and P7.00 for nonagricultural workers in Greater Manila, nonagricultural workers in the provinces and regular agricultural workers, respectively, are far below the level of subsistence.

Unemployment is more rampant than ever. Forty percent of the employable population is without employment. This exceeds the chronic level of 25 percent noted in 1970. Most of the unemployed are in the countryside, under the guise of being irregular farm workers. Many of the unemployed continue to flock into the cities to look for jobs that are not available.

There is no land reform whatsoever. It is a big hoax, obvious from the very start. The tenant masses have been merely offered to buy land from their landlords at prohibitive prices. The bogus land reform has been used as cover for divesting the tenant masses of their tenancy rights, for arranging high fixed land rent and promoting usury, for expanding corporate farming and for enriching Marcos-controlled corporations on fertilizer, pesticide and farm equipment sales contracts with the reactionary government.

U.S. and other foreign investors are encouraged to extract superprofits on their direct investments, loans and trade. Restrictions that should have fallen on U.S. investments upon the termination of the Parity Amendment and the Laurel-Langley Agreement have been overridden by obnoxious antinational provisions of the Marcos constitution and presidential decrees enlarging those privileges already available to foreign investors in those foreign investments incentives laws before fascist martial rule.

U.S. investments and assets amount to far more than the well-known figure of $3.0 to $4.0 billion and comprise 85 percent of all foreign investments. Ownership is often camouflaged by the various nationalities of U.S. multinational firms.

The U.S. monopoly capitalists, followed by the Japanese, have increased their direct investments especially in banking, investment houses, mining, oil exploration, foreign and local trading, plantations, repacking and reassembly, real estate and the like in accordance with their schemes of quick profit and misshaping the economy. The basic character of the economy remains as semifeudal as ever, restricted to being a producer of raw material and consumer of finished products from abroad.

Foreign loans with usurious rates of interest and other onerous conditions are being rapidly unloaded on the Philippines by the imperialists. Whereas the foreign debt of the Philippines stood at $2.2 billion at the end of 1972, accumulated through seven years of Marcos misrule, it now stands at more than $5.0 billion after only three years of fascist rule.

This is already far beyond the critical point. New and bigger loans have been incurred to pay old debts thus there is no end to the enlargement of the debts. What is most silly is that those who take most advantage of these loans are the foreign investors and the Marcos clique of big compradors and big landlords.

The deficit in the balance of trade has gone beyond the $1.0 billion level in comparison to the few hundreds of millions of U.S. dollars three years ago. It is still mounting. A greater volume of exports at lower prices is being made, while a greater volume of imports at higher prices is being made. With their tighter stranglehold on the local financial system, the foreign monopoly capitalists are using foreign trading more rapaciously than ever before to camouflage the remittance of superprofits.

The deficit on the balance of payments keeps on rising. It went beyond the level of $500 million at the end of 1975 and is now approaching the level of $1.0 billion. As usual, bigger foreign loans are resorted to in order to cover the deficit. Taking aside the private foreign exchange deposits in commercial banks, the international reserve fund of the

Philippines is composed almost entirely of foreign loans in the process of being rapidly spent and replenished by new borrowing.

A great deal of foreign loans incurred by the Marcos fascist dictatorship has been used to put up ill-planned and inflationary "infrastructure" projects beneficial essentially to the foreign investors and the local exploiting classes. The purpose is not only to make propaganda out of showy public works but also to enrich the fascist dictator and his henchmen through contract-pulling, kickbacks and real estate speculation. Marcos has controlling interests now in the major local construction firms and related companies.

The manipulation of public works is an old bureaucrat-capitalist method of self-enrichment which Marcos has indulged in an unprecedentedly colossal manner. "Infrastructure" projects are always priced high above the actual inflationary trend. A major part of the "cost" of every construction project represents the corruption of the fascist dictator and his top henchmen. The burden that is the fascist dictatorship's profligacy and corruption is always passed on to the people in the form of higher taxes and higher toll charges or service fees.

The tax burden has increased abruptly so many times. This increased from P6.6 billion in 1972 to P14.3 billion in 1974 and has continued to rise. And yet revenues of the reactionary government fall far short of expenditures. The budgetary deficit for fiscal year 1974–75 is P5.0 billion, almost equivalent to the total budget of only a few years ago. Aside from foreign borrowing, the fascist dictatorship has had to resort to heavy local borrowing. At P20.7 billion in fiscal year 1974–75, the local public debt is now rapidly approaching P30 billion, skyrocketing from the 1972 figure of P9.7 billion.

The new development in the budgeting of the reactionary government under fascism is the rapid increase of appropriations for the military and the number one position of military expenditures. Before fascist martial rule, expenditures for public education and public works always vied for the top position, with those for the military running a poor third. Out of the total 1974–75 expenditures of P18.5 billion, the share of the military is more than P4.0 billion, including some P1.0 billion for intelligence.

On the whole, the expenditures of the reactionary government has been mainly for beefing up the personnel and equipment of the reactionary armed forces, increasing salaries and privileges of military officers, purchasing office materials and vehicles, acquiring public works equipment, paying private contractors, maintaining the general payroll, servicing public debts and the like. In every money transaction involving the fascist dictatorship, there is the inevitable cost that goes for graft and corruption.

There is no economic development whatsoever. Deterioration is the precise word for it. The gross national product is no gauge for economic growth. The transactions of the reactionary government, the foreign monopoly capitalists and the local exploiting classes compose the bulk of this gross national product. Also, this can be no basis for per capita income. More than 90 percent of the people live the lives of the exploited workers and peasants.

2. Further Strengthen the Party and Rectify Our Errors!

We must further strengthen the Party ideologically, politically and organizationally. We have made some modest achievements on the basis of which we can advance further. But we have also had certain errors and weaknesses which we must rectify so that we will not be weighed down and dragged down by these and so that we will win more and greater victories.

The reestablishment of the Communist Party of the Philippines on the theoretical foundation of Marxism-Leninism-Mao Tsetung Thought constitutes a victory of profound and far-reaching significance in the Philippine revolution. We have set down and clarified the correct ideological and political line of the Party.

To set the Philippine revolution on the correct course, we have studied and researched into the history and circumstances of the Filipino people and the Party and put out the necessary documents and writings for the edification of all Filipino revolutionaries. In the process, we have successfully criticized and repudiated the long-standing revisionist lines of the Lavas and Tarucs which polluted and suffocated the old merger party.

We have disseminated the works and propagated the scientific revolutionary teachings of Marx, Engels, Lenin, Stalin and Mao and we have successfully criticized and repudiated Soviet modern revisionism and social-imperialism. Chairman Mao's works have been widely circulated because they not only deal correctly and elaborately with problems of a people's democratic revolution in a semicolonial and semifeudal country but also because they contain the latest and most comprehensive summing-up of the experience of the world proletariat and people.

To propagate the Marxist-Leninist stand, viewpoint and method, we have undertaken study courses, put out analyses of current national and international events, promoted further researches of national and regional scopes and required social investigations and criticism and self-criticism as methods for raising our ideological level and improving our practical work.

In our ideological rebuilding, we have had to lay stress on studying basic Marxist-Leninist principles and combating the modern revisionism of the Soviet and local renegades. We have had to rely considerably on books dealing with successful revolutions led by fraternal parties abroad. We ourselves have had to go through more revolutionary experience than what we started with in order to deepen our grasp of Marxism-Leninism. And quite a number of our Party cadres are of petty-bourgeois background who definitely have more book learning than experience.

Under these circumstances, the dogmatist tendency more than the empiricist has been most prominent among those ideologically in error. Instead of making concrete investigations and analyses in linking with the masses, there are some of us who would rather rest content with parallelisms, analogies, quotations and phrasemongering. There is even the notion that we do not deserve to be called revolutionaries if we cannot copy a successful revolution abroad.

There are also those who seem to grasp the basic principles and lessons derived from our criticism and repudiation of the Lavas and Tarucs but fail to grasp our own course of development and the different concrete circumstances that we are in. They fail to understand that we can advance only step by step and that we cannot apply on ourselves completely the same course of thinking and action demanded of the Lavas and Tarucs on the basis of forces available to them and circumstances obtaining at the end of World War II.

While the dogmatist tendency prevails among those in error, there are also those who remain immersed in their own narrow and limited experience either because they are given no chance of developing ideologically or are merely browbeaten or they systematically react to the dogmatist tendency with their own avoidance of theoretical study.

After more than seven years, our reestablished Party has gained enough experience to be in a new stage of knowing clearly the specific characteristics and specific requirements of our revolutionary struggle in the whole country and in the various localities. It is in this spirit that we call for rectification of ideological errors.

Those who have an advantage in book learning must link themselves closely to and learn from the toiling masses of workers and peasants and from our comrades who have an advantages in experience. At the same time, comrades who are of worker and peasant status must not shirk the responsibility of relating their experience to theory and asking that theory must be disclosed in a language easy to understand.

There is paucity of exchanges of worthwhile experiences within the Party, especially between our several regional Party organizations. To promote these, the Central Committee is putting out Rebolusyon as an internal and theoretical bulletin, exclusively for Party members. We intend to publish here, apart from statements and directives from the Central Committee, mainly documents emanating from regional Party conferences and articles that are the result of the application of Marxist theory in the course of concrete revolutionary practice, social investigations, study courses and criticism and self-criticism sessions.

We also intend to undertake conferences among representatives of various regional Party organizations and encourage the attendance in regional Party conferences of representatives of other regional Party organizations. In this way, the most detailed yet discreet exchanges of experience are made possible.

We urge all Party members to contribute to the general effort of giving Marxism a national form. We should disabuse ourselves of the idea that only a few theoreticians know theory and know how to apply it. We can triumph only if the entire Party consistently applies Marxist-Leninist theory on the concrete conditions of the Philippine revolution.

The Party has established its political leadership of the proletariat in the revolution by laying down, clarifying and carrying out the general line of people's democratic revolution. This is a great victory. We have made clear the character, the motive forces, targets and perspective of this revolution.

The character of the revolution is determined by its essential task, which is to liberate the people from foreign and feudal domination and establish an independent and democratic Philippines. Such a task can be accomplished only by waging armed struggle as the main form among the motive forces to isolate and destroy the target or enemy.

At the helm of the motive forces is the proletariat. It takes as its main ally, the peasantry whose demand for land is the main content of the people's democratic revolution and from which the main contingents of the people's army can be drawn. The basic alliance of the toiling masses of workers and peasants is the solid foundation for the united front which must win over the urban petty bourgeoisie firstly and the national bourgeoisie secondly.

The targets of the revolution are the comprador big bourgeoisie and the landlord class. Our current revolutionary struggle against the Marcos fascist dictatorship is more than a struggle against the ruling clique. In the course of fighting this clique, we must develop the strength to weaken the entire ruling system and then topple it in the end.

The perspective of the people's democratic revolution is socialism. The socialist revolution must begin upon the completion of the people's democratic revolution. Though we are ready to give concessions to the petty bourgeoisie and national bourgeoisie in a period of transition, we shall no longer pass through a full stage of capitalist development as in the case of the old democratic revolutions before the era of imperialism and proletarian revolution.

In line with the people's democratic revolution, we have established the New People's Army and launched the revolutionary armed struggle. Our strategic line is to encircle the cities from the countryside and through a protracted period of time develop rural bases from which to advance to seize political power.

Like the Party, the people's army started from scratch and immediately launched revolutionary armed struggle. The people's army has grown in strength step by step, won military victories against powerful odds and won the hearts and minds of millions by its heroic deeds.

The people's army has been the main instrument of the Party in organizing the peasant masses. Hundreds of thousands of people in the barrios have come directly under the barrio organizing committees organized by our guerrilla squads and armed propaganda teams. We have established small guerrilla bases and far more extensive guerrilla zones, carried out mass movements and initiated land reform.

In the face of the fascist enemy, we have continued to organize and lead large masses of people. Even when our barrio organizing committees collapse in one area due to a massive and prolonged enemy campaign, those in other areas increase to more than make up for the losses and even these losses are temporary, still open to recovery.

In support of the mass movement and armed struggle in the countryside, great mass movements have also been raised by the Party in the cities. The first quarter storm of 1970 and succeeding mass actions in Manila-Rizal and other urban areas have broadcast our revolutionary propaganda all over the country and have yielded to us a considerable number of Party and non-Party activists who have been shifted to the countryside or who continue to develop the revolutionary mass movement in the cities.

It is a matter of necessity in the countryside to expand at a rate fast enough to have a wide area for maneuver for our guerrilla forces. For the purpose, we have been setting up the barrio organizing committees. While we have required the organization of these committees to follow the policy of the antifeudal united front, many of these are so haphazardly organized that unreliable elements creep in, prevail over the poor and middle peasants and flaunt their functions while the enemy is not yet around.

The error of haphazard organizing oftentimes characterized by lack or insufficiency of social investigation and by yielding membership in the barrio organizing committee to whomever are the initial contacts in a barrio, leads on to another error. The work of consolidation is not attended to. The basic mass organizations for peasants, workers, women, youth, children and cultural activists are not organized and mobilized to ensure sustained all round mass support for the revolution. Thus, the surrounding waters may be wide but shallow.

When we cannot apply the principle of combining a few cadres from the outside with many local activists, it is even very likely that the scope of our political work is narrow. Thus, we must handle well the relationship of expansion and consolidation, of making the guerrilla zone and the guerrilla base a good fighting front for us.

In cases of errors with disastrous results, the principal tendency has been adventurism or "Left" opportunism. With mass support wide or narrow but shallow there are those who engage in military actions against enemy troops and then when enemy reaction rises, they do not know where to go or the enemy catches up with them. They fail to recognize that to support and ensure the success of any important action, military or otherwise, requires painstaking mass work.

There are petty-bourgeois elements who are still unremolded and who think that it suffices to beat the drum — make sweeping propaganda but forget to do solid organizational work among the masses — and who also think that the military action of a few courageous men must precede solid organizational work among the masses.

Relying on a mere committee dominated by unreliable but prestigious personalities has also spawned commandism. The chairman and the chief of defense of the barrio organizing committee often neglect to have any collective life within the committee. And in the absence of militant mass organizations, the trend is to order people around and make them do what is beyond their level of consciousness and organization.

While we oppose "Left" opportunism as the principal tendency among those of us in error, we must also be on guard against Right opportunism. Our insistence on taking the mass line, establishing the basic mass organizations and laying the foundation for a truly people's war should not be twisted to mean the indefinite postponement of tactical military offensives even when conditions for them are already ripe.

There have been manifestations of the Right opportunist tendency in the countryside. To consciously let in unreliable elements in barrio organizing committees and relax with the transitory advantages that they provide is one. To enjoy the conveniences of one barrio and fail to venture out and do mass work in another barrio is another. To remain fixed on going after local bad elements and fail to push forward the land reform and the armed struggle is still another.

In the cities, there is the "Left" opportunist notion prevalent among those of us in error that there can be no revolutionary struggle when there are no strikes, demonstrations and other conspicuous mass protest actions. They fail to recognize that it is perfectly revolutionary struggle to lay down the foundation for these higher forms of political action by doing solid organizational work among the masses.

There is also the notion among those of us in error that sweeping propaganda work suffices to mobilize the people. There is still another notion that the economic struggle of the workers can be slurred over, whereas we must grasp it at its own level and steadily raise it to the level of the political struggle.

There have also been instances of Right opportunism in a certain region. One is the proposal to superimpose the slogan demanding general election in the country on other slogans asserting the democratic rights and interests of the basic masses. Another is making flimsy demands to avoid even only basic trade union demands and the necessary preparations for pushing them forward.

While we have pointed out that sweeping propaganda does not suffice by itself in revolutionary work, we recognize that it is of great importance and that without it mass organizing is without an advance notice and also without direction. We need to step up our propaganda work if we are to enhance our all-round revolutionary work. Our capacity for propaganda and agitation will certainly rise as the basic masses are well organized and activists from their ranks increase.

The corrective measures that we need to undertake in our political work will be dealt with more thoroughly in succeeding sections of this statement.

The membership of the Party is drawn generally from the ranks of activists of the revolutionary mass organizations and Red fighters of the New People's Army. It is clear that our membership is closely linked with the masses and embedded in the revolutionary mass movement. But up to now, our Party is mainly a cadre party. We have thus remained a small party.

The Party started with less than a score of Party members coming from the old merger party and 75 prospective members in late 1968. The membership increased to several scores in 1969, to a few hundreds in 1970 and close to a thousand in 1971. Since 1972, we have had a few thousand members. But since 1973, we have had a slower rate of growth.

Our Party has become nationwide. Directly under the Central Committee, there were groups of Party members in Manila-Rizal, Central Luzon, Cagayan Valley and Southern Luzon in 1969 and 1970 with most members in the first two regions mentioned. Following the Second Plenum of the Central Committee in 1971, we started to build the regional Party committees and organizations. Now, we have nine regional Party organizations covering the whole country.

The majority of Party members are now under the regional Party organizations outside Manila-Rizal. In turn, the majority of these are in the countryside developing the revolutionary armed struggle. But the Manila-Rizal Party organization still remains the single largest Party organization. Though this regional Party organization has been giving cadres to the other regions, it has continued to grow.

We realize that the growth of the Party is quite slow if we relate it to the large numbers of masses being led by the Party. At first it looks flattering that so few could lead so many and that strict standards are being applied on recruitment. But there are unflattering reasons for the slow growth.

Sectarianism, poor tasking and check-ups, irregular and ponderous study courses and lack of recruitment planning are problems both in the cities and in the countryside which have restricted the organizational growth of the Party. We must solve these.

The outstanding reason for the failure of regional Party organizations outside Manila-Rizal to outstrip the membership of the Manila-Rizal Party organization is the failure to build the mass organizations and the mass movement in the localities. Without these, there can be no sound basis for establishing local Party branches. The mass organizations, aside from the people's army, should be the vast reservoir of revolutionary activists and Party members.

The Manila-Rizal Party organization should not be flattered and should not remain complacent about being the biggest single regional Party organization. In the last two years, there has been a tendency here for the membership to stagnate and even decrease. Just as we demand that local Party branches be set up among the peasants in the countryside, we demand that local Party branches be set up among the workers.

The fascist martial rule cannot be used as the main reason for the slow growth of the Party. The strictures of this tyrannical rule has been more than compensated for by the deep-going hatred and growing resistance of the broad masses of the people. In no year has the enemy struck down more than five percent of the membership of the Party. The Party should be able to achieve a high rate of growth because it is small but composed mostly of cadres, if only we grasp the necessity and importance of mass members of the Party from the ranks of the workers and peasants.

The Manila-Rizal based national bureaus served positively from 1971 to 1973 not only as administrators of the city-based national mass organizations but also as schools for a considerable number of new Party recruits. In the first year of martial rule, it also served positively to direct the orderly retreat of the mass organizations suddenly forced to go underground. But in 1974, it became very clear that the national bureaus had outlived their purposes.

It is admitted that the period of one year after the first year of martial rule and before their dissolution in July 1974 constituted a big delay which unduly restricted the disposition of good cadres for various regional Party organizations eager and ready to get them.

It remains our policy to expand the Party boldly on the basis of the revolutionary movement and without letting in a single undesirable. We must follow the reasonable standards set by the Party constitution and we must increase the number of Party members who are of worker and peasant status. In this regard, we must keep in mind that we do not wish to be an exclusively cadre party.

We want a large mass of Party members who are of worker and peasant status because this is a measure of the effectiveness of our revolutionary work, because we want to accomplish gigantic tasks that mainly concern and involve them and because we want to counteract and dilute the negative influences that Party members coming from other classes are liable to bring into the Party.

The Party upholds democratic centralism as its basic organizational principle. This is centralized leadership based on democracy and democracy guided by centralized leadership. By this principle, we can stand and act united and well informed on any important matter. We must apply this principle consistently.

The committee system at every level of leadership, from the Central Committee down to the branch executive committee, is the most important tool of the principle of democratic centralism. The leading committee at a certain level is the point of concentration for an entire Party organization on that level and for lower organs and lower organizations; and within the collectivity of the committee democracy, is carried over from the lower ranks.

With so few Party members taking on large tasks, there is a tendency for a far fewer Party leaders to take on large tasks. When the Party leaders are often attending to large tasks in different places and have difficulties in often coming together, there is always the danger that single Party leaders decide matters that should be taken up in a committee.

Thus, there are conditions for the phenomenon of one-man monopoly of affairs to arise. Indeed it has arisen in the Party and we have been combating this for a long time. Until now, it persists because the conditions for it to keep on arising persist.

The standard organizational solution to this problem is to have a smaller standing committee more easily convened than the full and large committee to act and decide on matters under the guidance of standing policies. For instance, there is the Political Bureau of our Central Committee, then there is the Executive Committee and still there is the General Secretariat. There is the executive committee of the regional committee and then there is the secretariat.

It takes good judgment based on experience and full grasp of policies for a Party leader to make a prompt decision on an urgent matter. He could be like an army commander in an emergency military situation. But always as soon as possible he must submit his decision or action to a collective body.

Any Party leader can initiate or propose a draft or anything, though it is the chairman or the secretary who is expected to perform this leading role. But there must be some preparatory meeting in a smaller committee before presentation of matters before the plenary meeting of a larger committee. In this way, there is thoroughness in preparation and in the entire process of decision-making.

Bureaucratism is also an error contravening the spirit of democratic centralism. Our cadres should not limit themselves to merely receiving reports but they should go down for worthwhile periods of time to lower levels and to the grassroots to investigate for themselves the basis for policies, verify reports and study the correctness or incorrectness of policies.

Going down to the grassroots is good for the remolding of high and middle level Party cadres. We do not mean to say that they abandon their functions in the leading organs but for them to perform these better. And we do not mean that they dissipate their efforts in going around to many places. But they must go down to investigate typical or critical situations (whatever is the main problem that needs close attention) and link themselves closely with the masses.

The central leadership no less has undertaken certain special projects requiring special detachment of personnel, heavy fixed investments and special methods of work that are not assured of effective or sufficient support by the masses in the vicinity of operation. These should no longer be undertaken because these easily meet failure and unduly preoccupy the leadership with matters of secondary importance to a self-reliant revolutionary movement.

At lower levels of the Party, there have also been instances of business and other projects that tend to distract Party leaders from their fundamental tasks. If these projects are beneficial to the revolution, they should be undertaken by trustworthy personnel without wasting the time of Party leaders and without risking the resources of the Party which are much needed for other purposes.

All leaders and members of the Party must be diligent and thrifty. Every moment must be seized to advance the revolution. Every centavo must be spent wisely. Upon our diligence and thrift, we can fruitfully carry out the policy of self-reliance.

In this period of fascist martial rule, the Party must not only be vigilant but extra-vigilant. We must have contempt for the enemy strategically but we must take serious, meticulous account of him tactically. The fact that the Party has always been underground and involved in armed struggle since the very beginning shows that it has always been prepared and equipped to face the worst of eventualities. But there are vulnerabilities that we must be aware of so that we can guard against them.

In the cities, we must be aware that the open activists of legal progressive organizations before fascist martial rule have been used by the enemy as unwitting tracers of the Party underground. Many of these activists have been apprehended and some of them are proven or merely suspected Party members. We must apply the policy of shifting or reassigning those Party members who can no longer effectively work in their present urban assignment.

In the countryside, the Party members on the manhunt list of the enemy should adapt to the fluidity of our guerrilla activity. The risks are also high in the countryside because we have mere guerrilla squads and at the most guerrilla platoons. But certainly, here we can rely on mass support that is bigger over wider contiguous areas than in the cities. Party members who cannot work freely in the cities can work here far more freely.

In both cities and countryside, a number of comrades have sacrificed their lives and limbs or have fallen into the hands of the enemy and have suffered the most excruciating torture and the torment of incarceration. These include some members of the Central Committee and various regional Party committees.

We honor and emulate our martyrs and heroes. And we convey to our comrades in prison to steel themselves further while in prison and turn the prison into a school. We should learn from their experience. So long as our regional Party organizations keep on growing through revolutionary struggle, there is always a basis for cadres to come forward and replenish as well as reinforce the Central Committee and the regional Party committees.

Only so few among those who have fallen into the hands of the enemy have become traitors or betrayers. There are also those few who cannot stand the difficulties of the struggle and drop out or surrender themselves to the enemy. All these renegades are only a handful and do not make even two percent of those who have fallen into the hands of the enemy. We should learn from their negative examples.

The Party reflects the iniquitous society outside. Thus, there are errors and weaknesses. And there are the few who go overboard completely and become traitors. It is clear that within the Party the law of contradiction and the law of class struggle operate. But our Party members in general are certainly good. The Party stands united to further strengthen itself.

3. Build the Revolutionary Mass Movement in the Countryside!

We must build the revolutionary mass movement in the countryside; and we must build the basic mass organizations for the peasants, youth, women, children and cultural activists to be able to generate it. Not much can be accomplished in mobilizing the great masses if our propaganda teams and guerrilla squads limit their organizing to the barrio organizing committees and small local armed groups.

The key point in our rural mass work is to arouse and organize the peasant masses in the shortest possible time and carry out the land reform movement step by step. In the course of focusing attention on the organization of the peasant association in a typical farming barrio, the other basic mass organizations can also be organized. The peasant activists can easily move the youth, women, children and cultural activists of their own class to accomplish their self-organization.

The farm workers' association, the union of nonagricultural workers and fishermen's association are also basic mass organizations that should be organized wherever there is a basis. In cases where there are already mass organizations positively working for the people's interests, all that we do is to adopt them and transform them further into revolutionary organizations.

There is really no point in feeling sorry that there is a paucity of Party cadres to attend to rural mass work. A propaganda team or guerrilla squad can rely on the local mass activists and can cover so many barrios, even as many as twenty within six months. It is even possible for one, two or three experienced cadres from the outside to work initially with the local mass activists and cover several barrios within a relatively short period.

The local mass activists emerging at every stage of the process of developing the revolutionary mass movement are themselves prospects for recruitment into the Party. Through this process, new Party members keep on arising and local Party branches can be established.

We must rely on and trust the masses. So long as we grasp their interests, needs and demands through social investigation and close contact with them, we can arouse and guide them to set themselves into motion. They can very well organize and mobilize themselves along the correct path. There are always enough activists arising from their own ranks to firm up the revolutionary direction of their movement.

There must be a series of careful steps in organizing the people in a barrio, especially under the present harsh conditions of fascist martial rule. There are four of these steps which culminate in the full organization of the basic mass organizations.

The first step is to get reliable contact men or liaison men in a barrio that we wish to organize. The number of these can range from three to ten. Within the shortest possible time, we should form them into what we may call the barrio liaison group. This has been called the "barrio organizing group" in Central Luzon and the "organized group of contacts" in Southern Tagalog.

Usually, we can get the contact men in a barrio because of our preceding mass work in an adjoining barrio. This is advancing wave upon wave. It is inevitable that the people in one barrio have relatives and friends in the next barrio. Sometimes too, we can reach a barrio where work must be done and get the contact men or liaison men because a Party member, a Red fighter or activist or any reliable person has relatives or friends in that barrio.

Preliminary social investigation can be done on a barrio in a day or a few days, depending on the reliability and knowledgeability of our initial contact men. The shortcomings of some of these contact men can be made up for by further contacts. We must gather all the general and specific information we need to start political work in the barrio.

There is expediency in forming the barrio liaison group from out of the contact men that we initially come to know through reliable intermediaries. Although we try immediately to put the best available men in the group, it may not be possible all the time to get the best representatives of the people in the barrio. After all, it takes time to develop revolutionary activists. Sometimes, the contact men may all come from only one part of sitio of a barrio or from only one section of the barrio population.

But we must make sure that the members of the barrio liaison group are desirous of revolution, are elements of the exploited classes, are known to be honest and good people, have extensive relations in the barrio, are intelligent and resourceful and are conscientious in performing the tasks that we give them.

The functions of the barrio liaison group include assisting us in social investigation, conducting initial propaganda among the people, putting us in touch with the positive forces and elements in the barrio gradually and secretly, and making sure that we are secure in our entry into, stay in and exit from the barrio. All these functions involve the smoothening of our initial relations with the people in the barrio.

The barrio liaison group replaces the barrio organizing committee. Some similarities between the two are apparent. But there are basic differences between them.

The barrio liaison group is no longer empowered nor expected to act as an embryo of people's government in the barrio. Its members do not have the unwritten vested privilege to becoming automatically the chief moving force behind the mass organizations to be established. We depart from the old pernicious practice of giving initial contact men this privilege and therefore we remove or drastically reduce the condition for unreliable elements to creep into the mass organizations.

The group is also under strict advice not to expose themselves as the organizers of mass meetings. At the same time, we take care that it does not know more than it should about the actual widening and deepening of organizational and political work being done in the barrio. Of course, the members of the group receive political education from us and are tested through work and at least some of them can advance from being mere contact men. But the group as a whole does not enjoy any automatic privilege of knowing details beyond its liaison work.

The second step is for our guerrilla squad, propaganda team or cadres to move from one part of the barrio to another or fan out to several parts at one time to conduct deeper social investigation and carry out study meetings among the people, especially the poor peasants, farm workers and lower-middle peasants. We should do everything possible to link ourselves closely with the exploited masses.

Our mass work should bear fruit initially in the form of the people's organizing groups. These include the peasant organizing groups for the poor and lower-middle peasants, the youth organizing group, the women's organizing group and such other organizing groups that have a basis. These are based on a division of territory (sitios and parts of the barrio center if much larger than the sitio).

The organizing groups should be able to win the majority of people in their respective fields and initiate activists to arouse and mobilize them. At this point, local activists should start to arise inside and outside the organizing groups. The cadres of the Party should make sure through propaganda and study meetings on the national democratic revolution that politics takes command of all activities.

We must grasp the antifeudal class struggle as the key link of our rural mass work and we must uphold the poor peasants, farm workers and lower-middle peasants as the most reliable and resolute revolutionary force in a typical farming barrio. But we cannot go far in the antifeudal struggle if we fail to link it well with the antifascist and anti-imperialist struggle not only by way of providing the basic antifeudal forces with the most comprehensive political view but also by way of bringing into active play all other positive forces in the countryside for the revolutionary cause.

The third step can be taken soon after the establishment of the people's organizing group in all or most of the parts of the barrio. There is already a wide and deep basis for establishing the people's organizing committees on a barrio-wide scale.

We have already found out who is fit for what function within each committee. The basic functions to be apportioned are those that pertain to organization, education, economy, defense and health. The apportioning of functions should be settled well within the committee by the members upon our guidance. The committees should be capable of raising the enthusiasm of the majority of the people in their respective fields for the revolution and coming into coordination with struggles launched over areas that include several barrios.

Like the organizing groups based on the parts of the barrio, which must be retained as their support, the people's organizing committees should be an underground force. They must know how to cover their activities with whatever legal and traditional organizations there are in the barrio and must know how to dissemble, use revolutionary dual tactics, before the enemy or unreliable elements.

As early as the successful establishment of the peasant organizing committees over a large area in the countryside, even only some scores of barrios, it is possible to take such a simple and easy first step towards land reform as the reduction of land rent through the systematic withholding of a certain part of the crop without the landlords' knowledge. The campaign to reduce interest rates and eliminate usury; arrange fair prices with the merchants; promote savings, mutual aid and simple exchange of labor and nonpayment of debts under Masagana 99; raise production and productivity; and the like can be pushed.

In cases where the landlords have cunningly abandoned the old practice of sharecropping on the bases of the actual crop and resorted to the "leasehold" system (the system of high fixed land rent) promoted by the Marcos fascist dictatorship and by the Lava revisionist renegades, the tenant masses should deliver only a part of the rent and claim bad crop or some plausible reason for the nonpayment of the full rent. If all the peasants claim the same reason, the landlords will be at a loss; they cannot threaten so many with eviction and they might as well simply write into their records the undelivered part of the rent as "debts".

Harvest after harvest, the process of peaceably outmaneuvering the landlords can be done until they come to terms with the peasants. The landlords' threat to deprive the tenants of credit for subsistence or production will be rendered naught by the peasants' gains from land reform, their thrift, mutual aid and simple exchange of labor and alliance with the well-to-do peasants who come under persuasion not to engage in usury.

Any despotic landlord who abuses his tenants is liable to be punished by the people's army or secret groups of peasants. It would not pay for him to refuse to come to terms with the peasants. It would be difficult for his overseers and for scabs to show their faces before the peasant masses.

Depriving the landlord of a part of the land rent and demanding fair terms from merchants and moneylenders can be achieved only if the peasant masses are well organized, united and have a high level of political consciousness.

In a typical farming barrio, the majority of the population are poor and lower-middle peasants (most tenants belong to these strata). On this basis, the peasant organizing committee plus the other people's organizing committees can have their way through the barrio councils of the reactionary government. Using the tactics of the united front, peasant organizing committees can enhance their strength.

The peasant organizing committees can actually control the barangay councils or any legal organization for purposes of holding public meetings favorable to the peasant masses and for revolutionary dual tactics in the face of the enemy. In effect, they can function as the embryo of the people's governmental authority on their own strength, supplemented with cooperation of their allies who are often very much their own relatives and personal friends.

The fourth step in organizing the barrio people is to fully organize the basic mass organizations. It would seem as if the people's organizing committees and groups are a skeleton taking full flesh. All members are enlisted and they elect the leading committees of their respective mass organizations. The peasant association includes mainly the poor and middle peasants.

Of course, like the antecedent organizing committees, the basic mass organizations cannot be fully organized all at the same time, say in one day or one night. There is the law of uneven development and differences of conditions. But we must strive that in one definite period in a barrio or group of barrios, all the basic mass organizations are fully organized. This requires planning and consistent work.

The fascist enemy has been more alert to peasant associations and far more intolerant towards them than the other mass organizations. We must be flexible in adopting legal forms for the peasant associations. We must use different names for them in different barrios. In handling them for the revolutionary cause, we must be good at combining illegal and legal methods. There must be open legal activities and clandestine illegal activities.

We should be fully aware of our strength and we should not overstep it. It is understandable if, for considerable period of time in a given group of barrios, the antifeudal movement is capable only of effecting rent reduction and other agrarian reforms in the manner that we have described in discussing the third step.

While experience has shown that mass organizations other than the peasant association are less suspected and less subjected to evil measures by the enemy, we must take the same precautions that we take in having the peasant association. Whenever the enemy comes to know that a mass organization is led by the Party, it is liable to be subjected to the most vicious attacks.

Even when we are still at the second step of organizing the people in a barrio, we should start to carry out Marxist ideological instruction and recruit into the Party the most advanced elements among the mass activists so that by the time we reach the third or fourth step, we shall have been able to establish the local Party branch in the barrio, with a group in every sitio and major part of the barrio center. At the fourth step, we shall also have Party groups within the basic mass organizations.

Upon the establishment of the basic mass organizations and the local Party branch, it becomes possible to establish the barrio revolutionary committee as the organ of democratic political power. It shall simply be a matter of putting together the representatives of the Party, the basic masses and allied forces.

In our old areas where the barrio organizing committees are reliable and are of sound character, we should work as fast as possible for their dissolution by establishing the basic mass organizations, the local Party branch and the organ of democratic political power. We can speak of working fast here, at least faster than in new areas, because we have known the people and worked with them long enough.

When the basic mass organizations flourish, the revolutionary mass movement can make great strides. Revolutionary studies and propaganda become more widespread and vigorous than before. Land reform becomes firm. The able-bodied volunteers from every mass organization can be formed into the local militia and given military training and duties. The campaign for higher production becomes effective. Every mass organization has a special agricultural plot or cottage enterprise to support the revolution. Cultural activities blossom and raise the people's fighting spirit against the enemy. Health work is also attended to on a mass scale.

Under these circumstances, the foundation for greater military victories by the New People's Army is laid. The people's fighting spirit is ever rising. There is abundant material support for the revolutionary armed struggle because of land reform, higher production and special production. The local militia are a powerful reserve and auxiliary force of the people's army. The Party becomes well-rooted in the localities by taking into its ranks the most advanced local activists.

4. Further Strengthen the People's Army and Carry Forward the Revolutionary Armed Struggle!

We must further strengthen the New People's Army as the main form of organization under the leadership of the Party and carry forward the revolutionary armed struggle as the main form of our people's struggle. We have established a good basis for the further strengthening of the New People's Army.

Our Red fighters have a high level of political consciousness and are closely linked with the masses. Every squad has a Party group within it and oftentimes the majority of the Red fighters are Party members. The Party branch is at presently based on the platoon.

The people's army has grown in rifle strength from early 1969 to the eve of fascist martial rule and from the latter time to the present. What it is now in armed strength is a far cry from the 35 rifles and handguns that it started with. The people's army now has guerrilla forces in all regions outside Manila-Rizal and has a total of twenty guerrilla fronts.

Each regional army organization is led by a regional Party committee. The nationwide expansion of the people's army under the direction of the Central Committee is a far cry from its beginnings in the second district of Tarlac.

Our army has gained invaluable experience and has become tempered. It has undergone the acid test of massive and prolonged enemy campaigns. We recall Tarlac of 1969–71, Isabela of 1972–73, Sorsogon of 1974–75 and Aurora of 1975. At the peak of his campaigns, the enemy always employs a number of troops more than a hundred times bigger than ours, with the support of paramilitary forces, heavy weapons and the most modern means of communications and air and land transport.

Our heroic Red fighters and Party cadres together with the masses have overcome tremendous odds. Despite all the enemy campaigns, marked by the most wicked forms of "population control," the people's army has on the whole grown in armed strength. We have suffered some setbacks. There is not a single regional army organization which has not suffered serious setbacks at varying times. But the expansion, shifting and recoveries by our guerrilla forces have more than compensated for the losses.

Because of the nationwide expansion of the people's army, the enemy cannot concentrate his combat troops on one region without risking the advance of our forces in other regions. So far, he has not had the pleasure of inflicting a total or strategically decisive defeat on all our forces in any single region. Within a region, the existence of several guerrilla fronts tend to weaken the enemy campaign whether directed against all or any of these.

Despite all our achievements in building the people's army, our overall armed strength is still so small in comparison to that of the enemy who is several hundreds of times stronger. The course of historical development and the current balance of forces, particularly our level of armed strength, determine the mode of our warfare, which is guerrilla warfare.

There is no course for us but to grow in strength step by step. Our revolutionary armed struggle is just and enjoys abundant support from the people. So long as we adhere to a correct strategy and tactics, we shall grow from small and weak to big and strong. To repeat, we shall do so step by step.

Our people's war is protracted. It shall take a long period of time to change the balance of forces between us and the enemy. We must recognize further that at the back of the local reactionaries is U.S. imperialism. This superpower will keep on supplying and assisting them at the least. It regards the Philippines as an important base for maintaining itself as a Pacific power and as a position of strength in Asia.

The worldwide decline of U.S. imperialism, especially after its failed war of aggression in Indochina, is definitely favorable to our revolutionary armed struggle. But we must also recognize that U.S. imperialism is at the moment hardening its position in the Philippines precisely as a result of its defeats elsewhere and, for a long time to come, only a deep-going people's war can strike effectively at its foothold.

Friendly forces abroad cannot extend military assistance to us as much as we may need or wish. We must reconcile ourselves to the irony that when we need such assistance most it is most difficult for us to get it. The single imperialist power dominating the country is not yet an easy pushover in terms of the next few years. And his prior hold on our small archipelagic country is a serious factor to contend with.

We have to maintain a high degree of self-reliance in our people's war. We must rely on ourselves most certainly to a degree higher than many revolutionary armed movements abroad. There is no course for us but to always raise our determination to get all that we need for the armed struggle from our people and from the enemy himself in the battlefield.

Our strategic line in our people's war is to encircle the cities from the countryside until such time that we become capable of moving on the cities from stable revolutionary bases in the countryside. For a long time, we have to develop guerrilla warfare on a nationwide scale so as to convert into our advantage the disadvantage of fighting in a small archipelagic country, whose countryside is so vast in relation to the cities but fragmented into so many islands.

We are at the stage of the strategic defensive and we are precisely at its early substage of developing guerrilla warfare from almost nothing. From almost nothing because of the revisionist line of the Lavas and Tarucs that threw away all previous revolutionary gains of the people.

We have only to look at how much armed strength we have in each of the eight regions outside Manila-Rizal to know the magnitude of hard work that we have to do to further increase our squads and platoons. Again it shall take another magnitude of hard work to advance from the present phase of squads and platoons.

In the whole country or in an entire region, we are on the strategic defensive in the face of the large enemy forces encircling us. But we are capable of tactical offensives. In parts and parts of the countryside, we can achieve local superiority. At a given moment and in a limited area, we can put a small enemy unit in the tightest bag and crush it.

We must launch tactical offensives as the most essential content of our strategic defense. We simply refuse to engage our small forces in any strategically decisive engagement with the far larger forces of the enemy. Not in any region or guerrilla front should this happen. Knowing that large forces of the enemy is divisible, as everything is from a Marxist viewpoint, we must take the initiative of maneuvering the enemy to divide his forces and then concentrating our small forces at only that part of the enemy which we are sure of wiping out at a given place and time.

We should accumulate the small victories from our ambushes and raids. Over a period of time, such victories should give birth to more guerrilla squads and platoons. Then our capacity to destroy the enemy will increase. The highest mark of initiative in our guerrilla warfare is annihilating the enemy and capturing his weapons. We should not waste our precious limited ammunition and we should plan well the disposition and intensity of our lines of fire on a given target. There is no point in killing enemy troops if it is not in the course of depriving them of the weapons which they would refuse to yield.

We must learn well the rudimentary tactics of guerrilla warfare. We disperse to do propaganda and organizational work among the masses. We concentrate a superior force to destroy the enemy. We shift or circle round to avoid a superior enemy force, learn more about it through the masses and through our own reconnaissance and move to an advantageous position politically and militarily.

We can apply our guerrilla tactics well only if we have the wide and deep organized support of the people and we have eliminated the enemy informers and bad elements who are incorrigible. With the organized masses screening out the enemy, rendering him blind and deaf, we can foil his attempt to concentrate his forces on our small forces. Even when he is still preparing to attack us, we can learn through the masses his strength and movements and as a result we can act appropriately.

When the enemy is on some short-term offensive and wants to move in on us in superior force, we must deprive him of a target and we let him punch the air and thereby exhaust himself. We can remain on the active side either by laying an ambush on a weak part of the enemy disposition, attacking the enemy in an entirely different area or simply going elsewhere to do mass work. We should never accept or undertake any battle that we are not sure of winning. We may not be able to smash an enemy offensive but certainly we can frustrate it.

In all our experience, it is the massive and prolonged army campaigns, marked by forced mass evacuation and all kinds of barbarities, that have been our most outstanding problem in the battlefield. The enemy has launched such campaigns in areas where we are relatively strong over a wide area. At the early stage of such enemy campaigns, when enemy control is not yet tight, we must make him pay as much of a heavy price as we can exact from him, without prejudice to the prompt shifting of our main guerrilla forces to an alternative guerrilla front or area.

Enemy campaigns, whether short-term or protracted, are very costly to the enemy. That is why the military budget of the fascist dictatorship keeps on rising. Repeatedly frustrating them and depriving them of a target will undermine the resources of the reactionary government and also undermine the morale of enemy troops who also suffer some deprivations for nothing.

There is nothing wrong about shifting when faced with enemy forces ten or a hundred times stronger. This is neither accepting defeat nor flightism. This is preserving our forces to destroy the enemy another day. The areas that adjoin or are a short leap from the area being encircled by the enemy and under his heavy concentration are also fertile soil for revolution. Besides, we can always recover any "lost" area after sometime.

So as not to be merely forced to shift to an uncertain destination by an enemy campaign, we should be prepared long beforehand for such an enemy campaign by developing alternate guerrilla fronts and by deploying propaganda teams in areas where guerrilla warfare is to be developed from scratch or is to arise upon the shifting of guerrilla forces from elsewhere.

The unpopulated forest areas are good passageways and offer good points for schooling and temporary retreats. But to simply wait out a massive and prolonged enemy campaign of about one year to two years in the forests is to fall for the siege tactics of the enemy. It is also artificial to bring a considerable number of unarmed masses with you in this kind of retreat. Movement will be hampered. Food will soon run out and isolated kaingins are easily detected by the enemy.

When the masses are being forced to evacuate, legal mass struggle should be launched to oppose and stop the evacuation. Even when the forced mass evacuation is already done these legal mass struggles can go on for the restitution of damage to their crops and homes, for better treatment and rationing at evacuation centers and for their early return to their evacuated homes.

Some of the masses or selected families can also be directed by us to shift mainly on their own and by different ways to the area where we are shifting. There are many of those who might have relatives and friends there. Or there are public lands there which they can open like other people do.

Whenever the time comes for us to recover an area previously abandoned by us and then abandoned by the enemy, we must disarm the "home defense units" left by the enemy and increase the weaponry of the people's army. We must clean up those who have blood debts And we must be alert for spies planted in the midst of the masses.

We have insisted that for a start in every region we must develop our guerrilla fronts on favorable terrain, that is to say, forested, mountainous and hilly terrain with population. It is in this kind of terrain where enemy rule and influence are usually weak and where we can establish our guerrilla bases within the shortest possible time at this stage. Here we not only have a wide area for maneuver but also easily achieve depth in our maneuvers. Here we can best apply the tactics of "luring in" the enemy. He can not come in without first exposing himself and alerting us. It would be easy for us to be on the look-out and prepare for his coming.

We have also directed that for a start in a region, two or three guerrilla fronts on such a terrain should be established. We have been concerned with the possible dissipation of our limited Party cadres and resources by a previous current that we should have a guerrilla force in every province. But any regional Party organization can have more than two or three guerrilla fronts, whenever development and conditions permit.

While we must take advantage of the most favorable terrain for our guerrilla warfare, we must strive to move forward from the mountain to the plains and coordinate the revolutionary forces in the mountains and in the plains as well as those in the barrios and in the towns. In dealing with the islands, we should attend to the major islands first and then the minor ones.

This early, we must also pay attention to the coastal areas. This is important inasmuch as we are an archipelagic country.

Conditions are not yet ripe for having a well-known central revolutionary base, where the Central Committee of the Party and the general headquarters the New People's Army are seated. We should keep the enemy guessing and ignorant where our principal leaders are in the countryside. But certainly at this stage, we should be firmly taking the steps towards creating such a base in the best possible location.

The emergence of the central revolutionary base presupposes the achievement of a higher stage in our people's war and takes into consideration the development of nationwide guerrilla warfare and international developments involving U.S. imperialism. We still have a long road to traverse in this regard. Of all the regional Party and army organizations, the most directly concerned in bringing about the conditions for the emergence of the central revolutionary base are Northwest Luzon, Northeast Luzon and Central Luzon.

It remains the long-term strategic task of the revolutionary forces of Luzon to destroy the main forces of the enemy. The day is certain to come when the forces from the north and south of Luzon will converge on Manila-Rizal in a general offensive. It also remains the long-term strategic task of the revolutionary forces of Mindanao and the Visayas to draw the forces of the enemy and disperse them. At certain times, the bulk of enemy forces can be drawn to Mindanao. The area for maneuver for us here is as wide as that in the three regions north of Manila-Rizal, and the people's army can either take advantage of or coordinate its efforts with the resistance of the Bangsa Moro Army, if integration of the latter is not possible.

We have repeatedly pointed to the present low level of armed strength of the New People's Army. To amplify this strength, we must give full play to the participation of the people in the revolutionary armed struggle. We should not limit this participation to merely providing for the material needs of the full-time Red fighters and watching out for the enemy.

We must give political-military training to as many able-bodied men and women from the mass organizations and from time to time get the required number of volunteers from them to participate in well-planned military actions where their inferior weapons can blend with more advanced weapons of the full-time Red fighters. In the hands of so many people inferior weapons can prove to be superior and yet we make sure that at the core of such weapons as bolos, spears, bows and arrows and homemade explosives are good guns.

When the people's combative spirit is kept high by continuous political education and military training, they will make do with any weapon and will use every trick and ruse to disarm the enemy even with bare hands. The most important thing is the people's revolutionary determination and wisdom. In the future, popular uprisings or insurrections will arise over extensive areas.

5. Build the Revolutionary Mass Movement in the Cities!

We must build the revolutionary mass movement in the cities by developing the trade unions, the community organizations, school organizations and others and engaging them in a broad democratic movement that is distinctly antifascist and anti-imperialist, a movement sympathetic to and supportive of the distinctly antifeudal movement in the countryside.

We must pay principal attention to the masses of workers and other urban poor. We must get the workers mainly through their workplace and trade unions and also through the communities, where they are linked with the other urban poor. We must also pay attention to the urban petty bourgeoisie, especially the student masses and their teachers.

In undertaking an open democratic movement in the cities, we can invoke the very laws of the reactionary state which contain hypocritical terms and reform concessions just to enable us to go into the midst of the masses. Among the masses, we can create a revolutionary underground and transform legal organizations or build new ones that can militantly yet legally carry forward the national-democratic line step by step.

Combining legal and illegal methods, we can develop the revolutionary mass movement in the cities. Our main tactic is to turn the table against the enemy or to use another metaphor, to take the enemy's fortress from within by stratagem (but preparations for this are protracted and cannot be separated from the progress of the revolutionary armed struggle in the countryside).

The open and legal democratic mass movement cannot be firm, vigorous and well-directed without the illegal Party at the core. The Party as an underground force must be the backbone of this movement. It must be the guide, nurturing the movement at every step and seeing to it that the next step is taken upon the ripening of conditions for it.

As in the countryside, there is nothing discouraging about the smallness of the Party amidst the large masses in the cities. So long as the mass movement develops, activists emerge and make themselves available for recruitment into the Party. Thus, the Party is strengthened to achieve more and assume greater tasks.

It is only through a reinvigorated mass movement that we can raise the new forces to tackle the new situation created by fascist martial rule. There is no other way to solve such problems as the constrictions and unhealthy conspiratorial tendencies of a narrow underground and the enemy's cunning in looking out for the Party by merely tailing known activists of days before martial rule.

In this time of severe economic crisis, the masses of workers are stirring and pushing forward their economic struggle. We must get into this economic struggle and raise it to the level of the political struggle so that the entire working class will not only be able to fight most effectively for its own interests but also link itself fully with the rest of the people in the powerful flow of the people's democratic revolution.

There are immediate conditions and issues which make easy the transformation of the economic struggle into a political struggle. As previously pointed out, the wage and living conditions of the workers are extremely pushed down and benefits put into law by virtue of several decades of workers' struggle have been drastically reduced by the fascist dictator. And to top these all, the workers are prohibited from exercising their right to strike in most enterprises just because they are categorized as "vital industries" and "export industries" by the fascist dictatorship. In the main, these are enterprises owned by U.S. and other monopoly capitalists and by the big comprador bourgeoisie and big landlords.

Whenever the employer gets wind of a plan among the workers to make a mass petition for the improvement of their conditions, the easiest thing for him to do is to make "preventive suspensions" and to call on the troops and police to show up and bully the workers. Of course, when the strike, slow-down, sit-down or any mass protest action is already on, the armed minions of fascism show up to make arrests and make all sound and fury about "subversives", "economic sabotage" and "national discipline".

The masses of workers have experienced the right to strike in times far better than the present. Their present experience of intensified oppression and exploitation is extremely intolerable to them. Thus, no amount of fascist intimidation has deterred them from mass protest actions. These have already developed into concerted strikes and street demonstrations.

We must promote the strike movement and must make it so widespread and so intense to demonstrate to the entire nation and people that the fascist ruling clique and big bourgeoisie are so puny and weak and so rotten to the core. We must promote the economic strikes and transform them into political strikes and political demonstrations. We must hit the big bourgeoisie (and foreign monopoly capitalists and the comprador big bourgeoisie) the hardest. The rate of exploitation is highest in their enterprises.

We are presently at the stage of making the economic strikes more widespread. Even at this stage, the political dimension of such strikes is already coming to the force. We must make solid preparations to bring great multitudes of workers to the streets and plazas for political demonstrations.

In the face of fascist martial rule yellow labor leaders have become more discredited than ever. The top labor aristocrats of the country have blatantly placed themselves in the payroll of the fascist dictatorship under the so-called Trade Union Congress of the Philippines. Others have been so cowed and discouraged by anti-union restrictions that they have turned to other occupations.

The trade union movement has become more than ever a fertile ground for the revolutionary work of the Party. The masses of workers are already aware that when the Party is in their midst their economic struggle becomes resolute and militant and they become equipped with a profound political understanding of their situation and with a wide range of tactics.

Our propaganda has had some effects. Normally, it should outstrip our organizational work. But our propaganda and prestige have too far outstripped what solid results there should be for our organizational work. We should solve the problem not by reducing our propaganda. On the other hand, we should ceaselessly increase and amplify it. We should intensify not only our written propaganda of a general character but also all forms of verbal and nonverbal agitation suited to the most specific conditions. But we must harvest the crop of propaganda and agitation.

We must conduct organizational work among the workers more vigorously than ever before in conjunction with our propaganda and agitation. Since long before the fascist rule, the Party has devised the workers' organizing committee as an underground force for organizational expansion among the workers. But learning from experience in the countryside, specifically in connection with organizing a trade union where there is none yet, we do not immediately form this committee from out of those workers whom we meet at the beginning.

We can go through a process akin to that in organizing the present masses. First step is to organize as a matter of expediency the workers' liaison group from out of those workers with whom we can have relations at the beginning. Second step is for members of this secret group to introduce to us more workers, coming from every major part of an enterprise, so that we can form a secret organizing group in every major part of that enterprise.

Third step is for us to draw representatives or the best elements from the organizing groups to form the workers' organizing committee. At every step, we must deepen our social investigation and provide political education and appropriate instructions to the workers that we come into contact with and organize.

The workers' organizing committee retains the organizing groups as its subsidiaries and improves their composition whenever necessary. By the time that the committee is established, it shall have been ready to draw up the list of workers' demands to which the majority of the workers are to be won over before the employers and his agents get wind of it. It takes only one, two or three capable Party cadres to work with the committee.

The workers' organizing committee can be formed ahead of the workers' organizing group only in cases where we are certain right away that reliable and capable members are on hand at the beginning at least for honest trade union work. Such cases occur whether the objective is to form a trade union where there is none, to transform an already existing one or to put up one trade union against a thoroughly discredited one.

In any case, the workers' organizing committee and its organizing groups are a good means for giving way to the emergence of worker activists within them and outside them. The process of winning over the majority of workers to a list of union demands, creating the militant unity necessary to pursue such demands and developing the political consciousness of the worker masses are conditions for the emergence of a considerable number of worker activists.

Even only at the stage of the workers' organizing committee and organizing groups, our Party cadres should draw into the Party the advanced elements from the ranks of worker activists. Those who are through with the mass course on the trade union work and the national-democratic revolution can be immediately introduced to Marxism, their very own class ideology to which they are very receptive.

The ideological, political and organizational work of the Party branch and the groups under it in the enterprise is the best guarantee that revolutionary politics is in command of trade union work. The Party branch forms and directs the Party groups embedded in the leadership of the trade union.

The workers' organizing committee and its organizing groups are dissolvable upon the establishment of the Party branch and groups within the enterprise and the absorption of all the worker activists into the structure of the trade union. The organizing groups can be converted into group stewards and certainly a number of their members can qualify to be members of the Party groups. More and more workers can be put into study circles organized by the Party.

It is necessary for some of our Party cadres to draw salaries and allowances from trade unions so as to devote their full time to trade union and political work. But Party members should not monopolize the high posts in the trade union, and the members of the secretariat of the Party branch should not necessarily become the highest leaders of the trade union. We must allow the democratic broadness of the trade union; there can be good union leaders who cannot yet comply with the requirements of Party membership. And moreover, we do not want to let the enemy cripple the Party branch by simply clamping down on the trade union or its open leadership.

In further consideration of tactics in the face of the fascist enemy, trade unions under the effective leadership of the Party should not be replaced under only one chosen legal labor federation. This is to prevent the enemy from singling out one nest for attack. Our trade unions can variably be independent or members of various labor federations. We must determine the best possible status of each trade union.

The Party secretly links and coordinates all our trade unions. Our "independent" unions can retain more income from membership dues and are somewhat saved from control by the reactionary trade union leaders. But when members of different labor federations, our unions have the advantage of enjoying close relations with other unions which the Party can gradually get into.

The Party branch in an enterprise should see to it that Party members and other worker activists, with the help of the mass of their workers, do systematic revolutionary work in the communities. We must expand the workers' revolutionary movement by promoting contacts among workers of various enterprises not only within labor federations, along industrial lines or through factory areas but also through the communities.

In communities, workers from all kinds of enterprises reside. The workers already organized and politicized by us can form secret study circles and work closely in community work with other workers. The result is that the latter will bring us to so many more enterprises. Our Party cadres should take firm hold of this possibility for expansion.

In community work, we must rely mainly on the masses of workers and other urban poor. They compose the majority of the people in most communities in the cities. If we place the focus on them in establishing the community organizing committees and either transforming the previously established mass organizations where they predominate or building new mass organizations, especially where there are none yet, it becomes relatively easy to strike roots in the community and reach the youth, women and other sections of the community.

We must consign to a secondary position the old pattern of sending youth activists, mainly student activists, into urban poor communities and then letting them deal mainly with the youth in the community. We must advance from that situation before fascist martial rule in which there were more youth and student youth organizations than workers' organizations under our direction. We do not wish to diminish youth organizing and discourage activists from schools from participating in local community work. But we wish to give full play to the workers' role not only in trade union affairs but also in community affairs.

The community organizing committee can be immediately formed when we rely on workers or a combination of workers and youth who are themselves residents of the community and have proven to be good activists elsewhere. Of course, we assume that they are led by Party cadres. Then, community organizing groups can be formed to cover the various parts of the community.

The community organizing committee should continuously conduct social investigation and expand its contacts to be able to do well its work at every step. Since there are mass organizations existing prior to our organizational work, the community organizing committee can draw activists from these to form the community organizing groups. These organizations usually include the neighborhood associations, youth clubs, women's associations, squatters' organizations, athletic clubs, groups of professionals, civic clubs, regionalist or provincial groups and the like.

The advantage in drawing activists from already existing organizations is that they are closely related to the people in the community and that we can cover effectively not only the parts of the community but also the already existing mass organizations. Though we can form new mass organizations with different names in different communities, there is a decided advantage, especially under conditions of fascist martial rule, to make use of the legality of already existing mass organizations and engage the soonest in activities by which we can go deep among the masses and gradually raise their political consciousness.

Because we rely mainly on the masses of workers and other urban poor and we take up their majority interests, it is not too difficult to transform certain already existing mass organizations. We develop a Party group within each of them and make political advances step by step. On this basis, we can maneuver or overwhelm even the "barangay councils" or "kabataang barangay" and other reactionary organs or institutions into becoming forums or channels for our revolutionary propaganda.

At every stage of the work of the community organizing committee and its organizing groups, we can draw into the Party the most advanced elements from the ranks of the revolutionary activists. In due time, the community organizing committee and its organizing groups can be dissolved because a Party branch has been established in the community and in the legal mass organizations. Mass work and Party work can so advance in the communities that the Party branch will be based eventually on the street.

It is a matter of course that the Party should be vigilant and look after its security all the time and everywhere, especially in the cities where enemy control and surveillance are tighter than in the countryside. But the Party should pay special attention to securing itself from infiltration by antisocial lumpen-proletarian elements though this be covered by our political work.

The urban petty bourgeoisie is a social stratum whose members are usually self-centered and dispersed. But their children are concentrated in universities and high schools and here they are receptive to revolutionary propaganda. The schools therefore merit the conscientious attention of the Party. These are next in importance to the factories and the urban poor communities.

The student masses and their teachers are an important force in bringing the intelligentsia and the entire urban petty bourgeoisie to the side of the revolution. They are the section of the urban petty bourgeoisie which has the most revolutionary potential. This fact has been proven repeatedly in our history; and the first quarter storm of 1970 and succeeding developments prove it. Students continue to join today's workers' struggles.

Quite a number of students and their teachers have gone so far as to strive remolding their outlook, engage deeply in revolutionary work and join the Party. Other students do not go as far but they accept the general line of the Party and spread this to the ranks of the petty producers and the professionals. The revolutionary fervor of the student masses could be such that even some children of the exploiting classes who are their schoolmates become attracted to the revolutionary movement.

In the course of community work, the owners of small stores and shops, professionals and white-collar employees are reached by our propaganda. Though they can render some service to the revolutionary movement, they are not as important as the student masses and teachers who are concentrated in great numbers in schools, are very capable of propaganda work and mass actions and are willing to coordinate their activities with the masses of workers.

The national-democratic organizations of the youth before fascist martial rule have done a great service to the revolutionary cause. Their work has been so fruitful in some schools and communities that there are now Party branches continuing revolutionary underground work here.

In schools where there are yet no Party branch and no Party-led mass organization, Party cadres should establish school organizing committees and organizing groups to develop the initial activists from among the students, teachers and other school personnel, push for the establishment of genuine student governments and publications, promote revolutionary ideas in old student organizations or build new ones as means of promoting such ideas and help develop unions among teachers and other school personnel.

Student activists developed by the school organizing committee and organizing groups should be directed to create as many secret study circles as they can among friends and classmates; and teacher activists should do likewise among co-employees, students and friends. The efficacy of their ideological and propaganda work should in due time result in political mass actions.

The student masses, teachers and other school personnel should link the issues on the campus with the deteriorating conditions of society in general. The progressive students of the University of the Philippines are showing the way to fight the Marcos fascist dictatorship, how to oppose antinational, antidemocratic policies and actions. They have started to make mass protests of their own and join those of the workers.

Even only at the stage of the school organizing committee and organizing groups, we can start to draw into the Party the most advanced elements from the ranks of the school activists. Eventually the Party branch should emerge in the school, and Party groups in the various parts of the school as well as in the mass organizations there. In large universities, it is possible for a section committee of the Party to lead so many Party branches that are based on the colleges.

We should continue carrying out the policy of deploying student activists for social investigation and mass work in factories and communities accessible to them. We should promote the closest links between the worker and student activists in the cities so that concerted mass actions of the worker masses and student masses will become possible.

The development of the democratic movement in Manila-Rizal and other urban areas constitutes powerful political support to the revolutionary struggle in the countryside. The people in the entire country become aroused and the enemy is shaken within his fortress.

The people in the cities should realize that the long-term development of the underground there and the steady growth of political mass actions and a preparation for the final day of reckoning for the ruling system, when their general uprising will come into coordination with the general offensive of the people's army. The Party should promote this revolutionary thinking and dispel notions that the people's army should now send its small but growing forces to the cities for some spectacular actions.

There are other kinds of support from the cities for the revolutionary struggle in the countryside. The Party organization in the cities can systematically dispatch cadres who still have legal status or who no longer have this to the countryside. Cadres of worker status or of student background can be sent to their native areas or where they are most needed. Funds, medicine, military equipment, medical equipment, communications equipment, clothes, revolutionary publications and other useful materials can also be collected and sent.

It is inevitable at the moment for our communication to pass through certain cities. For instance, communications between the Visayas and Mindanao on the one hand and the central leadership of the Party cannot bypass Manila-Rizal. There should be a reliable corps of couriers who can travel legally between the cities and the countryside and from one region to another.

There should be coordination between the revolutionary struggle in the cities and that in the countryside on so many things. The Party is the coordinator and should have special organs to attend to the requirements of coordination.

6. Realize a Broad Antifascist, Antifeudal and Anti-Imperialist United Front!

We must realize a broad antifascist, antifeudal and anti-imperialist united front under the leadership of the working class through its political party. As earlier pointed out, the foundation of this united front policy is the basic alliance of the working class and the peasantry.

Upon this foundation, we win over the urban petty bourgeoisie principally and the national bourgeoisie secondarily as additional allies. At the same time, we note well and take advantage of the splits among the reactionaries — the comprador big bourgeoisie and landlords who are now divided between the pro-Marcos and anti-Marcos sides.

The toiling masses of workers and peasants compose the overwhelming majority of the national population and, being the most oppressed and exploited, they are the most interested in a comprehensive antifascist, antifeudal and anti-imperialist movement. They constitute the main force of the united front. Only with such a force can we implement the policy of uniting the many to oppose the few and isolate and destroy the enemy.

Going deep among the workers and also among the peasants, the Party links and coordinates both classes for a united revolutionary struggle. At the stage of the national-democratic revolution, when armed struggle is the main form of struggle, it is of the highest importance that the Party in representation of the working class must do painstaking mass work among the peasants and build a peasant army.

It does not suffice to say that the peasantry is the closest and most reliable ally of the working class. Further analysis is required for the concrete application of the united front in the countryside. The peasantry is divided into three strata with various political attitudes on the basis of their economic status.

We must develop the antifeudal united front in the countryside. We must rely mainly on the poor peasants, win over the middle peasants and neutralize the rich peasants to oppose the evil landlord gentry. When we speak of the peasantry as the closest ally of the working class, we refer essentially to the poor peasants and middle peasants.

The barrio organizing committee was originally conceived as an organ of expansion and as the embryo of local people's government along the line of the united front. Now that we are laying it aside, it does not mean that we are dispensing with united front work in the barrios. We simply want to strengthen the poor peasants and lower-middle peasants together in their own mass organization and not simply mix them up with the rich peasants and other unstable elements in a committee.

Carrying out the united front policy and employing its tactics, we must deal properly with all those entities outside the peasant movement. We must step by step win over the entirety of the middle peasants into the association, we must deal with them properly as individuals or groups and still try to gain some support and cooperation from them.

The rich peasants are not so much interested in the antifeudal movement. But they resent the economic crisis, the arbitrariness of the fascist dictatorship and the increasing taxes and have some patriotic feelings. When the revolutionary peasant movement is strong and the people's army is around, they are quite a hospitable lot and may even offer to join the peasant association. It is upon the rise of reaction that their reactionary aspect comes to the fore.

There are usually traditional and legal organizations where peasants of all strata are mixed up. We cannot summarily ban or ignore these. We must study these carefully and apply the united front policy to make them truly beneficial to the poor and lower-middle peasants or helpful to the revolutionary struggle.

There are such associations or groupings as the elders' councils, the usually informal mutual aid and labor exchange groups, irrigation associations, farm workers' groups, cooperatives, youth clubs, athletic teams, carpenters' groups, the parents-teachers association, 4H club, women's club, religious sects and so on and so forth.

Even such tools of the reactionary government as the barrio or "barangay council", "kabataang barangay", "samahang nayon" and at certain times the rural police, ronda or "home defense"' unit may be neutralized, transformed or broken up, depending on the circumstances. The names of these associations can often be used for revolutionary dual tactics specifically for covering up what is revolutionary.

In the countryside, there are many other kinds of possible allies. There are the teachers and other professionals, the small and middle merchants and entrepreneurs, certain relatively big businessmen and some enlightened landlords. The teachers and professionals are good medium for spreading propaganda in the towns. Doctors and nurses can give much-needed medical services and medicine. The businessmen and enlightened landlords pay taxes or give contributions and sometimes provide facilities to us.

When conditions are ripe, we must establish the organ of democratic political power along the line of the united front. We have already pointed out that the full establishment of the basic mass organizations in the barrio is the precondition for the establishment of the barrio revolutionary committee. In the period before the establishment of the barrio revolutionary committee, the functions of local self-government can be performed with the peasant organizing committee or the leading committee of the fully-organized peasant association hewing to the Party's united front policy. In the cities, we must continue the policy of winning the support of the student masses and their teachers by way of reaching and winning over the entire urban petty bourgeoisie. Upon the success of this policy, we can also win over the national bourgeoisie as they become aware that a strong anti-imperialist movement is advocating independence and national industrialization.

Elements of the national bourgeoisie in areas within the jurisdiction of the people's army have extended support to us. In the cities, there are also members of the national bourgeoisie who have extended support to us, especially through the student and youth movement.

In the principal conservative and reactionary organizations in the country, best exemplified by the political parties like the now dormant Nacionalista and Liberal parties, the urban petty bourgeoisie and the national bourgeoisie have been mere tails of the ruling classes — the comprador big bourgeoisie and the landlord class.

This is true even in professional and civic organizations at the municipal, provincial and national levels. In the chambers of commerce and industry, the national bourgeoisie are also reduced to being mere tails of the big bourgeoisie and big landlords. We must form groups within these associations to consolidate the ranks of the national bourgeoisie and promote the national and democratic line.

The Preparatory Commission of the National Democratic Front and the regional united front commissions have projected and broadcast our united front policy; have succeeded in winning over groups and personalities who take the stand of the urban petty bourgeoisie and the national bourgeoisie and have established progressive underground groups, called national-democratic cells, within the most reactionary institutions and organizations. Some of these groups have helped us reach the basic classes that would otherwise be difficult to reach.

The aforesaid commissions have the special task of winning over the middle forces to the revolutionary cause and bringing to the main organization of the Party concrete assistance in reaching the basic forces of the revolution. Legal mass organizations and mass activities of a national-democratic character should be well undertaken. Close attention must be paid to this urgent task.

The door continues to be open widely for cooperation with those who are against the Marcos fascist dictatorship who may vary in degree of anti-imperialism and antifeudalism. We must unite with them but we must maintain our independence and initiative and we struggle with them on just grounds and with restraint all for the purpose of winning the hearts and minds of the people and advancing the revolutionary struggle.

The Lava revisionist renegades have long excluded themselves from the united front. By surrendering to the Marcos fascist dictatorship and actively participating in vicious counterrevolutionary actions, this handful of revisionist fascist criminals have become totally discredited even in the few small areas which they once boasted of as their bailiwicks. The Manglapus group, fancying itself as the "social democratic party", has also excluded itself from the united front by being no more than a tool of the Central Intelligence Agency.

As it is now taking shape, the main split among the reactionaries is between the Marcos fascist gang and an alliance ostensibly led by Macapagal. Though Marcos has a sizable number of agents within the interim national assembly and has limited its authority, especially under fascist martial rule, he refuses to convene it and intends to explicitly abolish it because he is afraid that it would become a forum for popular opposition.

Aware of Marcos' scheme, especially with Imelda already emerging as second-in-command and successor, Macapagal has called on the officers of the reactionary armed forces to make a countercoup and rule for a short period to pave the way for the convening of the interim national assembly. Obviously, he has already gotten the assurance of U.S. imperialism that he can openly lead the opposition loyal to the ruling system. The pushing out of certain inside men of the C.I.A. from Marcos ranks bears watching.

U.S. imperialism intends to be aggrandized, whichever direction events may take in the struggle between the Marcos and Macapagal factions. This single dominant power in the country wants two dogs to compete for the same reactionary purposes. The only difference there is from reactionary competitions before martial rule is the increasingly conspicuous role of the reactionary armed forces.

Under the circumstances, with both reactionary factions competing for the good graces of U.S. imperialism, it is clear that we become more determined to carry forward the national-democratic line against fascism, feudalism and imperialism and carry out the armed struggle relentlessly. As revolutionaries, we do not want to get bogged down in debates whether the Marcos constitution or the 1935 constitution is to be promoted. The point is to fight well the Marcos fascist dictatorship and the forces behind it and in the process carry the revolution forward.

A coup d'etat led by reactionary military officers can be as bad as or worse than the present Marcos fascist dictatorship even if it promises to pave the way for the interim national assembly. However, there is also the possibility that the coup d'etat will bring to power a civilian faction and really allows it to reverse Marcos' fascist excesses. We must be prepared for every possibility.

We must always remember that our united front work is in support of the revolutionary armed struggle. We must have reliable and long-term allies and we must also have unreliable and short-term allies. The most important thing is that we have allies to be able to reach, arouse, organize and mobilize the millions upon millions of people who are under various influences for the revolutionary cause.

7. Relate the Philippine Revolution to the World Revolution!

We must relate the Philippine revolution to the world revolution. We are proletarian internationalists. We are carrying out the Philippine revolution to contribute our own share in the struggle of the world proletariat and the entire mankind to defeat imperialism and bring about the dawn of communism.

We recognize at the same time all anti-imperialist struggles and advances of the revolution in other countries redound to the benefit of the Philippine revolution and favor its advance. These bring about conditions favorable to our revolutionary efforts. We receive powerful political support and boundless inspiration. We learn invaluable lessons. We see in the victorious national-democratic revolutions and socialist revolutions abroad our bright future.

The astounding revolutionary victories of the Indochinese peoples of Vietnam, Cambodia and Laos have signaled the irreversible decline of U.S. imperialism in Southeast Asia, in the whole of Asia, in the whole world and in its very homegrounds. We are enthusiastic that the peoples of small countries can deal so stunning a blow to U.S. imperialism and make so great a contribution to the world revolution.

The stable outposts of anti-imperialism in Southeast Asia have arisen and have raised the banner of socialist revolution and socialist construction. In all unliberated countries in the region, the people are more than ever determined to carry out revolutionary armed struggle against U.S. imperialism and its lackeys.

We are witness today to the abandonment of the ignominious Southeast Asia Treaty Organization, an outrightly U.S. military instrument, and a retreat into the Association of Southeast Asian Nations. This latter organization no longer flaunts the aggressive power of U.S. imperialism and even denies being an instrument of this superpower. But it admits openly that the three main concerns of its reactionary member governments are to suppress "insurgencies"; promote "peace, freedom and neutrality" and develop "regional economic cooperation". We must not fail to recognize that the main and essential character of the ASEAN is counterrevolutionary even as we observe that this organization reflects a certain trend that is merely the result of the crisis of the world capitalist system, the U.S. imperialist debacle in Indochina and the crisis plaguing each unliberated Southeast Asian country. Such a trend should remind us the more of our responsibilities as revolutionaries.

In our vicinity are the people of China surging forward in their socialist revolution and socialist construction and standing firmly against the two superpowers. The Korean people are engaged also in socialist revolution and socialist construction in the north and are facing up to U.S. imperialism and its lackeys in the south.

Far and wide, the revolution is rapidly advancing. The people of Asia, Africa and Latin America continue to wage powerful revolutionary movements against imperialism, colonialism and hegemonism. In all other continents, including the homegrounds of U.S. imperialism and Soviet social-imperialism, the people are engaged in revolutionary struggles. Revolution is still the main trend in the world today and Marxist-Leninist parties are steadily forging ahead.

The world revolution is advancing under conditions of intensifying superpower contention, grave crisis of the world capitalist system and the rise of the third world people and countries as the main force of the world anti-imperialist struggle. All basic contradictions are sharpening and all the ingredients of both revolution and war are achurning.

Despite their off-and-on "peace" and "detente" duets to lull the people of the world, the two superpowers are engaged in an ever-intensifying rivalry for world hegemony and are feverishly making arms expansion and war preparations. They are trying to push each other out and gain an advantage everywhere. It is clear that their imperialist rivalry is the source of the danger of war.

Though the two superpowers are over-extending themselves all over the world, Europe is their main bone of contention. Their clashing interests are most concentrated here. War is likely to start here. Troubles are now increasingly erupting here and in its vicinity. Should war break out in that part of the world, the beasts can finish off or weaken each other while we push forward the revolution in our country and in our region.

But while war does not yet break out in Europe, Soviet social-imperialism is trying to penetrate even such a country like the Philippines which U.S. imperialism considers a permanent preserve in this part of the world. Soviet social-imperialism calculates that it must make diplomatic and trade inroads to weaken U.S. imperialism in as many places as possible and push hard its new-tsarist ambitions of world hegemony.

U.S. imperialist domination in the Philippines can be removed only by a powerful revolutionary movement. But the Soviet social-imperialists nurture the illusion that someday their long-discredited local agents, the Lava revisionist renegades, will be able to do turns for them and commit far more treachery and mischief than they presently can as shameless tools of the Marcos fascist dictatorship. Even now, within their narrow circles, the Lava revisionist renegades do not tire of talking about getting more help from their imperialist master to do more mischief.

The reason is clear why Soviet social-imperialism even as enemy of U.S. imperialism cannot be our friend in any way. While we must oppose U.S. imperialism, we must be alert to Soviet social-imperialism and frustrate its scheme. We are well past the early sixties when Soviet modern revisionism could still deceive well-intentioned people.

The present crisis of the world capitalist system has been the worst since the end of World War II and continues to deepen and worsen. The inherent law of motion of capitalism, bringing about a crisis of overproduction; the monopolistic competition among capitalist countries, especially the leading imperialist powers; and the reduction of economic territory by revolutions and by the assertion of independence by hard-pressed countries have spelled the present world capitalist crisis.

The imperialists shift the burden of crisis to those whom they can. They do so through accelerated rates of profits on direct investments, usurious loans and unequal trade. The people resist. Even a reactionary government like that of the Philippines, while determined to remain a puppet of U.S. imperialism, has to maneuver for its own sake.

The third world countries have increasingly asserted their independence and demanded a new international economic order in the face of the world capitalist crisis and superpower machinations. Underlying the phenomenon of even reactionary governments posing to assert the independence of their countries is the growth of the revolutionary movement and at the same time the concern of the reactionary leaders that they must lessen or palliate the crisis that threatens them.

It must be made clear to the people that the Marcos fascist dictatorship has broadened the diplomatic and trade relations of the Philippines out of desperation and weakness even as it still clings to U.S. imperialism as its imperialist master. The circumstances in the emergence of better Philippine relations with the Middle East countries and China are clear.

As the fascist dictator claims credit for promoting the U.S. line of "interdependence" in the third world, we must criticize and condemn him for acting as an inveterate agent of U.S. imperialism within the third world and for putting a brake on the most meaningful participation of the Philippines in the anti-imperialist struggle of the third world. We must make our own projection of the demands of the third world in the terms especially of its revolutionary people.

The facts show that under the Marcos fascist dictatorship the economic stranglehold of U.S. imperialism on the Philippines has become tighter. Because of the Marcos constitution and the fascist decrees giving more privileges to foreign investors, there is practically no more need for any new economic treaty replacing the Laurel-Langley Agreement.

The fascist dictator has always asserted that U.S. imperialism should keep its military bases in the Philippines, provide a "nuclear umbrella" and guard the skies and seas. Negotiations on the US-RP military treaties have been an old ritual repeatedly resorted to in a futile attempt to deflect the people's anti-imperialist struggle.

The only new thing in current negotiations on such treaties is that the Marcos fascist dictatorship wants some rent on the vast tracts of land occupied by the U.S. military bases, relinquishment of some small sections of the land for Marcos' real estate speculation and assurances of more U.S. financial and military assistance. The question of sovereignty over the U.S. military bases has long been resolved; the point has always been to assert such sovereignty by deeds.

We must strive to have the Philippine revolution enjoy not only the political support of friendly forces abroad but also concrete assistance from them. U.S. imperialism has not stopped but has even stepped up the giving of congressional and extra-congressional military and other kinds of assistance to the Marcos fascist dictatorship.

Remaining a puppet of U.S. imperialism, the Marcos fascist dictatorship misappropriates such terms as "self-reliance" and "nonalignment" in the same fashion that he domestically misappropriates such a term as "democratic revolution" for the fascist counterrevolution. Snatching terms from the revolutionary movement is an old trick of the fascist thief. But reality speaks louder.

Unlike the reactionaries, we stand on the basic principles of independence and self-reliance. Foreign assistance should only be supplementary to our independent and self-reliant efforts. Even without any foreign assistance, we should be able to fight on and advance step by step. As already pointed out, practically everything that we need can come from the people and from the battlefield.

We should be able to draw support and assistance from as many foreign friends as possible, short of falling into any trap set by the U.S. imperialists and the Soviet social-imperialists. We appreciate most the kind of assistance that enhances self-reliance, our armed struggle and our propaganda.

Aside from developing the closest and most fruitful relations with the Marxist-Leninist parties and other revolutionary organizations, we should pay attention to our own Filipino compatriots abroad. Associations of our compatriots should extend every possible kind of support to the revolutionary struggle in their motherland and should win the widest possible support from their host people.

The half-a-million Filipinos in the United States have a very important role gathering support for the Philippine revolution not only from their own ranks but also from the American people. U.S. intervention and the possibility of another U.S. war of aggression in the Philippines must be effectively opposed with the support of the American people.

Overseas Filipinos are found in various parts of the world. Wherever they are, they should do what they can to help their people and should prepare themselves to join the ranks of the revolutionaries in the motherland. We assume that the most progressive among them study Marxism-Leninism and take appropriate interest in the revolutionary struggles in their host countries.

The conditions in the world which now favor the advance of the Philippine revolution are bound to become more excellent. The future for all revolutionary people is bright. That of the imperialists and the reactionaries is bleak.

Reaffirm our Basic Principles

Armando Liwanag
Chairman
CPP (Central Committee)
December 26, 1991

On the 23rd anniversary of the reestablishment of the Communist Party of the Philippines, let us reaffirm our basic principles and resolve to carry the revolutionary struggle of our people forward.

As set forth in the documents of the reestablishment of the Party, the basic principles are the following: adherence to the theory of Marxism-Leninism, repudiation of modern revisionism, the class analysis of Philippine society as semicolonial and semifeudal, the general line of the national democratic revolution, the theory of people's war and strategic line of encircling the cities from the countryside, the united front along the revolutionary class line, democratic centralism, the socialist perspective and proletarian internationalism.

We celebrate today the achievements of the Party under the guidance of the foregoing principles. We base ourselves upon these achievements in order to advance. At the same time, we face up to problems and solve them. In the course of doing so, we further temper and strengthen ourselves.

The overwhelming majority of our Party cadres and members are determined to follow the revolutionary principles and line set by the Party at its reestablishment. The entire Party is resolved to solve and overcome not only those problems posed by U.S. imperialism and the domestic ruling system and the enemy campaigns of suppression but also those problems due to major deviations and errors which we must identify, evaluate, criticize and rectify.

The enemy tries and expects to weaken and destroy the Party and the revolutionary movement in 1992 and 1993. But he will continue to fail and fail even more dismally as we further build upon the accumulated achievements of the Party, rectify errors and deviations, expand and consolidate our mass base and strengthen the Party and other revolutionary forces in an all-round way.

Under the leadership of our Party, the proletariat and the broad masses of the people are determined to throw off the yoke of oppression and exploitation; and fight to achieve national liberation and democracy against U.S. and Japanese imperialism and the local exploiting classes of big compradors and landlords.

The crisis of the domestic ruling system continues to worsen and provides the fertile ground for the armed revolution. The world capitalist system is in an ever deeper crisis and in increasing turbulence, notwithstanding the triumphalist U.S. claim of a new world order.

I. Further Strengthen the Party in an All-round Way

We must strengthen the Party ideologically, politically and organizationally. We cannot do so without taking stock of our strengths and weaknesses. We must assess and evaluate all these, identifying and understanding what are the major accomplishments and problems. Only then can we set forth our tasks correctly.

We must rectify the deviations and errors which violate our basic principles and negate the hard work, struggle and sacrifices of our Party, the people and the revolutionary martyrs. The central leadership of the Party is taking the initiative of carrying out a comprehensive and deepgoing rectification movement.

Study Marxist-Leninist Theory and Combat Subjectivism!

The Party has succeeded in integrating the universal theory of Marxism-Leninism with the concrete practice of the Philippine revolution. It has clarified Philippine history, the semicolonial and semifeudal character of Philippine society, the new-democratic stage of the Philippine revolution, the leading class, all the motive forces and adversaries, the strategy and tactics of people's war, the main tasks and socialist perspective of the Philippine revolution.

By clarifying these, the Party has been able to provide the theoretical and political guidance to the revolutionary movement as never done before in Philippine history. The revolutionary movement of the people has won victories surpassing those of the old democratic revolution and all attempts to resume the Philippine revolution before 1968.

The documents of the Party's reestablishment and subsequent basic documents of the Party are the study materials for the basic level of Party education. Further, there are the distinctive content and study materials of the intermediate and advanced levels of Party education.

The intermediate level studies more thoroughly than the basic level our own revolutionary experience, compares it with and draws lessons from the most significant and most relevant experiences abroad in terms of building the Party, the people's army and the united front in the new democratic revolution. This entails the evaluation of the revolutionary experience of our Party and that of others and gives due recognition to the significance and relevance of the Chinese, Vietnamese, Korean, Cuban and other revolutions to the Philippine revolution.

The advanced level provides the Party members with a comprehensive and profound knowledge of materialist philosophy, historical materialism, political economy, scientific socialism and the world revolution as taught by such great communist thinkers and leaders as Marx, Engels, Lenin, Stalin, Mao and Ho. This provides us with the most extensive and deepgoing understanding of the basic principles of the proletarian revolution and proletarian dictatorship.

All Party members are enjoined to engage in theoretical study not only through formal courses but also in the course of revolutionary mass struggle and in the course of Party life in leading organs and in basic units and to strive to raise their collective experience and practical knowledge to the level of theory. They must ceaselessly develop their Marxist-Leninist stand, viewpoint and method.

Since the late 1970s, however, there has been a gross neglect of theoretical education and a gross inadequacy of study courses and materials. Worse, there has been a departure from a structure of theoretical education that is based on our revolutionary experience, that is suitable to our situation and revolutionary struggle and that properly takes into account the significance and relevance of the advances of Marxist-Leninist theory and practice abroad.

We must be able to evaluate the significance and relevance or applicability of the teachings of all the great communist thinkers and leaders. We must know how the teachings can shed light on our conditions and struggle. We must know the historic conditions from which the teachings have arisen. We must not take any successful foreign revolution or any segment of it out of the concrete context of its own national history as well as of world history.

The works of one great communist thinker should not be dogmatically used to squeeze out those of another, especially if the works of the latter which are more relevant in terms of historical and social conditions and can shed more direct light on the Philippine revolution. Lesser figures of revolutions that do not reach the socialist stage should not be evaluated more highly than any great communist thinker in an eclectic or dogmatic manner.

The basic writings of our Party, which are based on the analysis of our own concrete circumstances and our revolutionary experience, should never be laid aside nor depreciated in the desire to copy some recent model that is believed to be the easy way to victory, without full consideration of the history and conditions of such a model. We must not fly away from the actual conditions and level of the development of our own revolutionary struggle by pursuing any foreign model, be it a complete revolutionary process or a mere part of it.

There has been the subjectivist wish of certain elements to hasten the Philippine revolutionary process and bring it abruptly far beyond its actual level of development. They focus on and take out of historical context such dramatic events as the Bolsheviks' Petrograd and Moscow uprisings of 1917, the Vietnamese uprising of 1945 or Tet offensive of 1968 and the Sandinista's final offensive of 1979 in Nicaragua. These examples are counterposed to the entire theory of people's war and to the entire process of developing people's war in stages and the strategic line of encircling the cities from the countryside.

The mere wish for achieving total victory and a share of political power in the offing, unwarranted by the existing strength of the revolutionary movement and the objective conditions, is passed off as "new theory" and has been turned into a reason for reorienting and rearranging the revolutionary forces for armed urban insurrection, the premature formation of larger but unsustainable military units as well as topheavy staffing in both urban and rural areas. In areas where this "new strategy" has been carried out, mass work is neglected and the enemy gains ground in forcing the revolutionary forces into a purely military situation.

The basic principles and basic line of our Party have been put under question or denigrated by elements who have a narrow, one-sided and fragmented view of things and processes in the country and abroad and who have not really studied both Marxist-Leninist theory and the history and conditions of our own revolutionary movement in a comprehensive and deepgoing way. Because of their failure to understand our own revolutionary experience, they do not even realize that they are actually seeking to resurrect and combine both the Sakdalista concept of insurrection of the 1930s and the Jose Lava adventurism of the 1950s.

The erroneous thinking that power can be seized or shared with the bourgeoisie, regardless of the actual strength of the people's army, by rousing and riding on the spontaneous masses has to be immediately cited because it has attacked the basic principles and line of the Party most systematically; and it has wrought the gravest damage _ unprecedented in the history of our Party and the ongoing revolutionary movement.

Since its reestablishment, the Party has been committed to a cogent antirevisionist line as a result of the study of the

Lavaite errors and the modern revisionism promoted by the Communist Party of the Soviet Union on a world scale since 1956. The Party has never abandoned its Marxist-Leninist line. No leading or staff organ can overturn the decision of a Party Congress. The basic antirevisionist line in the basic documents of the Party's reestablishment has never been erased, notwithstanding any previous current of thought among some elements that the revolutionary struggle would either stagnate or retrogress without the foreign assistance of Brezhnev and his successors.

The critical antirevisionist line of the Party is proven correct and vindicated by the disintegration and collapse of the revisionist ruling parties and regimes in the Soviet Union and Eastern Europe. There, capitalism and bourgeois class dictatorship have been blatantly restored after more than three decades of peaceful evolution (degeneration) from socialism to capitalism.

Gorbachov has the historical distinction of presiding over and carrying out the final stage of the destructive career of modern revisionism in the Soviet Union and Eastern Europe. The initial stage was that of Khrushchov who laid the foundation of modern revisionism by spouting bourgeois populism and pacifism and carrying out capitalist-oriented reforms in the economy. The middle and longest stage was that of Brezhnev who recentralized the bureaucracy and resources for the benefit of the new bourgeoisie as well as for the arms race and further promoted the so-called economic reforms of his predecessor.

The disintegration of the Soviet Union and collapse of the revisionist ruling cliques and regimes mean the total discredit of modern revisionism as well as that of its consequence _ undisguised capitalism _ that continues to wreak havoc on the lives of the peoples in these countries. Contrary to the mocking propaganda claim of our enemy, it is not our Party which is embarrassed and orphaned by the fall of the revisionist ruling parties and regimes. It is the Lava revisionist group and its successors.

As far as the Party is concerned, Marxism-Leninism stands brilliantly as the proven correct guide in the new democratic revolution and in the future socialist transformation in our country. The new challenge in theoretical work is the further development of the theory of continuing the revolution, combating modern revisionism and preventing the restoration of capitalism in socialist society and resuming the revolution where modern revisionism has prevailed or has already passed on to blatant capitalism in the anticommunist and antisocialist counter-revolution.

Mao Zedong started theoretical and practical work on the problem of modern revisionism. The failure of the proletarian cultural revolution, after some years of success, has not invalidated the theory of continuing proletarian revolution in the same way that the failure of the Paris Commune of 1871, after a fleeting success, never invalidated the theory of proletarian revolution. Persevere in People's War and Build the Mass Base!

There is no doubt whatsoever that under the oppressive and exploitative conditions of the semicolonial and semifeudal system the Filipino people have no choice but to engage in the new-democratic revolution under the leadership of the working class through its advanced detachment, the Party.

The people in their millions have been aroused, organized and mobilized by the Party as never before in Philippine history, in accordance with the general line of new democratic revolution. Through the revolutionary armed struggle and the united front, the Party has been able to lead the broad masses of the people in their millions.

By building the NPA and waging people's war, the Party has been able to arouse, organize and mobilize the largest oppressed class in Philippine society, forge the basic alliance of the working class and peasantry and answer the central question of the revolution.

There are now scores of guerrilla fronts in the countryside in the overwhelming majority of Philippine provinces. Here the mass base is being expanded and consolidated. Organs of political power are not simply being built above the heads of the local people but mass organizations of workers, peasants, fishermen, women, youth, cultural workers and others are being formed to realize the most active and strongest participation of the people in the armed struggle and all types of mass campaigns for their benefit.

The key campaign is land reform. What is generally being carried out is the minimum program of rent reduction, control of interest rates, improvement of the wages of farm workers, better prices of farm products and raising production through rudimentary forms of cooperation, improved agricultural techniques and sideline occupation. Land confiscation is carried out against despotic landlords and restitution of land to the rightful owners is carried out in cases of landgrabbing.

Let us continue to remind ourselves that our people's war is a revolutionary political mass movement within the framework of the new democratic revolution and that it integrates the armed struggle, land reform and building the mass base along the antifeudal line. This is being restated in view of a gross misrepresentation that the waging of people's war and the building of the people's army is mainly or primarily a military process.

The NPA has been able to preserve and strengthen itself through guerrilla warfare. The Party spreads the people's army like a fisherman's net to do mass work and draws it in to concentrate a force in order to wipe out the enemy forces piece by piece by surprise. If they are to fight effectively and self-reliantly and accumulate strength in the long term, the NPA guerrilla forces must rely on an ever expanding and consolidated mass base in view of the vastly superior military strength of the enemy.

At the present stage of the development of the people's war, it is wrong to absolutely concentrate any company or battalion within the short radius of one, two or three villages or in a forest camp when it is not on an offensive mode or on training exercise. If such units are not spread out to conduct mass work, they become bogged down with problems of their own maintenance and other internal problems, they become isolated from a dwindling mass base and end up fighting less and less and becoming more and more vulnerable to enemy encirclement and attacks.

There has been a gross deviation from the line of developing the people's war and the people's army in stages and of building the foundation of victory through painstaking mass work. This deviation has caused setbacks through a process of self-constriction and has inflicted unprecedentedly heavy losses in the strength of the Party and the people's army and gross reductions of our mass base. It has caused a reversal of what the Party has always been proud of: namely, when the enemy pours in his brigades and battalions on a particular area the revolutionary forces can flexibly fight back and grow in strength by leaps and bounds in so many other areas.

For nearly ten years, there has been the erroneous line of thought in certain parts of our Party that victory can be achieved sooner without so much the necessity of painstaking mass work and solid organizing by rapidly forming companies and battalions in absolute concentration and combining their offensive actions with urban uprisings of the spontaneous masses, the urban mass organizations and the armed city partisans. The armed urban uprisings, according to them, are the "highest form of struggle" that the movement is supposed to achieve. What is wrong and self-destructive about this deviation is that it argues against the necessity of developing the people's army in stages by encircling the cities from the countryside, disregards the current stage of the development of the revolutionary forces and in the name of "regularization" draws away cadres and resources from mass work and concentrates them into urban-based staff and staff of military units.

This erroneous current of thought and action has brought about the gravest setbacks and destruction to the Party and the revolutionary movement, first in one major island and subsequently on a nationwide scale. It has brought about the lopsided distribution of cadres and resources, the costly building of urban-based staff organs and topheavy military staff (which are vulnerable to the enemy), gross reductions of the mass base, the eventual isolation and passivity of the prematurely enlarged and unsustainable armed units, defeats and demoralization in a purely military situation and finally a wild surge of panic like the anti-informer hysteria.

This erroneous trend falls into the enemy's line of creating a purely military situation that allows him to effectively use his vastly superior military forces in his strategic offensive (war of quick decision) and blockhouse warfare (gradual constriction) in the countryside. The urban-based leading or staff organs which are supposed to coordinate and combine the urban and rural forces for the armed urban insurrection are also vulnerable to surveillance and punitive actions by the enemy, especially because many of the cadres are on the enemy manhunt list and can be easily identified.

In the exercise of its absolute leadership, the Party must in the first place decide the line and the strategy and tactics, and deploy cadres and resources correctly. No staff organ should be allowed to take away initiative from the comprehensive leadership of the Party in this regard.

The guerrilla forces of the New People's Army must develop under the principle of centralized leadership (especially ideological and political) and decentralized operations. They must create more guerrilla fronts and conduct guerrilla warfare on all types of terrain in order to effect extensive and intensive guerrilla warfare. They must be able to maintain initiative and flexibility and skilfully use the tactics of dispersal, concentration and shifting.

When the enemy concentrates his forces, he can grab a certain territory but in the process gives away more space to the guerrilla forces. When he disperses his forces, the dispersed parts become more vulnerable to guerrilla attacks. When he keeps on shifting his forces, he also opens his parts to attacks by the guerrilla forces. He cannot carry out the same war of fluid movement conducted by the people's army because he does not enjoy the popular support that the guerrilla forces have.

What spells victory for the NPA is the extensive and deepgoing mass participation and support, which keeps the enemy deaf and blind despite his superior military forces and war materiel. The people's army ceases to be what it ought to be when it concedes the people to the special operations teams, the paramilitary forces and other organizational devices of the enemy and fails to deploy the armed propaganda teams, local guerrilla forces and militia as well as to build the organs of political power and the mass organizations.

We must cast away illusions that we can capture and keep the cities without breaking the military backbone of the enemy in the countryside. The NPA must keep to the strategic line of encircling the cities from the countryside. And even in parts of the countryside where there are big and well fortified enemy camps which we cannot as yet raid and capture, we can wipe out part by part the small units that go out of such camps so long as we can encircle them with an extensive and powerful mass base.

We are on the strategic defensive. But we can launch the tactical offensives that we are capable of winning. We can carry out this strategy and tactics only by availing of the widest room for maneuver in the countryside and by constantly expanding and consolidating the mass base. We should not imagine that the U.S. and the local exploiting classes are easy pushovers in our country. We should ensure that we have the capacity to seize power and hold it when in the future we decide to take their citadel.

Build and Broaden the Revolutionary United Front!

The party has amplified its strength and expanded its influence by building the united front. The purpose of this united front is to broaden the support for and strengthen the revolutionary armed struggle and the legal democratic movement.

The revolutionary united front cannot exist without the leadership of the working class through the Party and without the basic alliance of the working class and the peasantry as the foundation. The Party branches, the people's army, the peasants' and workers' organizations, and the organs of political power built at the village level are the organized forms of the basic alliance of the working class and the peasantry.

The National Democratic Front has been essentially the underground united front organization of the basic revolutionary forces (i.e., those of the working class, peasantry and urban petty bourgeoisie) under the leadership of the working class through the Party. It is a united front for armed struggle and it serves to pave the way for the establishment of organs of political power, especially at levels higher than that of the village.

There have been proposals and attempts to erase the working class leadership and the leading role of the Party in the united front, to subordinate the Party to a specific formation of the united front and deny the independence and initiative of the Party and its allies and to negate the socialist perspective of the ongoing national democratic revolution.

Rather than try to attract more cooperating organizations within its fold by erasing the class leadership of the working class and the historical initiative of the Party in its formation and by diluting its new democratic program and socialist perspective, the NDF should maintain its character as the most advanced and most consolidated underground united front organization of the basic revolutionary forces under working class leadership and stay committed to the two stages of the Philippine revolution.

It must build its array of underground cooperating organizations, form conferential leading committees of representatives of such organizations and then proceed to invite worthy personalities from various organizations and trends to join the leading committees and commissions at various levels. Rather than have a federation, which subordinates the Party to the united front and runs counter to the principle of independence and initiative in the united front and which puts the Party and the NDF leadership on a potential collision course, the relations of cooperating organizations within the NDF framework should be consultative and consensual as should be the case in a united front.

In the legal democratic movement, there are sectoral and multisectoral alliances which take a patriotic and progressive stand on issues. These include mostly organizations of workers, peasants and the urban petty bourgeois. They have been effective in raising the political consciousness of the broad masses of the people in the entire country.

The national bourgeoisie is one of the positive forces, which include the basic revolutionary forces. But this stratum in the Philippines has a dual character; it has a progressive aspect being progressive as well as a reactionary aspect and it is weak and vacillating, especially because it does not own basic industries in the specific case of the Philippines. It has articulate spokesmen but no strong organization of its own.

The members of this stratum are in certain businessmen's organizations together with the big compradors and the representatives of multinational firms. However, the national bourgeoisie cooperate with the revolutionary movement in areas where it is strong or when progressive political currents are strong as during the antifascist and anti-imperialist struggle against the U.S.-Marcos regime in 1983–86.

The concept and reality of the united front can extend to a formal or informal alliance of the revolutionary forces with sections of the reactionary classes. We have had extensive experience in dealing with local officials of the reactionary government and enlightened landlords and businessmen who comply with the laws of the people's government on land reform, wages, business, taxation and so on. They have also cooperated with us in mass actions, elections and other events. In the 1983–86 antifascist movement, anti-Marcos reactionaries at all levels allied themselves with us, especially before they could secure full U.S. support.

To take advantage of the splits among the reactionaries is to be able to isolate and defeat the most reactionary faction at a given time. The policy of the Party is to fight and defeat one reactionary faction after another and in the process strengthen the revolutionary movement.

When we have reactionary allies, we must describe them as such to the Party rank and file and explain to them that these are unstable and unreliable allies so that there can be no confusion. We must neither lump them together with the petty bourgeoisie and the middle bourgeoisie under the category of "bourgeois reformists" nor describe any big comprador-landlord political party or regime as "liberal democratic". Errors have occurred in this regard.

The legal democratic movement based in the urban areas is of indispensable and great importance. As a matter of fact, this movement through its pronouncements and mass actions reaches and inspires people beyond those that the Party, the NPA and the NDF can reach directly at any given time. When we describe the legal form of struggle as secondary to the armed form of struggle, we are clearly addressing the question of smashing the bureaucratic and military machinery of the reactionary state and seizing political power. In this connection, the legal and defensive character of the democratic mass movement in the urban areas must be respected and must not be prejudiced. We should not give the reactionaries the excuse to smash it.

The organizations of the toiling masses of workers and peasants and the middle social strata are of great importance. We can wage all forms of legal struggle effectively if, in the first place, there is solid mass organizing at the basic level. Through the mass organizations, it is possible to mobilize more people and launch all kinds of democratic action in their places of work, communities, in halls, in the streets and in the premises of official structures or offices of the reactionary government.

We can build Party units within all kinds of legal organizations, including the reactionary organizations and institutions. Without being publicly known as such, these Party units can utilize the legal processes to promote patriotic and progressive ideas and forces. But bourgeois elections, particularly those previously staged by the Marcos fascist regime in 1978 and 1986, have been the occasions for heated debates on whether to "participate" in them or "boycott" them. In this regard, the question properly is: Can the Party utilize the process through Party cadres who are not publicly known as such and allies who take a patriotic and progressive stand?

Regarding these elections, the Party can correctly call them farces as a whole and in essence. At the same time, the Party undertakes measures to use these to promote the national democratic line and encourage progressive parties and candidates. This is in the exercise of revolutionary dual tactics to counter the counterrevolutionary dual tactics of the enemy.

The boycott error of 1986 was a major sectarian error separating the advanced section of the masses from the middle and backward sections of the antifascist mass movement and imposing the Party's puristic will on the legal progressive mass organizations for the duration of the electoral campaign period of December 1985 to February 7, 1986. The boycott decision of 1978, which practically remained unimplemented, was another major error insofar as it led to developments divisive among cadres and damaging to the Party organization.

Principal cadres of the national capital region refused to carry out the decision and were subjected to disciplinary measures. Worse, the Manila-Rizal regional and district Party committees were not properly reorganized and practically went into shambles. The upsurge of the urban mass movement, which was possible from 1978 onward, could not be realized until the 1983–86 period.

There are honest elements who criticize the errors of the Party involving electoral exercises staged by the reactionaries. But there are other elements who have overdrawn the boycott error of 1986 in order to promote a line of urban armed insurrection that is opposed to or subordinates the entire people's war to armed urban insurrection and to cover up the far more disastrous consequences of this erroneous line, which started to become clear in 1984 and extremely devastating from 1985 onward in one major island.

With regard to the forthcoming bourgeois elections, the Party describes them as farcical on the whole and in essence because these are controlled and monopolized by the political parties and agents of the exploiting classes. At the same time, we encourage and favor the most patriotic and progressive candidates in accordance with the revolutionary united front. We require all political parties and candidates to get safe conduct passes from the revolutionary forces before they can go into any area controlled by the revolutionary forces.

Since 1986, the question of peace negotiations has assumed a significance unseen in previous years of the Party. We have to learn lessons from the preceasefire talks and ceasefire agreement in 1986 and 1987. To this date, the enemy has clearly shown by his framework and actions that he wants the revolutionary forces to capitulate to his rule, his constitution and his armed forces; to split the revolutionary movement; and to surveil and attack the movement.

The NDF have clearly stated its willingness to negotiate with the reactionary government at the national bilateral level and in a proper venue abroad; and has presented the framework and strategic line for a just and lasting peace. These conform to the people's demand for national liberation and democracy. The refusal of the enemy to negotiate with the NDF can only mean that the revolutionary forces need to fight harder and win more victories in order to change the balance of forces. The question of peace talks should not be allowed to undermine our revolutionary will to fight.

The duly-authorized representatives of the NDF have repeatedly met abroad in Europe and Hongkong with officials of the Manila government on an informal and preliminary basis regarding the question of peace talks since 1990. But Aquino has so far failed to formally reply to the September 20, 1990 letter of the NDF national chairman offering a new round of bilateral peace talks, with the U.N. secretary general as an intermediary.

Since 1991, the European Parliament in a resolution has called for peace negotiations between the NDF and the Manila government and the Swiss government has offered to both sides its good offices and Geneva as venue for the peace talks. But the reactionary government has been intransigent. It has also repeatedly frustrated the urgings of peace advocates in the Philippines and abroad for the start of a peace process.

All revolutionary forces at all levels have correctly and strongly rebuffed the calls of the Aquino regime and the reactionary armed forces for localized dialogues, localized ceasefires and localized surrenders, with revolutionary statements and actions. They have called on the local officials of the reactionary government and military and police forces to surrender to the revolutionary movement or to make a common front against the regime seated in Manila. Uphold Democratic Centralism and Revive Basic Party Life!

The Party is a nationwide organization and is deeply rooted among the toiling masses. It has a few tens of thousands of members and thousands of cadres. It is supported by a far greater number of mass activists in the organizations of workers, peasants, women, youth, professionals and so on.

The organizational principle of the Party is democratic centralism. This means centralized leadership based on democracy and democracy guided by centralized leadership. There is a body of basic revolutionary principles to which all Party members must adhere. And there are the basic conditions and processes by which decisions and discussions are made democratically within the Party structure. These are thoroughly made clear in the Party Constitution.

A correct style of work is also demanded of all Party members. This involves adhering to the principle and practice of democratic centralism, belonging to a basic Party unit and performing basic tasks and functions, being closely linked with the masses and making criticism and self-criticism in order to improve work, rectify errors and strengthen the unity of the Party.

The overwhelming majority of Party members are dedicated and hardworking. But there are certain problems which we have to face up to in order to stop any trend of decreasing or stagnating Party membership anywhere so that we can perform the gigantic tasks in the revolution.

If there is any erroneous line that has resulted in the reduction of our mass base, we must do away with that line. Without an expanding mass base, we have nothing to consolidate and we become unfit to lead the revolution. A key point in consolidation is the recruitment of the advanced elements in the mass movement to the Party within the period of candidature made clear by the Party Constitution.

We have to increase our Party membership and strengthen basic Party life ideologically, politically and organizationally. We must build the Party branches and groups at the grassroots level in both urban and rural areas.

It is wrong to concentrate the majority of our Party cadres and members in urban-based staff organs, in Party groups above the grassroots level (even if these are in mass organizations) and in topheavy military staff organs in the countryside. The so-called regularization is bureaucratization which prevents a huge number of our Party cadres and members from doing mass work and having a basic Party life at the grassroots level.

Overnight we can further strengthen the Party and the mass movement in the local communities if we redeploy the Party cadres and members in the staff organs and let them attend to basic work at the grassroots level. Every Party member must belong to a basic Party branch. No Party cadre of whatever rank is exempt from membership in a basic Party unit. This is clear in the Party Constitution.

We must also stop the practice of recruiting advanced elements in the mass movement only to employ them as staffers and not developing them to become fullfledged Party members within the period of candidature set by the Constitution.

The source and base of bureaucratism is the accumulation of Party cadres and members in higher staff organs and their alienation from mass work and basic Party life at the grassroots level. Lower organs and basic units are depleted of Party cadres. And then the wrong attitude arises that no one in these lower organs or units can represent them in higher organs. Thus, there is the phenomenon of the one-person layer of authority, the "political officer" abolished in 1986 but persisting as the appointive "secretary" who acts as a top-down representative of the higher organ to the lower organ and whose best argument is either the supposed command from above or his interpretation of the decision of the higher organ.

The most dangerous, most costly and most absurd situation has arisen, with the basing and proliferation of staff organs in urban areas, the concentration of cadres in these staff organs and the mixing and frequent contacts of cadres who are in the enemy's manhunt list with surveilled former political detainees and with legal personalities of the legal mass movement (who are themselves the subject of enemy surveillance).

The illusion that the staff organs have to be "positioned" in the urban areas in anticipation of "sudden shifts" in the situation that would bring about the opportunity for armed urban insurrection must be cast away. The staff organs must be streamlined so as to release cadres for work in the countryside and at the grassroots level. This must be done before the enemy "streamlines" them out of existence. All cadres in the enemy manhunt list must be redeployed to the countryside. Staff organs that are appropriate to the countryside must be shifted. In the countryside itself, top-heavy military staff organs must also be streamlined to release cadres for work with the masses.

It is wrong to set up the straw figure that the Party has neglected urban work and to encourage Party cadres to stick to the cities and discourage them from going to the countryside. The peasant masses and the countryside cannot by themselves produce certain types of well-educated cadres, with ideological, political, professional and technical competence, required for the revolutionary work in the countryside.

The enemy has obviously surveilled the urban-based staff organs for long periods of time and has repeatedly hit these with precision raids and arrests. It now plans to launch a crackdown on these urban-based organs before May 1992. Since 1989, as a result of the 1988 arrests, the Party has issued comprehensive and detailed security guidelines. But these have been complied with only in a token and passing manner. The most absurd was the continued basing of the NPA general command in Metro Manila despite enemy actions in 1988 and onward.

Leading territorial organs as well as staff organs characteristically generate overly long meetings, debates and papers. Oftentimes, the presiding officer is a mere moderator and not a leader. There is no lack of discussion within these organs. Meetings on administrative and procedural matters eat so much time that no time is left for study or work. The disease of bureaucratism arises from the lack or inadequacy of basic Party life and the exaggeration of the top-down administrative structure, especially through the staff organs.

Bureaucratism has begotten ultrademocracy. In the long periods of noncontact with the leading territorial organs, staff organs acquire excessive discretion and authority and improperly issue policy directives, make major decisions and implement them without passing through the leading territorial organs to which these staff organs are subordinate and which they are supposed to assist. The leading territorial organs are made to chase after unauthorized acts, errors and debates of staff organs with other staff organs and even with some leading territorial committees.

When it suits them, certain staff organs invoke compartmentalization to shut off for long periods of time not only other staff organs but even the leading territorial committee of which they are mere appointive derivatives. Thus, there are unhealthy tendencies of "several centers", independent kingdoms and ultrademocracy.

There are staff organs and individuals that issue publications questioning and attacking the line of the Party. They are engaged in ultrademocracy or liberalism. They wish to turn the Party into a liberal debating club and ape the modern revisionists and anticommunists that have destroyed the revisionist ruling parties and regimes from the inside. They act as if the Party had no basic principles to uphold and were not in a life-and-death struggle with the enemy.

Any revolutionary party or any organization for that matter is bound to degenerate or disintegrate when it allows its members to cast doubt on, denigrate, revise and attack its basic principles and line. We have seen entire revisionist-ruled states and entire revisionist parties go this way. We still have to see a declared communist remaining as a member of good standing in any bourgeois party or a declared atheist remaining a member of the Catholic Church.

There are a handful of elements who are either unreconstructed petty bourgeois or with petty bourgeois tails whose idea of democracy is to be able to do away with the leading role of the working class and the Party in the new democratic revolution and other basic principles, including democratic centralism. They promote the theory of spontaneous masses, especially in connection with insurrectionism. And they are falling into an anti-Party conjuncture with petty-bourgeois populists, liberals, "social-democrats", "democratic socialists", pacifists, advocates of pacification, Trotskyites and the like. The Party must uphold democratic centralism. Inner Party democracy must be given free rein under the guidance of the basic principles of the Party and within the structure and confines of the Party and especially through an all-rounded basic Party life. There are both discipline and freedom within the Party. The Party does not allow any individual to enter the Party to attack its basic principles and general line and even use the personnel, facilities and resources of the Party against the Party. The Party is so guided by democracy that it recruits its members on a conscious voluntary individual basis and at the same time allows anyone to quit the Party when he can no longer accept its basic principles.

II. Domestic Conditions Are Favorable for Revolution

The domestic conditions are fluid, volatile and favorable for waging the new democratic revolution, especially through a protracted people's war. These are definitely and patently more favorable than the external conditions. In the case of the latter, we need to see through the apparent successes of imperialism and neocolonialism and see the essential further worsening of the crisis of the world capitalist system. The Socioeconomic Crisis Is Worsening

Since the reestablishment of the Party or from the regime of Marcos to Aquino, the basic characteristics of the Philippine social economy as backward, agrarian, preindustrial and semifeudal have deepened and have become ever more devastating to the people. The economic system is afflicted by a chronic crisis that keeps on worsening and ceaselessly lays the ground for the armed revolution of the people.

The economy is controlled by such local exploiting classes as the comprador big bourgeoisie and the landlord class and is an appendage of the world capitalist system. It is an economy whose principal means of production is agriculture, that is without basic industries and that is dependent on imported equipment, components and fuel for the production of agricultural and manufactured goods for local consumption and of raw materials for export.

The economy exports raw materials in the main in order to earn the foreign exchange for purchasing from abroad a wide range of essential producer and consumer goods as well as luxuries for the upper classes. Such low value-added exports as garments, semiconductors and toys bring a marginal amount of foreign exchange income. The export of labor power has earned far more foreign exchange than any single export commodity. But this has diminished since the contraction of the labor market in the Middle East.

The economy is not only in a state of recession but is in a state of depression if the real figures can be established. Even the official statistics declare that the gross national product has continuously gone down since the last quarter of 1990. The fall in GNP up to the last quarter of 1991 is considerable. And the statisticians of the IMF and the Philippine government are trying to manipulate the figures to produce a year-end GNP growth rate of 0.5 percent or one-half percent.

At any rate, the Aquino regime has completely failed to fulfill its promise of making the economy recover to the level of 1981, notwithstanding budgetary expenditures of nearly P/ 1.3 trillion, more than P/ 100 billion additional domestic public borrowing (83 percent of which is in short-term treasury bills) and increased foreign borrowing which is up by several more billions of dollars up to the end of the regime in June 1992.

The IMF is applying on the Philippine government a "stabilization" or austerity program to cut down deficit spending, impose a levy of five percent even on essential producer and consumer imports and ensure that foreign debt-servicing enjoys the highest priority. The austerity measures have resulted in the sharp reduction of local production, the breakdown of public services and the deterioration of the standard of living.

The balance of trade deficit continues to rise. At yearend 1991, the trade deficit was expected to go beyond the level of US$ 4.0 billion out of an estimated total foreign trade of US$ 20 billion, despite the attempts to discourage imports. The terms of trade for Philippine exports have ceaselessly deteriorated in general. The Philippine economy has to keep on begging for more loans in order to maintain itself at lower levels of operation or at one lower level of austerity after another.

The accumulated foreign debt of US$29 billion by itself has become a crushing burden. This official figure is misleading because rescheduled debts are taken out of public accounting. At any rate, foreign commercial banks continue to reduce their lending. Thus, the Philippine government continues to beg for and incur debts on a bilateral basis and from the multilateral financial agencies. The debt service reached the level of US$ 5.6 billion or 76 per cent of export income last year.

The budgetary deficits have increased from year to year. Local public borrowing has been resorted to cover these and has gone beyond the level of P/300 billion. The bulk of public spending is for the servicing of foreign and local public debt and for the military and police establishment, including the paramilitary forces. Foreign debt service accounts for more than 40 per cent of the budget and the military and police establishment, easily more than 15 per cent, in a more accurate accounting.

The military budget is made to appear small by the segregation of the amounts for "civil" though total-war related offices, programs and projects of the national defense, interior and other departments; the Philippine National Police and paramilitary forces; the National Intelligence Coordinating Agency, intelligence funds under various departments; military schools, etc. In addition to what the military takes from the Philippine government budget, it gets from the U.S. what is equivalent to 63 per cent of its total requirements for operations and equipment.

Government spending is largely nonproductive and characterized by corruption at various levels of the bureaucracy. Funds are dwindling for such basic social services as public health, education, housing and the maintenance of the infrastructure. Social relief and rehabilitation of victims of the long series of frequent major calamities (earthquakes, volcanic eruption, typhoons, floods and drought) have been grossly inadequate and further reduced by corrupt practices.

Aquino's term is coming to an end. There has been a general economic decline from 1986 to 1991. The current regime is notorious for not having a single industrial project, for retrogressing in land reform legislation and spending billions of pesos for the maintenance of a department of agrarian reform but only a few millions for token expropriation of land for redistribution and for allowing the deterioration of infrastructure and public services.

Seventy percent of the population or 7.4 million of the 10.5 million families (average of six persons each) in the country fall below the poverty line of P/ 4997 (US$ 185). Some 30 percent or 4.5 million families live below the P/2283 (US$ 84.50) food threshold. Eighty percent or one million families in the national capital region (Metro Manila) live below the poverty line.

There is massive accumulated unemployment, approaching 50 per cent of the total labor force of 27.5 million. As of the third quarter of 1991, the official unemployment rate is 17 per cent (4.5 million) and the official underemployment rate, 30 per cent (9.0 million). Those classified as underemployed are in fact unemployed. And among those considered employed, a sizable percentage do not have full and regular employment. There are false criteria that official statisticians go by in their random surveys.

There is hyperinflation in the country although the officially admitted rate is only 19 per cent as of the third quarter of 1991. It is cutting down the real income of the people even as wages are being pressed down. There is now an extremely wide gap between the rate of increase in the legislated wage rates and the official rates of increase in the prices of basic commodities. The official rate of inflation is understated by a manipulation of the basket of basic goods.

Essential producer and consumer goods are in short supply. Staples are in short supply and are being imported. The cost of fuel is ever rising and being passed on to the ordinary consumers and riding public. The price of oil is domestically kept above the level of the world price in order to assure the multinational firms of a hefty profit. Basic social services have broken down and are being priced far beyond the ability of the masses to pay.

Taxes are being increased to satisfy the IMF demand to cut down deficit spending. Interest rates have gone up to more than 23 per cent. Local entrepreneurs are discouraged from production by the high costs, including the levy on imported producer goods, and by the inflow of foreign commodities under the regime's policy of import liberalization.

With the ever deteriorating economic conditions, there is widespread and deepgoing social unrest. The legal democratic mass movement and the armed revolutionary movement can and must arouse, organize and mobilize the discontented masses.

The Political Crisis Is Worsening

The socioeconomic crisis continues to fuel the political crisis of the ruling system. The rivalries of the political parties and factions of the exploiting classes are becoming more bitter and more violent. The ruling system is increasingly being weakened internally as it escalates its attacks on the people.

The objective conditions for waging the armed revolution are better than ever. The crisis of the ruling system under the U.S.- Aquino ruling clique is far worse than under the U.S.-Marcos ruling clique. The current regime is thoroughly isolated. The people are desirous of a change of government; and they are in a revolutionary mood.

There is no doubt whatsoever that due to the chronic crisis of the system and the ceaseless aggravation of the crisis, the objective situation is fluid, volatile and favorable for bigger mass actions by the legal democratic forces and for accelerated tactical offensives by the people's army. It can also be said that the subjective forces of the revolution are certainly stronger than in the earlier periods of revolutionary upsurge (as, for instance, in 1970–72). But there are problems besetting the revolutionary forces that reduce their capacity and effectiveness to take advantage of the situation.

These problems need to be identified and solved through an all-round rectification movement in order to enable the subjective forces of the revolution to take advantage of the fluid crisis-ridden situation and cause the revolutionary mass movement to surge forward. There are deepseated and long-running problems that have reduced the capacity of the Party to lead the masses at the basic level in both urban and rural areas. These problems should not be glossed over by casuistic argumentations over whether it can be said that the objective conditions are fluid or not.

Since July 1990, the acutely critical conditions in the country have been favorable for an upsurge in the revolutionary mass movement in the urban areas. But neither sweeping agitation for an "immediate insurrection" to crack the ruling system nor the scheme to degrade the revolutionary forces by building a paper alliance (with peace negotiations as its main concern supposedly in order to swing the middle forces and the unpoliticized masses to the Left in preparation for an "insurrection that would lead to a sharing of power in a coalition government in the medium term") has brought about a great upsurge in the revolutionary mass movement. The revolutionary forces should neither be too far ahead (thus the need for the united front) nor too far behind (thus the need for revolutionary integrity) if allies and the masses are to be galvanized for an upsurge of protest actions on definite burning issues.

In the countryside, the objective of solving the problem of "regularization" and correcting the imbalances in the deployment of cadres and resources in favor of extensive and intensive guerrilla warfare on the basis of an ever expanding and consolidating mass base is precisely to enable the people's army to launch more effectively the tactical offensives within the strategic defensive. Our guerrilla fighters must wage only those battles that they are capable and sure of winning.

Although stimulated by the favorable objective situation, the subjective forces of the revolution, the Party and other revolutionary organizations, have to know the measure of their strength, rectify errors and shortcomings and undertake all necessary measures to preserve and further strengthen themselves. In leading the masses, the Party must arouse, organize and mobilize them. Consequently, it can launch legal mass actions and armed tactical offensives that can be won within the strategic defensive.

The rectification of insurrectionism does not mean that we stop calling for and undertaking those mass actions within our capability. Neither does the rectification of "regularization" mean that we stop calling for and undertaking increased tactical offensives within our capability.

There is a stampede by some eight political figures seeking to replace the already isolated president in the forthcoming elections. But the more potent of the various reactionary political forces are those that have a substantial share of government resources, access to campaign money from the big U.S., Japanese and Taiwan-Chinese firms and the local exploiting classes and have a considerable armed following inside and outside the reactionary military and police forces.

It is expected that money and blood will flow to decide which candidates will win at the highest level as well as at lower levels. The stakes are extremely high in the contest between the Aquino and the Marcos factions even as they seem to have made secret deals regarding the question of stolen assets and human rights violations. The most formidable competing teams in the elections are offshoots of the Aquino and Marcos factions. But there are also the other parties that wish to take advantage of the main split within the ruling system.

It is the notion of the U.S. and local reactionaries that a brief electoral campaign period, elections for a day in a multiparty circus and making a choice among candidates of the exploiting classes can delude the people and make them believe that there is democracy. Thus the elections are supposed to stabilize the neocolony. But in fact these elections split the ruling system. The fragmentation of the exploiting classes is such that the winning party and presidential candidate are unlikely to garner more than 50 percent of the electorate.

Whoever gets elected president from whichever party will have to work out compromises with allies but will be faced with powerful opposition within the system. If the Aquino ruling clique retains power through a dummy presidential figure and cheats in the elections, there will probably be some major political violence soon after the elections. And yet even if the current ruling clique prevails, the Aquino family will have increasing differences with whomever may be its presidential front man.

The ruling system will become more fractious, weak and volatile. The commanders of the reactionary armed forces will become more ambitious as the political and economic crisis worsens, even as the same reactionary military and police forces remain fragmented into several factions. At the moment, there are as many as five of these military factions: the Aquino faction, the Ramos faction, the pro-Marcos Soldiers of the Filipino People (SFP), the pro-

Enrile Rebolusyonaryong Alyansang Makabayan (RAM) and the Young Officers' Union (YOU). These factions will not disappear despite the efforts of the United States to reunify them and concentrate them against the revolutionary movement. The reorganization of the Philippine Constabulary and the local police forces into the Philippine National Police creates additional conditions for fragmentation and allows local executive officials to cultivate their own armed following within the PNP in so many fiefdoms.

At the moment, the AFP and the PNP continue to coordinate in launching campaigns of suppression against the revolutionary forces and the people. But there is a growing division between the military and police forces not only because of clashing loyalties to political groups but also because of clashing interests over criminal activities and tong collection from gambling, prostitution and other vices.

In conducting operations against the Party, the NPA and NDF, the military and police forces appear to coordinate very well only because there are crack intelligence units directed by U.S. and Filipino intelligence officers who take advantage of the urban basing of the staff organs of the revolutionary movement and the identifiability of revolutionary personnel who are on the enemy manhunt list and yet are in these staff organs. Upon the withdrawal of such personnel to the countryside, the enemy will be deprived of easy targets.

All Party members and Red fighters must grasp the point that when the military and police forces are fractious and the ruling clique feels threatened by a coup d'etat, it concentrates its forces in the citadel and therefore makes it difficult for revolutionary forces to seize this citadel before the backbone of the enemy military forces is broken in the countryside. The illusion of hastening the seizure of the cities mainly through urban activities and urban concentration of cadres, who are on the enemy manhunt list, must be cast away.

The very perseverance of the revolutionary forces and the people along the strategic line of encircling the cities from the countryside and accumulating strength through tactical offensives within the strategic defensive serves to weaken and crack the ruling system, as more and more resources are misdirected towards the military, police and paramilitary forces rather than towards other purposes. As the armed revolutionary movement and the legal democratic mass movement grow in strength, the ruling system weakens and cracks further.

The enemy is already under severe political and economic strain in pursuing his total war policy. He deploys brigades to concentrate on certain guerrilla fronts and in the process assaults and abuses the people but fails to destroy the guerrilla forces that are closely linked with the masses on a wide scale in far more guerrilla fronts than he can pounce on.

The broad masses of the people reject the ruling system and detest its military, police and paramilitary forces as they go on a rampage of killing, looting and burning to force the peasant masses to leave their homes and farms. The Aquino regime's six-year record of human rights violations surpasses any six years of the Marcos fascist record in terms of disappearances, assassinations, illegal detention, torture, arson, bombings, strafing, food blockades, strategic hamlets and forced mass evacuation of people.

More than a million people have been displaced and turned into refugees by military operations. The military forces use blind bombing, artillery fire and strafing, massacre people, burn homes and crops and compel the people to flee from targeted areas in different parts of the archipelago. Several tens of thousands of people have been rounded up and illegally detained in both rural and urban areas. Worse than during the Marcos fascist regime, the military, police and paramilitary forces can kidnap people at will under the Supreme Court doctrine of warrantless arrest. Thousands have been subjected to torture and extrajudicial execution. Others are languishing in prison because their right to bail is violated or nonbailable charges are maliciously filed against them.

Hundreds of priests and pastors, human rights lawyers, journalists, leaders of legal progressive political parties and other well-respected personalities have been assassinated or have been made to disappear. The military has been more brutal under the Aquino regime than under the Marcos regime in this regard. Thousands of leaders and activists of the working class, peasantry and youth have been murdered.

The Aquino regime has viciously attacked the patriotic and progressive forces that consistently fought against the Marcos fascist regime. And yet under U.S. auspices, the Aquino and Marcos political factions of the same exploiting classes try to exercise restraint in fighting each other and even forge agreements on stolen assets. There is certainly close kinship between Marcos and Aquino not only in corruption but also in the continuing violation of human rights.

But the people are not helpless. They are determined to fight for their national and democratic rights. The struggle between armed revolution and counterrevolution is still at the center of the stage. The guerrilla forces of the New People's Army continue to wipe out enemy units, inflict casualties and accumulate strength. They are resolved to expand and consolidate the mass base for their self-reliant revolutionary armed struggle.

Far more significant than the electoral farces and institutional games played by the already isolated ruling clique are the strengthening of the patriotic and progressive mass organizations and the launching of mass actions and campaigns to promote the rights and interests of the workers, peasants, fishermen, women, youth, professionals, small businessmen and other people.

The broad mass movement has taken up the issues of national independence and democracy. Among these major issues taken up by information campaigns and mass actions are the following: U.S. military bases, IMF economic policy dictates, foreign debt, oil price increases, wages and workers' rights, land reform, human rights violations, the regime's total war policy, women's rights, education, ecology and peace.

Strikes and protest rallies and marches have been carried out. The most outstanding of these in the year have been the demonstration of nearly a hundred thousand people in February at Mendiola bridge and the May First workers' rally and march on the U.S. embassy. On the issue of the U.S. military bases, the militant mass organizations and alliances have been able to inspire the majority of Philippine senators to reject the draft treaty agreed upon by the regime and the U.S. government.

The struggle against the U.S. military presence is far from over. The U.S. government is still in a position to deal with the next reactionary regime for the retention of the Subic naval base. The JUSMAG, the Defense Intelligence Agency, the Central Intelligence Agency and U.S. control over all radar stations in the country will persist until they are removed by the people's revolutionary struggle.

The legal democratic mass movement has high hopes of advancing further in the year ahead. The mass organizations and alliances have shown their determination to bring the struggle for national liberation and democracy to a new and higher level.

III. The World Is Fraught with Contradictions

In the consideration of certain developments abroad in 1991, it looks like the "new world order" proclaimed by U.S. President Bush earlier in the year is valid and true. For a moment in history, it seems that the world is under the unchallenged unipolar hegemony of the United States. In this regard, the clear message to the Philippine revolutionary movement is to be more than ever self-reliant and not to be dependent on any expectation of immediate assistance from abroad. After all, the Philippine revolutionary movement has never been dependent on foreign assistance.

By high-tech mass media, the United States has been made to appear as the leader of all nations championing the sovereignty of other nations, democracy and human rights. And by high-tech means of destruction, the United States has devastated Iraq and massacred hundreds of thousands of the Iraqi people, with impunity and without compunction. It is also proclaimed that the U. S. has overcome its Vietnam war syndrome.

Once more in history, the United States has gotten its way by the perverse logic that Kuwait, Saudi Arabia and the entire Persian Gulf had to be saved from Saddam Hussein by the most cruel methods just as the Philippines had to be saved from Emilio Aguinaldo who had been demonized beyond all proportions by the U.S. yellow press upon the outbreak of the Filipino-American war. The U.S. has tightened its control over the oil resources, military sales and the regional security system in the Middle East and is now arranging a Pax Americana for its own maximum benefit and for Israel at the expense of the Palestinian and Arab peoples.

Following the alleged coup attempt by certain Soviet officials to preempt the divisive "union" treaty and preserve the Soviet Union, the two anticommunist demagogues, Gorbachov and Yeltsin, have combined and competed to dissolve and dispossess the Soviet revisionist party and the central regime and to break up the Soviet Union and regroup the remaining centrifugal republics into some loose "commonwealth". Finally, the Soviet Union has basically gone the same way that the other revisionist-ruled countries have gone since 1989.

The revisionist party and regime have been abolished in favor of undisguised anticommunist bourgeois regimes as in Eastern Europe. Nationalism, ethnic conflicts, superstition and criminality are rampant. The worsening political chaos portend bloody ethnic conflicts and civil wars worse than that now raging in Yugoslavia, Georgia and Nagorno-Karabakh.

The economy of the former Soviet Union is in shambles, characterized by production breakdown and decline by as much as 20 percent; massive unemployment; privatization of public assets; profiteering; bureaucratic corruption; rapid increases of the money supply (100 percent in 1991); hyperinflation (already running at more than 300 percent and expected to accelerate when price decontrol takes effect on January 2, 1992); conspicuous consumption by the bourgeoisie; severe food shortages and begging for food aid from the West.

Within a short period of six years, Gorbachov and his band of capitalist restorationists have impoverished and turned the former Soviet Union into a full-fledged neocolonial client-state with a huge foreign debt of US$81 billion (starting at the level of only US$30 billion in 1985) that it has extreme difficulty in servicing. The borrowed foreign money has been used for importing consumer goods and also for lining the pockets of the bureaucrats through the joint ventures and private cooperatives.

The U.S. policy makers are confident that the bourgeois liberalization of the Chinese economy will continue to reproduce the Chinese bourgeoisie, corrupt the bureaucrats and generate an anticommunist intelligentsia and will inevitably result not only in the bourgeois liberalization of Chinese politics but the ultimate restoration of an undisguised bourgeois rule through peaceful evolution as in the Soviet Union and Eastern Europe. For the time being, the United States is using trade, financial and other levers to exert pressure on China and interfere in Chinese affairs.

The third world countries characteristically remain as neocolonial client-states, straining under deteriorating terms of trade for their raw-material exports and under heavy foreign debt burdens. The International Monetary

Fund continues to dictate upon them to adopt "austerity measures" and "multiparty democracy" ala Philippines. An increasing number of them are wracked by political violence. And they seem to have no way out of the world capitalist system.

Even those regimes which were previously described as socialist or socialist-oriented and used Marxist and anti-imperialist rhetoric have climbed down and have pleaded for capitalist investments and trade and loan concessions or have been replaced by unabashed puppets of imperialism. The Ethiopian and Eritrean revolutionary movements have won power through protracted people's war against the Soviet-supported regime but continue to face extreme difficulties due to domestic and international conditions.

Countries that are firmly resolved to remain socialist, like Cuba and the People's Democratic Republic of Korea, are under tremendous pressures and threats from the United States. The United States cannot conceal its glee over the opportunities provided by the disintegration of the former Soviet Union.

Amidst the social turmoil throughout the world, the capitalist powers appear to be consolidating their positions and neatly redividing the world among themselves. The U.S.-Japan combination is supposed to have Asia as its sphere of influence. The United States is to remain dominant in its own backyard, Latin America, and in the Middle East. With Germany and France as the prime movers, Western Europe is building its economic and political union while the Soviet Union has disintegrated. The European Community is taking charge of the Soviet Union and Eastern Europe and most of Africa as spheres of influence.

However, it is not enough to look at the appearances of the world situation within a short period of time. We have to see through these ephemeral appearances. A certain aspect may be conspicuous or may actually be dominant in a given period of time. But it is inextricably linked to another contradictory aspect which resurges precisely at the moment that the dominant aspect is or appears to be overwhelmingly or unquestionably dominant.

Indeed, the world today is under the unquestionable dominance of capitalism. This is stressed by the obvious retreat and even disintegration of the anti-imperialist and socialist forces in several countries. But once upon a time, capitalism enjoyed dominance, with practically no serious opposition, until the great October Socialist Revolution of 1917 came.

This revolution came about as a result of the capitalist crisis of overproduction and interimperialist war. It confirmed the thesis of Marx that large-scale machine commodity production under capitalism leads to the crisis of overproduction and interimperialist rivalries and wars. The high technology that is in the hands of the capitalist powers today generates far more rapidly than the electromechanical processes of the past the crisis of overproduction.

There Is a New World Disorder

In fact, high technology has already created an unprecedentedly severe crisis of overproduction and continues to wreak havoc on the lives of billions of people and causes rising levels of social turbulence, mainly in the South and East of the world in the meantime. There is a new world disorder.

The United States continues to be in strategic decline. It cannot solve its problem of huge budgetary and trade deficits, without generating severe social tensions within American society and without upsetting the balance among the capitalist powers. The U.S. decline can only be temporarily overshadowed by the disintegration of its former superpower rival, which is paying for the misallocation of resources for the arms race and overconsumption of the new bourgeoisie under the Brezhnev era.

The trumpeted end of the cold war is generating a demand from the American people for the so-called peace dividend. But the United States cannot easily draw back from its own high-tech military-industrial complex to pay for the overconsumption of the past which was done through massive foreign borrowing. Every kind of financial instrument has been scandalously abused by the United States in connection with military overspending and overconsumption.

The trade deficits of the United States are the trade surpluses of Japan, Germany and a handful of "newly industrializing" economies in the third world. As the U.S. tries to save and invest in the more efficient production of goods tradable in the world, it throws both white collar and blue collar workers out of jobs and goes through spasms of recession and unleashes economic problems in countries that have taken advantage of previous U.S. overconsumption. As a matter of fact, the U.S. economy is in prolonged recession, already in its third year.

There is a fragility in the economies of the other major capitalist powers like Germany and Japan. Germany is suffering from indigestion as a result of the reunification of East and West Germany and also from having to lend capital to Eastern Europe and the Soviet Union which clearly have limited capabilities of paying back. Japan has expanded only at the sufferance of the United States and Western Europe.

U.S. President Bush has made another significant statement this year to the effect that trade war has replaced the cold war. This is a succinct reflection of the frustrating negotiations among the capitalist powers (within the Group of Seven, OECD and GATT) regarding trade and financial policies. The growing differences among the capitalist powers revolve around the question of "free trade" in all types of agricultural and industrial goods and around the question of sharing the responsibility of lending money to the countries that have no way of servicing their accumulated foreign debt, except by incurring more debt.

At the moment, in our part of the world, it looks like the United States and Japan are still cooperating very well in exploiting the people. Due to its serious budgetary and trade deficits, the United States is pushing Japan to share military burden and to increase its military forces under the pretext of peacekeeping under the U.N. flag and is trying to break open the well-protected Japanese market to U.S. products.

The United States and Japan are the closest foreign partners today in keeping the Philippines as a neocolony in economic and political terms. As the United States continues in strategic decline, Japan is increasing its economic and indirect military role in the Philippines and in the entire Asia-Pacific region.

The United States still has the edge over Japan in accumulated investments in the Philippines and expects to retain the Subic naval base after the 1992 elections as well as control over all the radar and communications stations dotting the country. But Japan has outstripped the United States in the rate of investments, trade and "development aid" and the thrust of new investments is to achieve direct control over land and natural resources.

Japan is taking advantage of the United States' own plea for military burden-sharing and the United Nations flag for building its forces of military aggression under the guise of peacekeeping. Within the decade, we shall see the U.S.-Japan cooperation in the domination of the Philippines and the Asia-Pacific region turn into rivalry. We are still fighting the United States as the main imperialist power and opposing the U.S.-Japan combination. But we must also anticipate the U.S.-Japan rivalry that is bound to develop and become conspicuous within the decade.

It is of great importance that the Philippine revolutionary movement is closely linked with the peoples and revolutionary movements in the neighboring countries in both Southeast Asia and Northeast Asia (China, Korea, Japan, etc.) and in North America as well as with the governments that continue to be or are likely to become anti-imperialist when violent interimperialist rivalries reemerge in the region.

Whether China remains socialist or not, it has built up a powerful industrial capacity and is among the countries in the region with their political independence and a higher capacity for resisting U.S. or Japanese imperialism than before World War II. China is the largest imponderable factor in the forthcoming rivalry between the United States and Japan in the region. Recently, China and India made a joint statement opposing oligarchy in world affairs.

In all capitalist countries today, there is the dramatic resurgence of the problem of stagflation. This was previously put under control through the mechanism of lending large amounts of money to countries in the third world and Eastern Europe since the 1970s and to the United States, China, India and the Soviet Union since the 1980s. Now, this mechanism has broken down as the economies of most debtor countries have deteriorated and have been unable to pay back the loans. In the capitalist countries, there is the sticky problem of unemployment and the cutbacks on social welfare and social services. Social tensions are manifested in contradictory currents, the perseverance of progressive organizations and the surge of racism and neofascism, now directed against migrants from the third world.

The success of neocolonialism is its own failure. It has succeeded in putting the world, especially the countries of the South and the East, under control principally through economic and financial means. But the failure lies in ultimately constricting the world capitalist market.

The general run of the countries of the South has been restricted to the production of raw materials for export, subjected to the ever deteriorating terms of trade, overburdened with foreign debt that cannot be paid back and afflicted with military overspending, bureaucratic corruption and conspicuous import-dependent consumption of a few. These third world countries suffer from a crisis of overproduction in raw materials rather than in finished products. The Philippines belongs to this group of countries.

Political Violence Is on the Rise

There are consequently rising levels of political violence in the third world countries. There are repeated food riots, coup attempts and counter-coups, ethnic and religious conflicts and civil wars. These are occurring on a widening scale. The passing illusion of world peace pertains mainly to the disappearance of the bipolar confrontation between the United States and the Soviet Union and to the debilitation and defeat of political entities previously dependent on the Soviet Union.

The Persian Gulf war between the U.S.-led alliance and Iraq is actually a manifestation of the limits and crisis of neocolonialism. The United States was compelled to resort to the classical violence of modern imperialism (this time using hightech weapons of mass destruction effectively on the peculiar terrain of Iraq) on a recalcitrant neocolonial client-state, which had been driven by the costs of the Iran-Iraq war (instigated by the U.S.) and by the world oil glut to come into conflict with another neocolony, Kuwait.

Under socialism, certain countries of Eastern Europe were able to establish basic industries even while the Soviet Union overconcentrated on military production and channeled scientific research and high technology to arms production. But as they increasingly adopted capitalist-oriented reforms, they took on the ills afflicting the neocolonies. Even before the revisionist ruling parties and regimes were replaced by undisguised bourgeois parties and regimes, based on an anticommunist intelligentsia, the corrupt bureaucrats and private entrepreneurs, they had already become hooked to patterns of production and consumption dictated by the West and most of them had already been burdened with foreign debt which they could not pay back. To this day, the East European countries in varying degrees can export only agricultural, steel and textile products which are overproduced by the industrial capitalist countries and the newly-industrializing economies.

The capitalist wonderland has not at all come to the Soviet Union and Eastern Europe. Such ills of third world capitalism as unrestrained bureaucratic corruption and privatization, blackmarketeering, massive unemployment, lack of social guarantees, hyperinflation, fuel shortage, shortages of basic necessities and so on are rampant. Only the upper five percent of the population relish the new conditions.

In so short a time, capitalism is in total disrepute among the broad masses of the people in the Soviet Union and Eastern Europe. The new regimes, which are bureaucratic combinations of long-time anticommunists and a large number of overnight excommunists, are proving to be worse than the regimes in the pre-Gorbachov period. The advantage for genuine communists who are now under persecution in these countries is that the downfall of revisionist ruling parties and regimes that used to maintain communist and socialist facades, has put the responsibility squarely on the new bourgeoisie.

The main civil exports of the former Soviet Union are oil, natural gas and gold. But the production of these has broken down as a result of continuing misallocation of resources, political chaos, ethnic conflicts, previous withholding of funds from the center by the republics and general strikes. At the same time, the former Soviet Union has already abused foreign borrowing in so short a time. This has been used mainly for the importation of Western consumer products and not for the retooling and expansion of production facilities. The successor states of the Soviet

Union can sell weapons for hard currency. But the capitalist powers discourage them from doing so.

In brief, the full integration of former revisionist-ruled countries of the East into the world capitalist system is not an undiluted blessing for it. These countries do not have export-products in high demand in the West. At the same time, there is a shortage of capital for lending to those who have patently limited capacity to pay pack. Besides, in the current shrinkage of the world capitalist market, the capitalist powers cannot be too eager to allow these countries to become additional industrial competitors.

Multinational firms have preferred to export their surplus finished products to these countries and have invested only in the most profitable lines of business, which often do not involve new production facilities nor retooling of old ones. There is in fact a process of de-industrialization, involving the closure of industries and the redirection of manpower and resources away from industrialization.

A study of Yugoslavia is useful to illustrate the total bankruptcy of modern revisionism. Yugoslavia has had the distinction of being the first country (since 1948) to be ruled by modern revisionism. It has not grown into a strong industrial capitalist country under the new bourgeoisie. Neither have the capitalist powers heavily invested in it in order to develop it industrially. It has even been worse than the Philippines as an overconsuming and overborrowing country. Now, it is in the throes of disintegration and rebalkanization. It is rent asunder by a civil war, arising from the nationalism and separatism of the dominant ethnic and religious communities in the various republics and the rising passions of deepseated ethnic conflicts.

Regarding the former Soviet Union, what the capitalist powers are most worried about now is the dispersed location of 28,000 nuclear warheads in four independent republics (Russia, Ukraine, Byelorussia and Kazakhstan) and the probability of civil wars bigger than the current ones. At the moment, these republics are preoccupied with replacing the old Soviet center with a "commonwealth of independent states". The strong currents of nationalism, the interrepublic and intrarepublic ethnic and religious conflicts, the gross differences in economic development, the breakdown of the economies, the border disputes of the republics and the presence of large foreign enclaves (especially Russian) in non-Russian territory are likely to generate more turmoil and civil wars.

There is potential civil war between a Great-Russian chauvinist center or a central military command dominated by Russians and a republic that possesses nuclear weapons and refuses to follow the dictat from the Russian or military center and is accused of mistreating the Russian enclave in its territory. The republics with nuclear weapons can also take opposing sides in the various conflicts of republics and the ethnic and religious communities within republics. Because of their economic interests and fear of the possible mishandling of the nuclear weapons, the capitalist powers would be more prone to intervene in civil wars in the former Soviet Union than in the current ones in Yugoslavia.

A civil war in the former Soviet Union, similar to that in Yugoslavia but gravely dissimilar due to the factor of nuclear weapons in the equation, is not a farfetched possibility. Great-Russian chauvinism is likely to arise to oppress and exploit the other nations and use the Russian enclaves within the other republics to exercise Russian domination. After the demagogues of today shall have passed away (and they will do so soon because of the overwhelming economic crisis and political chaos), the rise of fiercer nationalists and military fascists can run ahead of the resurgence of the revolutionary forces.

In several respects, the status of Eastern Europe and the former Soviet Union has been degraded to that before World War I. There can be no complete duplication of any previous period in history but there can be comparisons of historical periods in certain respects and under precise qualifications. At any rate, the leaders and strategists of the capitalist powers have started to fear that there is a greater possibility of a war breaking out in Europe than during the cold war period as a result of the disintegration of Soviet power. The current ravages of capitalism can give way to unbridled nationalism and military fascism.

However, the proletariat and the people in the Soviet Union and Eastern Europe have come to know what is socialism, modern revisionism and undisguised capitalism. They have made great achievements under socialism, while disguised and undisguised capitalism has degraded them. They certainly abhor their disempowerment by the bourgeoisie and the scandalous private appropriation of the social wealth created by them in more than seven decades. The great legacy of Lenin and Stalin cannot be totally extirpated. The genuine communists who are now under persecution and the oppressed and exploited proletariat and people are certain to fight back and wrest back the power appropriated by the bourgeoisie. The resurgence of the forces of socialism is bound to come.

The Filipino Communists Are Among the Bolsheviks

In taking an overview of the world today, the Communist Party of the Philippines considers itself as being among the proletarian revolutionary parties adhering to the revolutionary essence of Marxism and persevering in revolutionary struggle mainly on the ground of the domestic crisis, like the Bolsheviks in the period when capitalism was expanding and developing into modern imperialism and the Second International was dominated by the classical revisionists who ultimately became embarrassed and disintegrated in 1914. Soon after the collapse of the Second International, the Bolsheviks won the Great October Socialist Revolution in 1917.

Another dark period for the anti-imperialist and socialist movement arose when fascist regimes wiped out communist parties in the period before World War II; and the forces of fascism invaded and wrought havoc on the Soviet Union in World War II. From that dark period, several socialist countries would emerge and the national liberation movements would forge ahead in an unprecedented way.

The anti-imperialist and socialist movement is bound to resurge at a new and higher level because of the insoluble crisis of the world capitalist system, the lessons from more than three decades of peaceful evolution of socialism to blatant capitalism and the irresistible demands of the proletariat and the people for national liberation, democracy and genuine socialism.

History goes into twists and turns. It will not end until the earth goes into a blackhole. Capitalism is not the end of history but is the forerunner of socialism. As proletarian internationalists, we must link up with all revolutionary parties, movements and peoples in all countries and work together with them in bringing about the resurgence of the anti-imperialist and socialist movement.

For the Central Committee
Communist Party of the Philippines

MARXISM LENINISM MAO ZEDONG THOUGHT AS A GUIDE TO THE PHILIPPINE REVOLUTION

Armando Liwanag,
Chairman,
Central Committee,
Communist Party of the Philippines
November 6, 1993

Proletarian revolutionary cadres reestablished the Communist Party of the Philippines on December 26, 1968 and proclaimed Marxism-Leninism-Mao Zedong Thought as their theoretical guide. The CPP armed itself with the most powerful ideological weapon of the world's proletariat for analyzing the revolutionary history and circumstances of the Filipino people, for resuming the new-democratic revolution through people's war and for looking forward to the socialist future up to the threshold of communism. Marxism-Leninism-Mao Zedong Thought is the microscope and telescope of the Philippine revolution.

After the crushing defeat of the revolutionary movement in 1950 and for nearly a decade afterwards, the revolutionary road had been enveloped in darkness both by the power of U.S. imperialism and the local exploiting classes of big compradors and landlords and by a long chain of unrectified grave errors and shortcomings. Were it not for the adoption of Mao Zedong Thought as its theoretical guide, the Communist Party of the Philippines could not have been reestablished and the revolutionary movement of the Filipino proletariat and people could not have been resumed. Mao Zedong Thought served to illumine the road of armed revolution.

The great victory of the Chinese revolution in 1949 breached the imperialist front in the East in a big way and resounded in the Philippines. But this was also the time that the revolutionary forces were being brought to destruction by the Left opportunist Jose Lava leadership of the old merger party of the Communist Party and the Socialist Party. What followed the defeat of the revolution in 1950 was a decade of intense reaction, made more acute by the Cold War and McCarthyism.

In the period of defeat, the Jesus Lava leadership of the old CP-SP merger party swung to a Right opportunist line and the followers of this line continued to be influenced by the Browderite line of "peace and democracy" and were further influenced by the rise of Khrushchovite modern revisionism. The proletarian revolutionary cadres therefore faced tremendous odds in striving to continue the unfinished Philippine revolution along the new-democratic line.

The works of Comrade Mao Zedong were scarce in the Philippines before the decade of the 1960s. As early as the late 1930's and during World War II, some of his works on the united front and armed struggle were already available to the comrades in the Chinese bureau in the Philippines. But these remained in the Chinese original. It would be through the efforts of the proletarian revolutionary cadres themselves that the works of Comrade Mao Zedong became readily available, with the assistance of Indonesian and Chinese comrades, at the time of the Great Leap Forward and subsequently the Great Proletarian Cultural Revolution.

The Filipino communists necessarily read and studied the works of Marx, Engels, Lenin, Stalin and Mao. They recognized that the teachings of Mao proceeded from the basic principles laid down by his great predecessors and were a further development of the revolutionary theory of the proletariat in the particular conditions of China as well as the world. They also recognized in 1966 that the stage of Mao Zedong Thought could be reached because of the earlier stages of Marxism and Leninism.

Marx and Engels laid the theoretical foundation of Marxism by putting forward for the first time the basic principles of dialectical materialism; the critique of capitalist political economy; and scientific socialism in the era of free competition capitalism. Lenin further developed the three components of Marxism in confrontation with the bourgeois subjectivists and classical revisionists and together with Stalin realized the stage of Leninism through the establishment of the Soviet Union as a proletarian dictatorship and through the sustained process of socialist revolution and construction until the emergence of several socialist countries in the era of modern imperialism and socialist revolution.

Mao Zedong Thought emerged as the third stage in the development of Marxism when Mao confronted the problem of modern revisionism and capitalist restoration already evident in the Soviet Union and Eastern Europe as well as in the manifestation of the same problem in China. He put forward the theory of continuing revolution under proletarian dictatorship in order to consolidate socialism, combat modern revisionism and prevent the restoration of capitalism and successfully put the theory into practice for the first time, from 1966 to 1976.

But the teachings of Mao pertaining to the new-democratic revolution had the most powerful immediate influence on the Filipino proletarian revolutionaries for the simple reason that those teachings had a strong relevance to the social conditions in the Philippines and showed the way to make the new-democratic and socialist stages of the Philippine revolution. Further on, Mao Zedong Thought provides the theory and practice of continuing revolution under proletarian dictatorship until it becomes possible to defeat imperialism and attain communism on a global scale.

Marxism-Leninism-Mao Zedong Thought is the most comprehensive and profound guide of the Filipino proletarian revolutionaries, the reestablished Communist Party of the Philippines and the Philippine revolution with regard to the analysis of Philippine history and society; the first great rectification movement from 1967 to 1969; the reestablishment of the Communist Party of the Philippines; the revolutionary struggle from 1968 to 1980; the revolutionary struggle from 1980 to 1991; the second great rectification movement from 1992 onward; the Philippine revolution in the new world situation; and the socialist and communist future of the Filipino people.

I. The Analysis of Philippine History and Society

In 1959, a few young men and women, independent of the old merger party of the Communist and Socialist Parties, started forming study circles to read and study the works of Marx, Engels, Lenin, Stalin and Mao Zedong that could be gotten from secret collections. They initially did so amidst the open and legal studies about the problems of national independence and democracy. The Marxist-Leninist works that they read included the Communist Manifesto, Socialism: Utopian and Scientific, Wages, Prices and Profit, The Three Sources and Three Component Parts of Marxism, Imperialism: The Highest Stage of Capitalism, Two Tactics of Social Democracy, State and Revolution, The Foundations of Leninism, the Analysis of Classes in Chinese Society and Talks at the Yenan Forum on Art and Literature.

The most avid students of Marxism-Leninism read and studied Das Kapital, The Dialectics of Nature, Materialism and Empirio-Criticism, History of the CPSU (Bolsheviks), Short Course; the first edition of the Soviet-published Fundamentals of Marxism-Leninism and the Selected Works of Mao Zedong. The volumes of the selected works of the great communists began to reach the Philippines in 1962. To get hold of Marxist reading materials in the period of 1959–62 was by itself an achievement in view of the anticommunist hysteria and repressive measures since the end of World War II.

The objective of the beginners in the study of Marxism-Leninism was to seek solutions to what they perceived as the fundamental problems of the Filipino people, use Marxism-Leninism to shed light on the history and concrete circumstances of the Filipino people and find ways to resume the Philippine revolution and carry it out until victory. In the study of Marxism-Leninism, with special reference to the Philippine revolution, they sought to grasp the three components of Marxism, which are materialist philosophy, political economy and scientific socialism as laid down by Marx and Engels, developed by Lenin and Stalin and further developed by Mao Zedong.

The beginners in the study of proletarian revolutionary theory were exceedingly receptive to Mao's teachings because of their proven correctness and success in so vast a country neighboring the Philippines and their recognized applicability to the Philippines. The most read works of Mao Zedong were On Contradiction, On Practice, the Analysis of the Classes in Chinese Society, The Role of the Chinese Communist Party in the National War, Problems of Strategy in Guerrilla War Against Japan, On Protracted People's War and On New Democracy.

In the light of Mao's teachings, the Filipino proletarian revolutionaries could define clearly the periods of Philippine history; the precolonial communities until the 16th century; the colonial and feudal society until the end of Spanish colonialism; the colonial and semifeudal society under U.S. imperialism until 1946; and the semicolonial and semifeudal society which has continued to this day since 1946.

The semicolonial and semifeudal character of present-day Philippine society is basically similar to that of China before the 1949. This is a society ruled by the joint class dictatorship of the comprador big bourgeoisie and the landlord class, which are subservient to the foreign monopoly bourgeoisie. The basic oppressed classes are the working class and the peasantry, which in the main produce the surplus product appropriated by the basic exploiting classes. The intermediate social strata are the urban petty bourgeoisie and the middle or national bourgeoisie.

The social economy is mainly agrarian, semifeudal and preindustrial. There is some import-dependent manufacturing undertaken by the imperialists and the big compradors but there are no basic industries producing basic metals, basic chemicals, machine tools and precision instruments to qualify the Philippines as a "newly industrializing country". The economy is principally dependent on agricultural production for domestic staples and exports; and secondarily on the production of raw minerals for export. Even today, import-dependent and low value-added manufacturing for reexport is a showy but negligible part of the economy, providing little or no net income for the country because of transfer-pricing.

Correspondent to the semicolonial and semifeudal character of Philippine society, a national democratic revolution is required in order to liberate the Filipino people from foreign and feudal domination. It is a democratic revolution of a new type because it is no longer led by the bourgeoisie but by the proletariat in the historical context of modern imperialism and proletarian revolution or the world proletarian-socialist revolution; and it can proceed from the democratic revolution to the socialist revolution under the class leadership of the proletariat.

The motive forces of the revolution are the working class comprising about 15 percent of the population; the peasantry, at least 75 percent; the urban petty bourgeoisie, about 8 percent; and the middle bourgeoisie, about one percent. These are the motive forces of the revolution fighting to overthrow such class enemies as the comprador big bourgeoisie and the landlord class that comprise fractions of one percent of the population.

The working class is the leading class because it is the most advanced productive and political force. For this class to carry out its historic mission, it must have an advance detachment such as the Communist Party of the Philippines, armed with the revolutionary theory of the proletariat and pursuing the general political line that can arouse, organize and mobilize the broad masses of the people against the enemies of national and social liberation.

The proletariat through the Party overcomes its being a minority in the population and draws the overwhelming majority of the people to the revolutionary cause by linking up with the peasant masses in order to develop them as the main force of the revolution and form the basic worker-peasant alliance encompassing at least 90 percent of the people. The proletarian revolutionary cadres deployed in the countryside rely mainly on the poor peasants, lower-middle peasants and farm workers, win over the middle peasants and neutralize the rich peasants, take advantage of the splits between the enlightened and despotic landlords in order to isolate and destroy the power of the latter.

In pursuing the antifeudal class line, the proletarian revolutionary cadres and the peasant masses must fulfill the main content of the new-democratic revolution, namely the solution of the land problem. To do so, they have to carry out revolutionary armed struggle, land reform and mass-base building as integral components of the protracted people's war in the new-democratic revolution.

The semicolonial and semifeudal society is in chronic crisis. On the basis of this concrete fact, the armed revolution can and must be waged. The peasant masses are an inexhaustible source of support for the people's war led by the proletariat through its advance detachment, the Communist Party. The countryside provides the revolutionary forces with a vast field of maneuver for its growth in stages and accumulation of strength until it becomes possible to seize the cities. Even while the enemy is still well entrenched in the cities, Red political power can be built in the countryside.

The urban petty bourgeoisie is a smaller minority of the population than the proletariat. But this stratum of the bourgeoisie is highly instrumental in assisting the exploiting classes to rule society. It is highly influential in society. It is therefore absolutely necessary to win over sections if not the entirety of it in order to tilt the balance in favor of the revolutionary movement. The urban petty bourgeoisie is relatively the most exploited stratum of the bourgeoisie. In going over to the side of the revolution, it can become a basic force of the revolution.

The middle or national bourgeoisie is another bourgeois stratum, far thinner than the urban petty bourgeoisie. It is economically and politically weak, particularly in the Philippines, due to the lack of basic industries. It has a dual character. In pursuit of its legitimate but selfish interests, it is capable of opposing imperialism and feudalism. But at the same time, it participates in the exploitation of the working classes, wishes to gain power for itself and distrusts the masses. However, it can still be induced to become a positive force of the revolution, if the proletariat through the Communist Party of the Philippines has, in the first place, successfully built the basic worker-peasant alliance and, in the second place, won over the urban petty bourgeoisie.

It is also part of the revolutionary class line in the armed struggle and the united front to take advantage of the splits among the factions of the reactionary classes of the big compradors and landlords. The internal contradictions of the exploiting classes weaken their class rule and indirectly aid the advance of the revolutionary movement. When internecine conflicts arise among the reactionaries, it becomes possible to further isolate and range the widest array of forces against the ruling clique, which is usually the most reactionary and the most subservient to the foreign monopoly capitalists.

In the simplest of terms, the program of the new-democratic revolution is to overthrow foreign and feudal domination and to effect national liberation and democracy. Upon the nationwide seizure of political power, the new-democratic revolution is basically completed and the socialist revolution can begin. We therefore speak of two stages in the ongoing Philippine revolution: national democratic and socialist. These are continuous but distinct stages.

In the course of winning power through the new-democratic revolution, the prerequisites for subsequently making socialist revolution are prepared and developed. The state that arises after the nationwide seizure of political power takes the form of people's democracy which is founded on the basic worker-peasant alliance. But the new state is under the leadership of the proletariat and at its core is the proletarian dictatorship.

The capital and landed assets of the imperialists and the local reactionary classes are nationalized or put into the public sector. All strategic enterprises, main sources of raw materials and main lines of distribution are likewise put into the public sector or placed under state ownership. The agrarian revolution is completed and cooperativization is carried out in stages. Socialist industries are built and socialist education is carried out. Concessions are extended to the petty-bourgeoisie and the middle bourgeoisie for a certain time but the consistent and relentless objective is to realize the socialist transformation.

In most of the 1960's the proletarian revolutionary cadres learnt the principles of the new-democratic revolution from the teachings and successful experience of the Chinese revolution led by Comrade Mao Zedong. These encompass the character of Philippine society and the current stage of the revolution, the motive forces and targets, the tasks, and the socialist perspective of the revolution.

II. The Gestation of the Communist Party of the Philippines, 1959–68

It is quite easy for anyone with a high degree of book learning to read Marxist-Leninist works; but to absorb the revolutionary ideas and apply them on the concrete conditions of the Philippines is another matter. The proletarian revolutionary cadres who studied Marxist-Leninist works sought from the very beginning to initiate the revolutionary mass movement. They knew that it was the only way that the revolutionary ideas could become a material force in the Philippines.

The period of 1959–68 may be described as that of rekindling the anti-imperialist and antifeudal mass movement and gestating a new communist party. These had been destroyed in the 1950s. In the absence of the revolutionary mass movement, the U.S. imperialists and the local reactionaries were unchallenged in promoting all sorts of organizations to preempt its resurgence.

The single event that broke the long period of reaction and began to inspire the resurgence of the mass movement was the demonstration of 5000 students, mostly from the state university, to oppose and stop the anticommunist witchhunt in 1961. The witchhunt was an attempt to enforce the antisubversion law which had been enacted in 1957 to threaten with the death penalty anyone who dared to propagate Marxism-Leninism and resume any communist activity. Ironically, the law challenged and incited the youth to rise up in protest and to take interest in what would emerge as the national democratic movement.

The young proletarian revolutionaries initiated the mass protest action, without direction from the underground remnant of the old merger CP-SP party. Following their success, they expanded their study and organizing activities from the University of the Philippines to other Manila universities and proceeded to take leadership over student governments and campus publications. While openly promoting the general line of the national democratic revolution they also secretly organized Marxist-Leninist study groups.

Taking notice of the militant progressive movement and the initial efforts of the youth militants to link up with the progressive workers' and peasants' organizations, the general secretary of the CP-SP merger party, Jesus Lava, invited the representative of the youth militants and the representative of the progressive trade unions to become members of the old CP-SP merger party and also to become members of the executive committee which he formed in late 1962. Following the Lava's dynastic tradition, he also appointed to the five-person committee two of his nephews who were not at all linked to any kind of mass movement.

The young proletarian revolutionaries linked up in earnest with the veteran cadres and masses in the progressive trade unions and peasant associations. The mass movement of the youth, the workers and peasants, grew steadily. The Kabataang Makabayan was formed in 1964 as a comprehensive mass organization of students, young workers, young peasants and young professionals. Two legal labor federations and several unions became militated under the banner of the Workers' Party in 1963 (renamed Socialist Party in 1964). The peasant movement reemerged under the name of Masaka in 1963.

The young proletarian revolutionary cadres were the most active in promoting the study of the works of Marx, Engels, Lenin, Stalin and Mao and in creating Party groups within the mass organizations and Party branches in localities to serve as the revolutionary core of the mass movement. They were also the most militant in launching workers' strikes and mass actions to expose and oppose the antinational and antidemocratic policies of the reactionary government.

The Progressive Review started to be published in 1963 and had a circulation of only 1000 to 2000 copies; but it was the most important periodical in clarifying economic, political and cultural issues along the national democratic line. As separate speeches in pamphlet form or in the 1967 book form, Struggle for National Democracy, using the Marxist-Leninist stand, viewpoint and method, became the most important material for propagating the national democratic line. Also of great significance in reflecting the mass struggles in the 1960s were the leaflets and pamphlets issued for various mass actions. A compilation of these will show comprehensively the march of progressive events along the national democratic line.

Despite the estrangement of the Lava clique in the old CP-SP merger party from the remnants of the people's army that disobeyed Jesus Lava's 1955 policy of liquidating the people's army, the young proletarian revolutionaries developed relations with the cadres and commanders of the remnant people's army by supplying them with revolutionary propaganda and with Marxist-Leninist works, especially of Comrade Mao Zedong. The strongest Kabataang Makabayan chapters outside Manila in the 1960s were in Central Luzon. Thus, it was possible for the young proletarian revolutionaries to keep in touch with the remnants of the people's army, despite the Lavas' aversion to them.

In the old merger party, the young proletarian revolutionary cadres who studied and acted according to the teachings of

Comrade Mao Zedong succeeded in taking the ideological, political and organizational initiative. They created Party branches and caused the revolutionary mass movement to resurge. For a time, the scions of the Lava dynasty pretended to go along with the revolutionary line. But in December 1965, inner Party struggle began to simmer over fundamental issues when the representative of the young proletarian cadres presented the general report which the executive committee had assigned him to draft.

The general report appropriately sought to present and analyze the history of the old merger party and to explain the major errors and shortcomings that had led to the debacle of the revolutionary movement in the 1950s. Its main thrust was to rectify the serious errors and shortcomings and point to the necessity of resuming the armed revolution. Although the report was openly and honestly presented in accordance with the assignment, the scions of the Lava dynasty reacted bitterly and one of them made a motion to make the report a mere memorandum supposedly to assist him in making a new draft which he would never do. And worse, he proceeded to spread intrigues against the drafter of the report and against the revolutionary line.

The inner-Party struggle revolved around the issues of Lavaite subjectivism and opportunism, and Soviet-centered modern revisionism. Inspired by the Great Proletarian Cultural Revolution, the proletarian revolutionary cadres held their ground even more firmly and upheld the line of Marxism-Leninism-Mao Zedong Thought. It became inevitable that in April-May 1967 the proletarian revolutionary cadres decided to leave the old CP-SP merger party and to start preparing for the reestablishment of the Communist Party of the Philippines under the theoretical guidance of Marxism-Leninism-Mao Zedong Thought.

At this juncture, it is helpful to review certain points in the history of the original Communist Party which was established in 1930 and which became the CP-SP merger party in 1938. The reestablished CPP highly respects Comrade Crisanto Evangelista, the founder of the original CPP. He was the most formidable leader of the trade union movement in his time. Credit must be accorded to him for having had the wisdom and courage to pioneer the formation of the revolutionary party of the proletariat and for seeking to integrate the theory and practice of Marxism-Leninism with concrete Philippine conditions.

However, he had limited opportunities and therefore limited achievements in building the CPP ideologically, politically and organizationally. Soon after its establishment, the Party was outlawed and came under severe repression. Evangelista wrote propaganda about the class struggle between the proletariat and the bourgeoisie in general terms, about the factories as command posts of the revolution, and about the "communist paradise" to come but he was not able to define clearly the line of the new-democratic revolution and to build a nationwide revolutionary party of the proletariat. He tended to concede that the struggle for national independence was already being satisfied by the decolonization process being undertaken by the U.S. and the local reactionaries. He saw the peasant struggle as a struggle for reforms but did not yet see the peasant masses as the main force for carrying out a new-democratic revolution through people's war under the leadership of the proletariat.

In 1935, the underground Communist Party was joined by Dr. Vicente Lava who had learned his Marxism from the Browderite Communist Party of the USA. He eventually became the leader of the second line of leadership which was supposed to replace the first line led by Crisanto

Evangelista in case this would be wiped out by the enemy. The notion that the struggle for national liberation could be accomplished through parliamentary struggle was reinforced. So was the notion that the struggle for democracy was one of demanding civil liberties and had nothing or little to do with the substantive democratic question of land.

In 1937, the CPP was legalized, as a result of domestic and international calls by communist and bourgeois-democratic forces for a Popular Front against fascism and also as a result of the pretense of the Commonwealth government for a program of social justice amidst the grave economic crisis generated by the Great Depression. The CPUSA played a key role in pressing for the legalization of the CPP and the release of its leaders from domestic exile. In 1938, the CPP merged with the Socialist Party of the Philippines, which had arisen in 1932 and had continuously remained legal, essentially as an agrarian party. This merger was fraught with problems as it automatically incorporated into the CPP so many peasant militants who had not undergone any study of Marxism-Leninism.

The CP-SP leaders who constituted the first line of leadership were all arrested by the Japanese fascists in Manila in February 1942. They suffered martyrdom after refusing to call on Party members to capitulate to and register with the enemy. Thus, Vicente Lava, the first of a series of three brothers who became general secretaries, assumed the position of general secretary in March 1942. He conceived of the barrio united defense corps and presided over the formation of the people's army against Japan on March 29, 1942.

But Vicente Lava was basically a Right opportunist. After the Japanese military onslaught on Mt. Arayat in whose vicinity the squadrons (companies) of the people's army were concentrated, he pursued the "retreat-for-defense" policy, which concretely meant the excessive fragmentation of the Huk squadrons into small teams of three to five armed members and merely echoed the "wait-and-see" policy dictated by the United States on pro-U.S. Filipino guerrillas to serve merely as the eyes and ears of the U.S. military intelligence and not to actively wage armed struggle far ahead of the return of the U.S. military forces.

Until September 1944, the most successful fighting Huk units were the platoons that disobeyed the "retreat-for-defense" policy. The Central Committee of the CP-SP merger party corrected this wrong policy but only when the U.S. military forces were about to land in the Philippines. The Huk squadrons were re-formed to take advantage of the retreat of the Japanese troops to the mountain provinces of Northern Luzon and to seize power at the municipal and provincial levels in Central Luzon just before the arrival of the U.S. troops.

Lava admitted his error and agreed to its correction. But he pushed another Right opportunist policy — that of welcoming the U.S. military forces, the formal grant of national independence, the installation of a neocolonial puppet republic; and preparing for the conversion of the people's army and armed peasant movement into a veterans' organization and a legal peasant organization for the purpose of waging parliamentary struggle.

Lava pushed the line of "peace and democracy" and Right opportunist leaders of the CP-SP merger party and the Hukbalahap ran for positions in the big comprador-bourgeois and landlord congress under the banner of the Democratic Alliance in 1946 when the United States shifted from direct colonial to semicolonial rule. But even as they genuinely won their seats in Congress, these known leaders of the CP-SP merger party and their allies were kicked out from their seats in Congress on trumped-up charges of fraud and terrorism.

In the countryside, the U.S. Counterintelligence Corps, the Philippine Constabulary and the civilian guards perpetrated massacres in order to wrest back political power and put the land back under landlord control in Central Luzon. Right opportunists worse than Lava (Pedro Castro and Jorge Frianeza) gained the upper hand in the leadership of the CP-SP merger party, pushed the line of collaborating with the Roxas puppet regime and agreed to the registration of Hukbalahap fighters.

Under these conditions, Jose Lava, the second of the Lava brothers to become the secretary general of the CP-SP merger party, took the initiative of fighting the Right opportunists and called for the resumption of the revolutionary armed struggle in 1948. But he failed to clarify the strategy and tactics. Inconsistently in 1948 and 1949, the Huk commander-in-chief Luis Taruc was allowed to negotiate for general amnesty. Following the discovery of the scheme of the reactionary regime to murder the underground leaders who surfaced under the amnesty agreement, Jose Lava pushed the line of "all-out armed struggle" against the Quirino puppet regime in 1950. He spelled out his line of achieving military victory within two years, imagining a geometric progression of spontaneous popular support and banking on armed uprisings promised by the Nacionalista Party politicians — the former Japanese puppet president Jose Laurel and Eulogio Rodriguez.

The battalions and companies of the people's army were renamed People's Liberation Army in 1950. They added up to some 3000 fighters with rifles. Two thousand of these were concentrated in military camps in the unpopulated forests of the Sierra Madre mountain range. In August 1950, they launched coordinated attacks on enemy forces on a wide scale. But in October 1950, the entire Political Bureau led by Jose Lava was captured in Manila. The second coordinated offensive slated for November 1950 could no t be carried out. Instead, the 30 army battalions newly equipped and trained by the United States were taking both strategic and tactical offensives against the forest military camps of the people's army in a purely military situation favorable to the enemy.

The "Left" opportunist Jose Lava leadership never bothered to work out the line of the new-democratic revolution and the integration of revolutionary armed struggle, land reform and painstaking mass work for a protracted people's war. After the 1950 debacle, Jesus Lava (brother of Vicente and Jose) became the Party general secretary. He also failed to consider and work out the requirements of a protracted people's war. Both Jose and Jesus Lava suffered from the petty-bourgeois mentality of wishing for an easy way to seize political power without fully and seriously studying the realities and weighing all the necessary factors in the revolutionary struggle.

In the case of Jesus Lava, he briefly wished to continue armed struggle and then took a Right opportunist line and proceeded to adopt policies seeking to liquidate the people's army and subsequently the CP-SP merger party. He tried to liquidate the remnants of the old people's army in 1955 by calling on them to turn themselves into "organizational brigades" for parliamentary struggle and, subsequently, the Party itself by devising in 1957 what he called the "single-file" policy of dissolving every Party collective and ordering Party members to form single files and receive his political transmissions from his isolated Manila hideout.

The old merger party practically ceased to exist in late 1950s. There was not a single existing Party branch in late 1962. The general secretary Jesus Lava was completely isolated from any mass movement. He had been drafting his political transmissions from 1955 to 1962 on the basis of clippings from the bourgeois press. He had no significant connections with any mass movement or with the remnants of the people's army which continued to exist as roving rebel bands in the plains of some provinces in Central Luzon.

Meanwhile, among the remnants of the people's army, there were the cadres and commanders who persevered in serving the peasant masses and there were also others who degenerated into banditry and running protection rackets in Angeles City adjoining the U.S. Clark Air Force Base and compromising with the landlords in the class struggle between landlords and peasants. This latter type of the remnants of the people's army, most represented by the Taruc-Sumulong gangster clique, also became the target of criticism and repudiation by the proletarian revolutionaries and by the New People's Army.

There was the crying need to reestablish the Communist Party of the Philippines and the people's army. This was realizable only because the proletarian revolutionaries had already grasped the theory of Marxism-Leninism-Mao Zedong Thought through which they could make the correct analysis of Philippine history and society and the criticism and repudiation of previous grave errors of the Lava brothers and the Taruc-Sumulong gangster clique and proceed to wage the new-democratic revolution.

III. The Revolutionary Struggle, 1968–1979

The Lava revisionist renegades wished to impose their line of indefinite parliamentary struggle on the proletarian revolutionaries and the people. Their line was engendered by their own bourgeois subjectivist and opportunist world outlook and by the line of the Soviet revisionist renegades. The two-line struggle between the proletarian revolutionaries and the Lava revisionist renegades became so intense that the latter threatened to inflict physical harm on the former. It was necessary for the proletarian revolutionaries to break away from the counterrevolutionary revisionists in April 1967, to wage a vigorous campaign of criticism and repudiation of the Lava revisionist renegades and reestablish the Communist Party of the Philippines under the theoretical guidance of Marxism-Leninism-Mao Zedong Thought.

It took more than a year to prepare for the reestablishment of the Party. The preparations included consolidation meetings of the proletarian revolutionaries, consultations with Party members and mass activists and drafting of the documents of reestablishment: Rectify Errors and Rebuild the Party and the Constitution and the Program of the CPP. The Congress of Reestablishment had only twelve delegates (one in absentia) representing only a few scores of Party members and candidate-members in the trade unions and the youth movement. They had the support of a few hundreds of advance mass activists and an urban mass base of nearly 15 thousand workers and youth. Soon after the reestablishment of the Party in 1968, the proletarian revolutionaries linked up with the good part of the remnant people's army with a rural mass base of 80 thousand peasants in the second district of Tarlac in Central Luzon.

On March 29, 1969, on the 27th anniversary of the founding of the people's army against Japan, the Party established the New People's Army and promulgated the Rules of the NPA. This entailed the criticism and repudiation of the Taruc-Sumulong gangster clique which had discredited the name of the armed revolutionary movement with its unprincipled and criminal activities. The NPA started with only sixty fighters, with nine automatic rifles and 25 inferior firearms. Expansion cadres for Northern Luzon, Southern Tagalog and the Visayas were trained from February to May 1969. The first expansion team was dispatched to Isabela province. In May 1969, the Central Committee of the CPP held a plenum to study further the strategy and tactics of people's war and also the peasant movement, and to include in its ranks peasant cadres and battle-tested Red fighters. The plenum decided that Tarlac and the whole of Central Luzon would serve as the resource base for nationwide expansion.

In both urban and rural areas, the reestablished CPP inherited the fine revolutionary tradition of the proletariat as well as the senior and middle-aged cadres of the long-drawn workers' and peasants' movement. The mass organizations of workers, peasants and youth condemned both the Lava revisionist group and the Sumulong gangster clique and fully criticized and repudiated the long unrectified grave errors of subjectivism and opportunism and the blatant degeneration of these renegades. The Lava revisionist renegades prated about parliamentary struggle as the main form of struggle but it was the proletarian revolutionaries who actually continued to lead the legal democratic movement. In fact, the revolutionary armed struggle inspired and served to strengthen the legal struggle.

From the very beginning, the objective of the proletarian revolutionaries was to create a nationwide Party organization with a cadre and mass character, deeply rooted among the working people and building a people's army waging protracted people's war and recruiting most of its fighters from the peasantry. The proletarian revolutionaries recognized that the people's army would be in a vulnerable position if it existed only in a small part or even in a much larger part of the plains of Central Luzon. They understood the necessity of developing guerrilla zones at various strategic points in the Philippine countryside and archipelago as soon as possible. Thus, from the very outset, members of the Party Central Committee were assigned particular regions to pay attention to and cadres for nationwide expansion were given politico-military training.

Even as it resumed the revolutionary armed struggle in earnest, the Party continued to lead the legal democratic mass movement in the urban areas. All sorts of legal mass organizations sprouted among the workers, peasants, youth, women, cultural activists, teachers and other professionals. In April 1969, the Party led a legal peasant demonstration of 15,000 in Manila and another one of 50,000 in Tarlac. In the first quarter of 1970, it was able to conduct weekly converging marches and demonstrations against the U.S.-Marcos regime over a comprehensive range of domestic and international issues, including the U.S. war of aggression in Vietnam. The participants ranged in number from 50 thousand to 100 thousand youth and workers per mass action. The First Quarter Storm of 1970 served to strengthen all the patriotic and progressive mass organizations, especially the Kabataang Makabayan, on a nationwide scale. The timely statements of the Party, later compiled in the book The First Quarter Storm of 1970, gave direction to the militant urban mass movement.

The urban-based Kabataang Makabayan acted as the seeding machine of the national democratic revolution all over the archipelago. It became the most important source of cadres who were immediately deployable for mass work. The Party accelerated its urban mass work. It encouraged the formation of new progressive unions and trade union federations such as KASAMA and PAKMAP and the transformation of reactionary unions into progressive ones. It built mass organizations among the urban poor and among the poor fishermen. It enlarged the KM chapters in urban poor communities as well as in colleges and high schools. It formed various types of organization among teachers, creative writers, artists, scientists and technologists, health workers, lawyers and other professionals.

Simultaneous to the militant mass actions in Manila and scores of other cities, the NPA intensified its armed tactical offensives in the second district of Tarlac. This enraged the enemy which accelerated search-and-destroy operations with the full force of a division and a wide network of paramilitary units against the barely 200 fighters of the NPA. By December 1970, the enemy declared that the NPA had been finished off. The NPA in Central Luzon was indeed in an extremely difficult situation due to the overwhelming concentration of enemy military strength. But unknown to the enemy, the work of expansion in Cagayan Valley had already resulted in a far wider mass base in Isabela and which extended to Nueva Vizcaya and Quirino. Also, revolutionary work had started in the Cordilleras.

Amidst the fierce revolutionary struggle, the Party was able to run courses of study on Marxism-Leninism-Mao Zedong Thought and on the basic documents of the Party. It would be able to reproduce eventually seven volumes of its own selections from the works of Mao Zedong as well as the works of Marx, Engels, Lenin and Stalin. It was able to put out Ang Bayan which published reports on and analyses of the ongoing revolutionary struggle in the Philippines and abroad and made critiques of the ruling system and U.S. imperialism.

After the reestablishment of the Party, the earliest and most sustained work that emerged from the revolutionary struggle was Philippine Society and Revolution (in its 1969 mimeographed form). Inspired by Marxism-Leninism-Mao Zedong Thought and using the Marxist-Leninist stand, viewpoint and method, the book traced the basic strands of Philippine history, defined the basic problems of the Filipino people and clarified the class strategy and tactics of the new-democratic revolution.

The ideological struggle against modern revisionism was kept up against the Lava revisionist renegades, the American revisionist renegade William Pomeroy and against their Soviet revisionist renegade masters, Khrushchov and Brezhnev. The sizeable collection of antirevisionist articles by the CPP is now a major part of the treasury of the proletarian revolutionary struggle.

As a result of the decisions taken by the August 1970 meeting of the Political Bureau in the forest region of Isabela, The Organizational Guide and Outline of Reports was formulated to explain the principles and methods of making social investigation, building the Party, the people's army, mass organizations and organs of political power and making reports on the situation and activities. The Organization Department of the Party took vigorous efforts to recruit Party members from the ranks of the revolutionary mass activists that had emerged from the First Quarter Storm of 1970 and ensuing mass actions and to urge the new Party recruits and the mass activists to take assignments in the rural areas. In the urban areas, Party recruitment and education among the youth was done mainly through the schools for national democracy, undertaken by organization-education teams of the Kabataang Makabayan and other organizations.

In April 1971, the Central Committee held its Plenum in the forest region of Isabela. As a result of this, the Rules for Establishing the People's Government and the Revolutionary Guide to Land Reform were formulated; and the work of nationwide expansion of the Party and the people's army was pushed further. The membership of the Party had risen to more than 1000 members. The mass base in Cagayan Valley was already 300,000. The revolutionary armed struggle was started in the Partido district of Camarines Sur. By 1972, expansion cadres were creating Party organizations and guerrilla zones in eight regions of the country: Northern Luzon, Central Luzon, Southern Tagalog, Bicol, Eastern Visayas, Central Visayas, Western Visayas, and Mindanao. United front work at various levels assisted the emergence and development of the revolutionary armed struggle.

Following up the suspension of the writ of habeas corpus in 1971, the U.S.-Marcos regime imposed martial rule on the Philippines in 1972 and suppressed all the aboveground progressive mass organizations. Hypocritically, Marcos announced that he wished to "save the republic" and "build a new society" in the face of the severe crisis of the ruling system and the newly-emergent armed revolutionary movement. At this point in time, however, the Party had only 2000 Party members, the NPA had only 300 full-time fighters with automatic rifles, hundreds of militia units, thousands of part-time guerrillas and local militia and a rural mass base of less than 400 thousand under local organs of political power and an urban mass base of some 50,000.

With the outlawing of the progressive mass organizations and the manhunt for their leaders, the Party decided to deploy to the countryside the Party members and mass activists who had been forced underground. However, the capacity of the rural Party organizations and the people's army to absorb them was limited. So, quite a number were encouraged to further develop the urban underground or start underground work in their home provinces, irrespective of the presence or absence of revolutionary forces. In 1973, the Preparatory Commission of the National Democratic Front adopted the 10-point program of the NDF and provided a framework for uniting the progressive mass organizations which had been forced underground as well as other possible allies.

Some petty-bourgeois commentators with superficial and partial knowledge of CPP history denigrate the people's war being waged by the reestablished Party as merely a dogmatic copy of that led by Mao Zedong. They cannot grasp that in accordance with the teachings of Mao Zedong, the CPP applies the theory of Marxism-Leninism on the concrete conditions of the Philippines and consequently the concrete development of the Philippine revolution has its unique features. There are indeed, basic similarities and common adherence to basic principles. The social conditions in the Philippines and pre-1949 China are basically similar and therefore the corresponding character of the revolution is similar. There are the common basic principles such as that painstaking mass work must be done and popular support must be gained as the inexhaustible and invincible base of the Party and the NPA, that the people's army must grow from small to big and from weak to strong over a protracted period of time and follow a probability course of strategic defensive, strategic stalemate and strategic offensive. And while the NPA is on the strategic defensive, it must wage tactical offensives in order to accumulate strength and build Red political power in the countryside until it becomes possible to seize political power in the cities and on a nationwide scale.

At the same time, there are marked dissimilarities between the Philippine and Chinese people's war, such as that the NPA had to start with guerrilla squads and not with large forces breaking away from the national army of the CPC-KMT alliance, that the main form of struggle in the strategic defensive is guerrilla warfare and not regular mobile warfare, that the minimum land reform program of rent reduction and elimination of usury is being carried out before the maximum program of land confiscation, that a single imperialist power overextended all over the world dominates the Philippines and not several imperialist powers at odds with each other inside the country through their respective puppets as in China, that China is a vast country where the Long March could take place while the Philippines is a medium-sized archipelagic country in which the short marches can add up to long marches and that, of course, international conditions are now different.

The CPP made timely criticisms of both dogmatism and empiricism and both adventurism and conservatism in the revolutionary struggle. It criticized the formalistic and ritualistic use of Marxist-Leninist terminology without providing the concrete facts on the basis of social investigation and mass work. It also criticized adventurist tendencies and the tendency of some cadres to look to foreign military assistance as a decisive factor in winning victory as well as tendencies of conservatism in mass work and armed struggle. It constantly called for a self-reliant revolutionary armed struggle, integrating armed struggle, land reform and mass base building and coordinating urban and rural work within the framework of the new-democratic revolution.

In 1974, it was clear that the great overall achievement of the Party was building itself and the NPA on a nationwide scale. Party membership rose to 4,000. The Party had well-consolidated guerrilla zones at so many strategic points favorable for guerrilla warfare on a nationwide scale. It had a wealth of experience in people's war in terms of positive and negative experiences and overall success. The isolation of the main military units of the NPA in Isabela due to heavy enemy concentration and due to the grave error of keeping these units in the forest region after the enemy's forced mass evacuation of the people was more than compensated for by the nationwide expansion of the Party and the people's army.

On the basis of social research and the abundant experience in the armed revolution, Specific Characteristics of People's War in the Philippines was written in 1974. This was a comprehensive and thoroughgoing application of Mao Zedong's theory and strategic line of protracted people's war in the Philippines. It carried a number of propositions that clarified the way to wage armed revolution in the Philippines and raised the fighting confidence of the Party members and Red fighters to a new and higher level. Among the important propositions were that, aside from the use of the countryside and the rough terrain as a wide room for maneuver, the archipelagic character of the country can be converted from being a disadvantage to being an advantage for further dividing the forces of the enemy so long as the correct revolutionary class line and mass work are carried out in the struggle. The slogan, "major islands first, minor islands next," was put forward. The principle of centralized leadership, ideological and political, and decentralized operations was adopted.

Open mass work and secret Party work flourished in the trade union movement from 1969 to 1972. Under conditions of martial rule, the progressive labor federations and trade unions were suppressed. So, work in the trade unions were carried out underground from 1972 onward. But in 1974, the workers' strike movement came to life, starting with the La Tondea strike and spreading to 300 workplaces all over the country. It became clear that the workers' movement would become the main force in forthcoming mass struggles in the urban areas. The urban poor communities were also becoming militated, uncowed by frequent enemy zoning operations or raids.

The student movement began to stir anew, demanding democratic rights and the restoration of student governments and publications which were suppressed by martial rule. Simultaneously, the capacity of the Party organizations in the rural areas to absorb manhunted Party personnel and mass activists increased greatly. Thus in 1974, the Party could dispatch more of them to the countryside.

By the end of 1975, Party membership nationwide had risen to 5000 and the NPA had 1000 full-time fighters with automatic rifles and a thousand more with inferior firearms. On the basis of the discussions and decisions of the plenum of the Central Committee in December 1975, a comprehensive and deepgoing summing-up and rectification document, Our Urgent Tasks was drafted in 1976 and published in the first issue of Rebolusyon in the middle of that year. This systematized the principles, methods and steps in building the mass organizations, the local organs of political power, the people's army and the local Party branches. This document distilled the most successful experiences of the revolutionary cadres and combated the wrong ideas and wrong methods in carrying out the armed revolution. The draconian situation in the country persisted.

By 1976, it was clear that the NPA on a nationwide scale was approaching the phase in which guerrilla fronts would multiply, with platoons as centers of gravity, and in which frequent and widespread platoon-size offensive operations could be launched against the enemy. Previously, these were rare and could be launched in only a few places. Well-consolidated guerrilla zones and even stable guerrilla bases were becoming more defined in contrast to the guerrilla zones in areas of expansion. Previously, guerrilla zones meant a cluster of a few barrios. Now, entire municipalities had become guerrilla zones. These guerrilla zones or several municipalities comprised the guerrilla fronts.

One squad of the NPA often sufficed to effect control of a municipality and often divided into armed propaganda teams in order to do mass work. This was possible because the rural municipality usually has a police force of ten to twenty-five men and the regular troops of the enemy (constabulary and army) simply do not have the force to maintain superior presence in every one of the 1500 municipalities and cities of the Philippines. On the basis of the expansion and consolidation of the mass base and the multiplication of the NPA guerrilla squads over time, it became possible to form platoons as centers of gravity and as strike forces in guerrilla fronts.

Since the beginning of the armed struggle, the creation of new guerrilla zones or expansion work had been the most challenging and most dangerous work. It could be done best only when there was a consolidated guerrilla zone from which to expand or, in a completely new area, when mass work was done without the premature show of arms. Errors in carrying or showing arms without prior mass work were paid for in blood by comrades, as in Zambales from 1969–71, Negros in 1969, Antique in 1972 and Mindanao in 1972, to cite only a few cases.

From 1970 onward, there were cases of grave errors involving the premature formation of absolutely concentrated companies, the purely military viewpoint and mountain-stronghold mentality. The first one was that of a premature company-size formation in 1970 in the sparsely wooded areas of Tarlac-Zambales which was completely wiped out in one tactical encirclement by the enemy resulting in the loss of at least 60 high-powered rifles. In 1973, an ill-armed company formation disintegrated under the blows of the enemy in Nueva Vizcaya. The remnant platoon proceeded to Quirino province and built itself up into a full company formation through rapid armed tactical offensives but without consolidation and expansion through mass work. Eventually, this company failed to withstand the counteroffensive of overwhelmingly superior enemy forces in 1975. In Sorsogon province in 1974, another full company which had rapidly grown from armed tactical offensives, but without solid mass organizing, also failed to withstand a powerful enemy counterattack.

The worst cases of prematurely concentrated company formations included the case of two well-armed companies in the Isabela forest region from 1972 to 1976. The regional Party committee and army command (especially those who were members of the Central Committee) insisted on staying in the forest region, despite the forced mass evacuation of the people. The two companies put themselves in an isolated and passive position, allowing the enemy to use the Cagayan river to cut them off from the masses, despite the instructions of the Central Committee for them to follow the example of the NPA platoon in Tumauini, slip out of the enemy encirclement, redeploy into smaller units and move towards the masses in Cagayan Province. In the Northern Luzon Party Conference in 1977, a thoroughgoing criticism of the error was made by the Central Committee and by the cadres and commanders of the region themselves.

Up to 1979, the regional Party organization and people's army in Eastern Visayas (particularly Samar island) showed the way to create a wide and deepgoing mass base and to build the revolutionary forces on this basis: Each guerrilla zone was taken care of by an NPA squad and on the scale of the guerrilla front, platoon-size tactical offensives were frequently undertaken. Municipal police forces and paramilitary units were disarmed and small detachments of regular troops were wiped out frequently. Thus, the Party and the people's army in Samar island became the model of revolutionary armed struggle throughout the country.

On the whole, the CPP was successful in waging the armed revolution from 1968 to 1979. The growth of the revolutionary forces was gradual and steady but cumulative. The municipal police forces, the paramilitary units at the barrio level and small detachments of regular enemy troops became the prime targets of NPA operations. Never was there an instance that a regional Party or army organization was decimated. In the twists and turns of the armed revolution, there were separate instances when grave losses were incurred by leading organs at various levels and by particular local forces. But on a nationwide scale, the revolutionary movement grew in strength and advanced from year to year. Even during the exceedingly difficult period of 1972–73, when martial rule had been recently imposed, the Party and other revolutionary forces were able to preserve themselves and grow on a nationwide scale.

While the decade of the 1970s was characterized by revolutionary successes from year to year, there were already certain unhealthy tendencies manifested at the level of the NPA national operational command. There was the notion spread by the head of the NPA national operational command up to 1976 that no stable base areas could arise in the Philippines before the total liberation of the country and that foreign military assistance was an absolute necessity for winning victory. At the 1975 Plenum of the Central Committee, there was also a Rightist demand from another cadre to withdraw Marxism-Leninism-Mao Zedong Thought from the masthead of Ang Bayan as well as the categorical term, anti-Marcos reactionaries, previously used to refer to such big comprador-landlord politicians as Benigno Aquino. From his previous insistence in 1976 that small teams of three to five armed fighters (reminiscent of the 1942 "retreat-for-defense" policy) should be the model for mass and guerrilla work, still another prominent cadre of Central Luzon swung in 1977 to the "Left" opportunist line that a company be concentrated out of the measly total of 105 armed personnel of the entire region.

Also in 1977, the questioning of the Marxist analysis of Philippine society as semicolonial and semifeudal started. A few cadres were impressed by the big-comprador infrastructure-building and fake land reform programs of the U.S.-Marcos regime and misconstrued these as promoting urbanization and industrialization. They even considered the export of cheap Filipino labor and engineering skills to the Middle East as an overflow of Philippine economic development. These comrades could not see that Marcos was not putting up basic industries and not carrying out land reform but was aggravating the agrarian, semifeudal and preindustrial character of the Philippine economy.

The U.S.-Marcos technocrats, with their theory of development; the Lava revisionist renegades, with their theory of noncapitalist development; the exponents of dependent capitalism; and the recipients of funds from the Australian Trotskyites were active in spreading the notion that the multinational firms and banks were out to turn the Philippines into a foreign-owned industrial base. All these served to stimulate the tendency of some Party cadres to speculate that the analysis of Philippine society as semicolonial and semifeudal was already outdated, notwithstanding the actual deepening and aggravation of the semifeudal character of the Philippine economy due to excessive foreign borrowing for anti-industrial purposes.

In 1978, the thrust of the questioning of the Party's correct description of the character of Philippine society was to put forward the idea of making a leap from the early substage of the strategic defensive to the advanced substage and accelerating the victory of the Philippine revolution by deploying more cadres for armed city partisan warfare and for a potential urban insurrection. The 1945 uprising and the 1968 Tet offensive in Vietnam and the 1979 final offensive in the Nicaraguan revolution were taken out of historical context and used to denigrate the theory and strategic line of protracted people's war. Although the NPA had only around 1500 full-time Red fighters with automatic rifles, the Central Committee declared that preparations had to be made for the leap from the early to the advanced substage of the strategic defensive. Thus, it designated "war fronts", administratively coalesced guerrilla fronts and created new command levels (even if unnecessary). This line of thinking ran counter to the need for multiplying platoons as centers of gravity and multiplying the number of guerrilla fronts.

From 1976 to 1980, there was a rapid nationwide growth of the Party, the people's army and the mass base as a result of the strong foundation built under the guidance of Marxism-Leninism-Mao Zedong Thought and such definitive documents as the founding documents of the Party and the NPA, Philippine Society and Revolution, Specific Characteristics of People's War in the Philippines and Our Urgent Tasks. As regards the NPA, its Red fighters with automatic rifles grew in number up to 2000 or by 100 per cent because of the tactical offensives carried out by platoons and oversized platoons. They benefited from an expanding and consolidated mass base in which land reform and other mass campaigns for the benefit of the people were conducted.

Abroad during this period, the essentials of Marxism-Leninism-Mao Zedong Thought were being negated and reversed in China. The depreciation of Mao Zedong in his own homeland tended to influence a few Party cadres in the central leadership. Although no member of the Central Committee ever dared to frontally attack the theory and strategic line of people's war, it became fashionable for a few members of the Central Committee and some central staff organs to propose the "innovation" on the strategic line of protracted people's war by putting forward the line of urban insurrectionism and the premature formation of absolutely concentrated NPA companies.

At the same time, the U.S. Central Intelligence Agency financed and instigated its Filipino assets in Katipunan ng Demokratikong Pilipino in the United States to spread the propaganda in the Philippines that the way to victory in the Philippines was to drop Mao's theory and strategic line of protracted people's war. To camouflage their U.S. imperialist connections, they proposed having the military and financial assistance of the Soviet Union as the decisive factor in the victory of the Philippine revolution.

IV. The Revolutionary Struggle, 1980–1991

Regarding the period of revolutionary struggle from 1980 to 1991, the most recent comprehensive and important documents of the Communist Party of the Philippines to read and study are: Reaffirm Our Basic Principles and Rectify Errors, General Review of Important Events and Decisions, 1980–1991 and Stand for Socialism Against Modern Revisionism. These documents approved by the 1992 Plenum of the CPP Central Committee strongly reaffirm Marxism-Leninism-Mao Zedong Thought as the guide to revolutionary action under the leadership of the CPP as well as to the current rectification movement, the second great one since the first in the period of 1967–69, for the purpose of overcoming deviations, errors and shortcomings and reinvigorating the Party and the revolutionary mass movement.

In the period of 1980–83, the revolutionary movement advanced at a rate faster than in any year in the 1976–79 period. Party membership increased annually by almost 4000. Basic Party units were established in the barrios, factories, schools, communities, in the people's army and mass organizations. In 1982, there were 34 platoons as centers of gravity of guerrilla fronts and more than 200 squads at the base, doing mass work. An annual average of 800 to 900 rifles were confiscated from the enemy by squads and platoons. By the end of 1983, the armed strength of the NPA was 5000 automatic rifles. To this day, the record shows that most of the NPA's weapons have been seized from the enemy by the squads and platoons.

In 1982–83, guerrilla fronts covered almost entire provinces and big portions of regions. Those of Mindanao, Samar, Negros and Bicol covered two-thirds to three-fourths of the total land area and total number of barrios. All guerrilla fronts in the country extended to well-populated areas, including environs of town centers, along highways, seashore and plains. In 1983, the majority of regions had two or three big and relatively stable guerrilla fronts. Tactical offensives by the NPA echoed each other all over the archipelago. Land reform and other mass campaigns thrived in the guerrilla fronts.

In the 1980–83 period, the legal democratic movement in both urban and rural areas steadily developed. Then it rose rapidly to an unprecedented level in the entire history of the revolutionary movement in 1983, following the assassination of Benigno Aquino and continued to surge until the Marcos fascist dictatorship was overthrown in 1986. It continued to grow until 1987. The contradictions within the ruling clique had led to the assassination in 1983 of Marcos' arch political rival Aquino and consequently the split of the reactionary armed forces between the Marcos-Ver and the Enrile-Ramos factions.

The rapid advance of the revolutionary armed struggle and the legal democratic movement and rapid increase of armed strength was the result of a number of factors: (1) the strong foundation of the revolutionary movement developed in the 1970s; (2) the perseverance of the revolutionary forces along the correct line in most regions, in accordance particularly with the founding documents of the Party, Specific Characteristics of People's War in the Philippines, Our Urgent Tasks and the Basic Party Course;

and (3) the rapid worsening of the crisis of the ruling system, which exacerbated not only the contradictions among the reactionaries but even within sections of the ruling clique.

Throughout the period of 1980–91, the correct line was upheld by the overwhelming majority of Party cadres and members and in most regional Party committees and organizations. But certain erroneous currents, which had started in the late 1970s to run among a few elements in the Central Committee and certain central staff organs, took shape and force through certain "Left" and Right opportunist lines in the 1980 Central Committee Plenum to challenge, undermine and reverse the correct line. In this Plenum, much time was devoted to questioning the Party's long standing analysis of Philippine society as semicolonial and semifeudal with the end in view of modifying the strategic line of protracted people's war, giving more importance than ever to revolutionary work in the urban areas and effecting the leap from the early to the advance substage of the strategic defensive through urban insurrections. It was asserted that the Philippines was more industrialized and urbanized than pre-1949 China and that therefore urban revolutionary struggles had a bigger role to play in the Philippines than in China in the past. The urban population of 40 per cent was arrived at by adding the population of the chartered cities and poblaciones (town centers).

In the 1981 meeting of the Political Bureau, the tasks of accomplishing both the leap from the early to the advance substage of the strategic defensive and moving on to the "strategic counteroffensive" and "regularization" were laid down. In 1982, the Mindanao Commission adopted the line of urban insurrectionism and military adventurism under the inspiration of the 1981 Political Bureau meeting. In its

1983 meeting, the Political Bureau, elaborated on the line of "strategic counteroffensive" and "regularization". It presupposed the accomplishment of the advance substage of the strategic defensive, described it as the second substage and called for carrying out the strategic counteroffensive as the third and final substage. Third and fourth class municipalities were classified as urban areas and as initial targets for uprisings.

The term "strategic counteroffensive" was a misnomer which meant the "Left" opportunist wish to accomplish far more than what the given forces of the revolution could permit. It overrated the role of armed urban insurrections in opposition to the strategic line of encircling the cities from the countryside. In fact, third and fourth class municipalities are categorizable as rural. Even the city of Yenan was rural relative to the city of Sian or faraway Shanghai. The line of "regularization" meant creating more layers of the Party bureaucracy and filling up the positions with Party members, without undertaking the corresponding theoretical and political education. It also meant — for the people's army — additional levels of command and further staffing, premature formation of larger units and aiming for an intensification of the war through regular mobile warfare, irrespective of the general level of development. The term "full-time Red fighters" was reinterpreted to mean separation from mass work and preoccupation with military tasks.

Even while the central leadership pushed the wrong line, the overwhelming majority of Party cadres and members adhered to Marxism-Leninism-Mao Zedong Thought, studied the founding documents of the Party, the basic Party study course along this line, studied Specific Characteristics of People's War in the Philippines and Our Urgent Tasks. In 1982, a definitive article, On the

Philippine Mode of Production, argued against the misconception about the character of the Philippine economy. In 1983, another article, "On the Losing Course of the Armed Forces of the Philippines", argued against premature verticalization of the people's army and pointed out its potential damage to the mass base. These articles were circulated to oppose the wrong line.

It took some time before the wrong line from the central leadership could be put into practice extensively. In the early 1980s the revolutionary forces in Samar and Negros continued to demonstrate that it was possible to intensify armed struggle while attending to mass work. Running counter was the attempt to put up a battalion in Samar. But the central leadership decided to disband it and redeploy the most capable cadres to other regions. Learning lessons from bitter experiences in the 1970s, the forces in Northern Luzon, Bicol, and Western Visayas paid close attention to mass work and gradually developed their armed strength by launching tactical offensives with platoons and squads. Even the forces in Mindanao generally followed the pattern of the other regions until 1982. With the exception of two platoons, the forces of Central Luzon persisted with squads and small teams in carrying out revolutionary work in the plains.

The line of "strategic counteroffensive" and "regularization" encouraged the more blatant militarist line of combining urban insurrectionism with military adventurism in Mindanao from 1982 to 1984. This line exaggerated the urbanization and industrialization of the Philippines in general and Mindanao in particular, in effect wrongly praising the U.S.-Marcos regime for supposedly developing and industrializing the country. It also wrongly presupposed that the Party had neglected urban revolutionary work, notwithstanding the fact that the Party had consistently developed and led the urban-based legal democratic movement. It put forward the idea that urban insurrection, prepared by armed city partisans and by sweeping propaganda and ultimately accomplished by the spontaneous masses, was the highest form of political struggle and that the people's army was a purely military force and was secondary to the armed urban insurrection. It also exaggerated the international work of the Party as a decisive factor for winning the revolution.

The erroneous line of combining urban insurrectionism and military adventurism was aggressively carried out in Mindanao from 1982 to 1984. Sweeping contact and propaganda work was done in the urban areas, armed city partisan warfare was intensified and people's strikes were carried out by busing in peasants or using NPA units to set up "checkpoints". Solid mass organizing was neglected and underground cadres in the narrow and small provincial cities exposed themselves to the enemy. In the countryside, fifteen absolutely concentrated NPA companies were rapidly formed from 1983–85. Fifty percent of the Red fighters were absorbed by the main regional guerrilla units (companies) and another large percentage were absorbed by secondary regional guerrilla units (usually platoons). These left a very few squads doing mass work, especially because they were converted into supply units of the main units. By 1984, the prematurely formed companies in absolute concentration had been put in a passive and isolated position both by the self-imposed drastic shrinkage of the mass base and the intensified strategic and tactical offensives by the enemy. Most of the time, these companies were preoccupied with logistical problems and were vulnerable to enemy attacks.

As a result of precision raids by the enemy on the urban underground and the military defeats of the absolutely concentrated NPA companies, the "Left" opportunists explained away the setbacks as the work of deep penetration agents. Thus, hysteria set in and led to the Ahos campaign in 1985. This bloody witchhunt was approved by the 1985 Executive Committee of the Mindanao Commission and was carried out by the so-called caretaker committee. It allowed the torture and execution of suspects without sufficient evidence. It victimized hundreds upon hundreds of Party members, Red fighters, mass activists and allies. At no time had the enemy killed as many CPP members, NPA fighters, mass activists and allies in so short a time and demoralized so many others. Party membership in Mindanao dropped from 9000 to 3000, the mass base decreased by more than 50 percent and the armed strength of the people's army fell from 15 companies and 30 platoons to two companies and 17 platoons.

There were definitely some deep penetration agents because of the loose recruitment policy along the wrong line of combining armed urban insurrectionism and military adventurism. But Ahos campaign was not the way to pinpoint them. On the other hand, it was the way for the real enemy agents to cause further destruction and to conceal themselves. Above all, the Party cannot permit the violation of the basic rights of Party members and Red fighters as set forth by the Party Constitution and the Rules of the New People's Army as well as the basic democratic rights of the people guaranteed by the Bill of Rights in the Rules for Establishing the People's Government.

In 1984, the first national military conference was held by the national military staff of the NPA. It adopted the line of urban insurrectionism and military adventurism, which was already resulting in gross setbacks in Mindanao. The line was pushed chiefly by the chief of staff who had just been promoted from his position as NPA commander in

Mindanao on the basis of the false reputation of having achieved great military victories. The Executive Committee and Military Commission uncritically approved the results of the military conference.

The NPA chief of staff and the members of the Executive Committee of the Mindanao Commission who were at the same time members of the Central Committee withheld from the 1985 Central Committee Plenum information about their erroneous line, the gross setbacks in 1984 and the Ahos campaign. They misrepresented themselves as cadres of a successful line and arrogantly demanded the withdrawal of the strategic line of protracted people's war in favor of the line of combining urban insurrectionism and military adventurism. The Central Committee repulsed the demand by invoking the fact that the strategic line of people's war was still in the Constitution and Program of the Party but failed to withdraw and correct the line of "strategic counteroffensive" which fathered the disastrous "Left" opportunist line in Mindanao. Instead, the Plenum put forward a three-year program of "developing/making" the NPA "as a regular army", building the factors of regular mobile warfare, maximizing the advantages of guerrilla warfare and "intensifying the war" towards the "strategic counteroffensive". In effect, the strategic line of protracted people's war was discarded, despite lip service to it.

In the absence of a factual assessment and correct evaluation of the situation in Mindanao, the highest officials of the Executive Committee of the 1985 Mindanao Commission kept their high positions and were promoted to higher positions of central leadership (Political Bureau, Executive Committee and Military Commission). Thus they gained the position which enabled them to further push their erroneous and disastrous line on a nationwide scale, especially because they bandied about their line as exceedingly successful in Mindanao. Their obsession was to create 36 absolutely concentrated companies and several battalions throughout the country by 1987. In July-August 1987, the NPA general command bypassed the territorial Party committees and ordered a so-called nationally coordinated offensive. It consisted of 600 big and small attacks on enemy hard points and wasted ammunition and other resources.

From 1986 to as late as 1990, one regional Party organization after another was pushed to adopt a variant of insurrectionism or putschism. In the formation of the premature and unsustainable larger military formations, the mass base drastically shrank and the situation became purely military as the enemy launched brigade-size offensives and at the same time fielded "special operations teams" (SOTs) to conduct psy-war and intelligence operations in the guerrilla fronts. The enemy could effectively carry out its war of quick decision and gradual constriction because in the first place the "Left" opportunist line had played into his hands. The gross error of the "Left" opportunists can be seen in the fact that they had reduced the number of squads and armed propaganda teams doing mass work and therefore reduced the mass base as the area of maneuver for the people's army, while the enemy was the one fielding "special operations teams" in order to create his "mass base" with the help of the local reactionary government, local police, paramilitary forces and religious fanatical cults. Since 1984, the enemy had been deploying brigades to concentrate on areas known as bastions of the NPA, to try to "clear and hold" and then to "consolidate and develop" them through small-unit operations. But the enemy left unattended far larger areas of the country and has never achieved control without gaps over any guerrilla front.

The loss of mass base meant the loss of political and material support of the masses for the people's army as well as the loss of capability to collect taxes from the relatively enlightened sections of the exploiting classes. The resulting loss of self-reliance strengthened the notion among the "Left" opportunists that the revolutionary movement could be supported by gangster activities in the urban areas and by foreign military and financial assistance. While still the NPA commander in Mindanao up to 1984, the 1984–91 head of the NPA national military staff conducted gangster activities, combining NPA armed city partisans with elements of criminal syndicates to carry out robbery hold-ups and kidnap-for-ransom. These were not authorized by the Party at the appropriate level. He spread the wrong notion that the people's army had a separate machinery from the Party. He also considered foreign military assistance as the factor that would decide the fate of the revolutionary movement and that without such assistance, the revolutionary movement would suffer stagnation or retrogression.

From 1984 onward, the national military staff (later called "general command") of the people's army based itself in Manila in accordance with the line of combining urban insurrectionism and military adventurism. The head of the national military staff preoccupied himself with so-called special operations, including gangster activities in Manila and other urban areas in the country, and seeking foreign military and financial assistance. After the overthrow of Marcos in 1986, he further justified his basing in Metro Manila by claiming to be ever on the alert for "a sudden turn of events" for "seizing opportunities" towards urban insurrection. In fact, he was overseeing and participating in gangster activities and in corruption at the customs bureau of the reactionary government. He sought to separate the people's army from the absolute leadership of the Party and pretended to command the units of the people's army all over the country by radio transmissions from Manila. Later, he escalated gangster activities independently or in collaboration with certain elements in the Manila-Rizal Party committee and the Visayas Commission.

By 1985, there was already a conspicuous degree of ideological degeneration among some members of the Central Committee. This was the result of the sheer disappearance of Marxist-Leninist study courses and reading materials, the rampancy of eclecticism, the depreciation of Mao Zedong Thought, the baseless questioning of the Marxist-Leninist analysis of Philippine society, the underrating of the Philippine revolutionary experience in people's war and the propagation of urban insurrectionism and military adventurism. Elements who never seriously studied and applied Mao Zedong Thought rated the examples of movements for decolonization and against despotic rule higher than the accomplished two-stage Chinese revolution and the already rich experience of the new-democratic revolution with a socialist perspective in the Philippines.

The line of seeking foreign military and financial assistance from the Soviet party and its allied parties had been pushed since 1982. It had a "Left" opportunist objective of accelerating the victory of the Philippine armed revolution through the importation of heavy military weapons. But in fact it had a Rightist content as it meant deviating from the antirevisionist line of the Party. As early as 1984, the "general command" of the NPA was already dispatching couriers to contact pro-Soviet parties abroad to seek military and financial assistance without full information given to the Executive Committee of the Central Committee.

In 1985, a proposal was made at the 9th Plenum of the Central Committee to consider the Soviet Union a socialist country. But the Central Committee decided to subject the proposal to further study. However, there was already a paper of the International Liaison Department as well as a study commissioned by the central leadership picturing the Soviet Union as a socialist and no longer a social-imperialist country and the Soviet party as a Marxist-Leninist, no longer a revisionist party. The Brezhnev ruling clique was hailed as a champion of proletarian internationalism. It was praised for achieving military parity with the United States and for giving assistance to national liberation movements and third world countries.

The "Left" opportunists who pushed the line of combining urban insurrectionism and military adventurism at the central and regional levels of the Party based themselves in the urban areas, notwithstanding the development of consolidated and stable guerrilla base areas and their proclaimed desire to build companies and battalions. The urban-basing is a clear manifestation of the greater value given to urban insurrectionism; it was the clearest point of departure for violating the strategic line of protracted people's war. If the "Left" opportunists had been more interested in building larger military formations, even if premature, than in wishing for an armed urban insurrection, they would have positioned themselves in the countryside rather than in the cities.

While the revolutionary forces in Mindanao suffered gross setbacks between 1984 and 1986, those in Luzon, (especially Northern Luzon) and the Visayas regions continued to make advances in the revolutionary armed struggle until 1987 and made up to a great extent for the big losses in Mindanao. However, the overall rate of growth for the entire movement declined from 1984 to 1987. As a result of the nationwide promotion of the "Left" opportunist line of combining urban insurrectionism and military adventurism, the revolutionary forces registered overall negative growth from 1987 to 1990. Relative to 1986, Party membership declined by 15 percent, the number of barrios covered by local organs of political power by 16 percent and, worst of all, the membership in rural mass organizations by 60 percent as a result of both errors and enemy action. The rifle strength of the NPA continued to grow but the rate of growth dropped to that of 1976–78. Cadres at the provincial, front and district levels were lost. A large percentage of the consolidated barrios were also lost.

From 1986 onward, one interregional or regional Party committees after another was pushed to build absolutely concentrated companies and adopt some insurrectionist and putschist plan. But most of the interregional commissions and regional Party committees and army commands eventually complained of the unreasonable targets imposed on them by the "Left" opportunists with regard to the formation of NPA companies and launching of offensives. Some of them were forced by circumstances to make adjustments in the years 1988–91. As late as 1987, the Political Bureau endorsed the rapid increase of absolutely concentrated companies and considered peasant uprisings within two years as the way to advance the peasant movement. In 1988, however, the central leadership noticed the decline of the mass base and heeded the demands of certain regions to allow them to redeploy the Red fighters and pay attention to mass work. Thus, it had a strong basis for starting to criticize the imbalances in revolutionary work and call for painstaking mass work and solid mass organizing.

The 1988 Party anniversary statement, which briefly summed up the 20-year history of the Party, criticized the imbalances in revolutionary work. In 1989, conferences on mass work were held at regional and interregional levels and a large portion of the NPA forces were redeployed for mass work, especially for recovery and expansion. The 1989 Party anniversary statement called for rectification, the further strengthening of the Party and the intensification of the people's revolutionary struggle. Like that of 1989, the 1990 Party anniversary statement clearly identified and criticized the errors of "regularization" and verticalization of the forces at the expense of developing the horizontal forces in stages and called for extensive and intensive guerrilla warfare on the basis of an ever widening and ever deepening mass base. The struggle between the proletarian revolutionary line and the bourgeois opportunist line intensified within the central organs of the Party. The "Left" and Right opportunists tried and succeeded in certain regions to block the documents of the central leadership which carried the correct line.

In 1990, the Political Bureau nullified the erroneous concept of "strategic counteroffensive" and put a stop to its implementation; but inconsistently it approved the results of the National Military Command Conference due to pressures by the "Left" opportunists. The trend in 1990 and 1991, however, was for the proletarian revolutionaries to defeat the wrong line and unscrupulous maneuvers of the "Left" opportunists. The Military Commission of the Central Committee and the Political Department of the NPA, in cognizance of the problems confronting the people's army, moved to hold the First National Conference on the Political Work of the New People's Army in March-April 1991, which basically adhered to the proletarian revolutionary line. In 1990 and 1991, the rapid narrowing of many guerrilla fronts was stopped. The people's army was further redeployed for mass work. There was a significant recovery of the mass base.

By the middle of 1991, the "Left" opportunist line was basically defeated at the level of the central leadership on the basis of the incontrovertible facts about its disastrous character and results and as a consequence of the assertion of the proletarian revolutionary line. But defeating the "Left" opportunist line also involved defeating the Right opportunist line in 1990 and 1991 because the most persistent and most malicious elements pushed the Right opportunist line of class collaboration, reformism and capitulationism for the avowed purpose of reaching the "Left" opportunist goal of armed urban insurrection irrespective of or even without the development of the people's war.

The questioning and denial, since 1968, of the character of Philippine society as semicolonial and semifeudal society in chronic crisis gave rise not only to the "Left" opportunist line of urban insurrection and military adventurism but also to the Right opportunist line of "regularization", "strategic counteroffensive", reformism, capitulationism and liquidationism. Some of the chief opportunists could flip-flop from one type of opportunist position to another or make schemes which metaphysically combine the two, usually pushing a Right opportunist line in practice and at the same time wishing for an armed urban insurrection at the expense of the revolutionary mass movement in both urban and rural areas.

In common with the "Left" opportunists, the Right opportunists gave the utmost importance to urban legal struggles and to urban-basing. They considered urban-based legal struggles — not the revolutionary armed struggle — as the principal form of revolutionary struggle.

As early as 1978–79, one group of Right opportunists in the Manila-Rizal Party organization provoked a struggle with the central leadership by insisting on the participation of the Communist Party of the Philippines in the farcical elections held by the U.S.-Marcos regime.

The debate was erroneously formulated as one of choosing between participation and boycott. The central leadership failed to resolve the debate at a level of principle higher than the boycott-participation dichotomy which certain elements in the Manila-Rizal Party committee wanted to dictate. The Party could have declared the 1978 elections as a farce and still allowed the legal progressive forces to use the elections as an opportunity to expose and oppose the fascist dictatorship. Disciplinary measures were meted out to the elements in the Manila-Rizal Party organization who generated struggle mania and ultrademocratic actions and made physical threats.

These elements disrupted the Manila-Rizal Party organization. After the disciplinary actions were taken against these unruly elements, another group of Right opportunists in charge of the urban mass movement and the united front was able to seize the opportunity to push its own Rightist line in the national capital region (NCR). They strengthened their position by their access to Western bourgeois and religious funding agencies and by using these funds to create urban-based offices and promote the line that sheer urban legal struggle and building urban institutions and coalitions could advance the revolution.

The Plenum of the Central Committee in 1980 encouraged the exponents of "Left" and Right opportunism to espouse urban insurrectionism and parliamentarism, respectively, by allowing both opportunists to spread doubts about the strategic line of people's war. The Politburo meeting in

1981 went further in favoring both types of opportunism. The "Left" opportunists were allowed to lump together and reject both liberal democrats (petty-bourgeois) and the anti-Marcos reactionaries (big comprador-landlord politicians) as "bourgeois reformists" along the line of monopolizing victory in the antifascist struggle, which was anticipated as forthcoming. At the same time, the Right opportunists were allowed to spread their own notion of "broad legal alliances" which aimed at playing down the revolutionary forces and tailing after the anti-Marcos reactionaries.

In 1981, the Right opportunists were already proposing the replacement of the vanguard proletarian party with a "vanguard front" called the New Katipunan. But the Party repulsed this blatantly liquidationist proposal. At any rate, the Right opportunists proceeded to realize their concept of "broad legal alliance", which meant denying or concealing the role of the Party in the antifascist struggle, kowtowing to and carrying the sedan chair for the anti-Marcos reactionaries and diluting the national democratic program. They preoccupied themselves with high level meetings and sweeping propaganda calls. They drew cadres from the countryside to the cities and recruited those whom they called "national democrats" to staff their offices.

The Right opportunist line ran so deep that "national democrats" (those who accepted the general line of the new-democratic revolution) from the ranks of the mass activist were enrolled into the Party without any Marxist-Leninist education and that only a few of these recruits were sent from the cities to the countryside. Party recruitment and education were sparsely undertaken in the course of the flow of the legal democratic movement in the period 1983–86 which occurred due to the long pent-up popular hatred against the fascist dictatorship and the sustained public outrage at the Aquino assassination.

Instead, cadres were attracted and drawn from the countryside to the cities and from work at the grassroots level in both urban and rural areas to higher levels, without replenishment at the grassroots level.

Following the overthrow of the Marcos dictatorship, there were recriminations within the Party over the boycott policy taken by the central leadership, particularly the Executive Committee of the Central Committee in the 1986 snap presidential elections. The Political Bureau decided that the boycott policy was a major tactical error and the Party chairman was compelled to resign. But the Right opportunists continued to insist that the error was a strategic one that occurred due to the commitment of the Party to the strategic line of people's war and not due to a "Left" opportunist and sectarian illusion that the Party could win victory through a boycott. In collaboration with anti-Party pseudoprogressive petty-bourgeois groups, they insisted that the Party should de-emphasize or stop the revolutionary armed struggle as the main form of struggle and emphasize the legal forms of struggle in the new situation in order to be in a better position to gain power sooner through elections or insurrection.

Among those who also took this line were the "Left" opportunists who had committed grave errors resulting in the 1984–86 disaster in Mindanao. They overstated the boycott error as the biggest error in the entire history of the Party in order to conceal their far greater errors and crimes in Mindanao. They even went to the extent of saying that the Party could have seized or taken a major share of political power had it been prepared for the Edsa uprising and had it not been obsessed with the strategic line of people's war. Subsequently, from 1986 onward, they used the Edsa uprising as an argument for both parliamentarism and urban insurrectionism and as a possible model for effecting social revolution.

They failed to understand the Edsa uprising as merely an anti-authoritarian uprising and not a social revolution. It was a phenomenon whose course and outcome were chiefly determined by the U.S. and the reactionary forces even as the forces of the Left and the spontaneous masses hated the tyrant and participated in his overthrow. The proletarian revolutionaries put forward Philippine Crisis and Revolution and Continuing Struggle in the Philippines to expose the counterrevolutionary character and weaknesses of the U.S.-Aquino ruling clique and to clarify the line of the revolutionary struggle amidst the confusion whipped up by the "Left" and Right opportunists. The Party study course on Lenin was also put forward to counter the opportunists and was combined with the study of the people's war in China. But this was sporadically undertaken and was not followed up by a more comprehensive and thoroughgoing campaign of Marxist-Leninist education.

From 1986 onward, the Right opportunists who advocated parliamentarism pure and simple as well as those who combined parliamentarism with urban insurrectionism collaborated with the promoters of anticommunist petty bourgeois currents outside the Party, such as the Christian-democrats, bourgeois populists, the pro-imperialist liberals, the old-type revisionists and the Trotskyite petty-bourgeois socialists in caricaturing and attacking the Party's strategy of people's war. By 1988, the Right opportunists began to openly adopt Gorbachovite revisionism and to babble about the "marginalization of the class struggle" and the need to get rid of working class leadership and the revolutionary principles of Marxism-Leninism to achieve "openness" and "democracy".

It was from 1986 onward that the limits of peace talks with the enemy, electoral politics, parliamentary struggle and foreign-funded NGOs became clearly demonstrated as the pseudoprogressive petty-bourgeois groups remained marginal and inconsequential and became no more than tails of the big comprador-landlord politicians. But the Right opportunists became more aggressive from year to year in pushing their reformist, pacifist and capitulationist line and in attempting to undermine the legal democratic movement. By 1988, it was clear that they had already sabotaged the legal mass movement in conjunction with the exponents of urban insurrectionism with whom they collaborated in drawing away personnel and resources from solid organizing among the basic masses and from Marxist-Leninist education.

The legal democratic movement peaked in 1986 and began to slow down in 1987, especially among the workers, peasants, fishermen, urban poor, women and teachers. The Right opportunists specialized in misdirecting personnel and resources towards building foreign-funded institutions and coalitions out of the same pool of legal organizations and steering them towards parliamentarism and reformism. The most talented youth were also influenced to veer away from the mass movement. At the same time, the "Left" opportunists in the urban areas departed from solid mass organizing and concentrated on forming small groups of armed city partisans and ordering these to go into indiscriminate killings that provoked the enemy to assassinate mass activists and suppress the most militant mass organizations, especially in urban poor communities in 1987 and 1988.

However, from 1988 onward, upon the increasing frustration and bankruptcy of the "Left" opportunist line of combining urban insurrectionism and military adventurism, a conspiratorial, factionalist and splittist bloc of Right and "Left" opportunists increasingly promoted Gorbachov's revisionist line in certain central staff organs, certain regions and Party groups within certain institutions.

In 1990, the Right opportunists tried to usurp the authority of the central leadership and sought to liquidate the Party and the revolutionary movement through a series of maneuvers. They tried to do away with the Executive Committee of the Political Bureau as the daily collective leading organ of the Party. They sought to replace the Party as the center of the revolution with the NDF. At the same time, they tried to change the NDF program from one of new-democratic revolution into one of bourgeois nationalism, pluralism and mixed economy; and convert the NDF from a united front or alliance into a mix-up of member-organizations and individual members.

They peddled the concept of the "anti-imperialist democratic front" which meant combining the Left, Middle and Right against the U.S.-Aquino regime. They pushed the line of going Right supposedly in order to reach the goal of urban insurrection (medium-term plan) and promoted the line of capitulation and pacifism on the question of peace. They also tried hard to entrap the legal progressive forces into the capitulationist framework of the "multisectoral peace advocates" and people's caucus and convert them into a "third force" between the revolutionary movement and the reactionary government. They tried to remove the Central Committee as publisher of Ang Bayan and used a number of issues to espouse the Right and "Left" opportunist lines and actions and to hail Gorbachov as "a communist renewing socialism" even as he was already unmasking himself as an anticommunist completely restoring capitalism.

Within the organs of the central leadership, the proletarian revolutionaries struggled against the ideas of the "Left" and Right opportunists who tended to support each other. From year to year on one major issue to another since 1988, the opportunists were beaten through reasoning on the basis of the facts of the disastrous results of their erroneous ideas. In 1990, they took advantage of the dislocation and difficulties of the central leadership due to enemy pressure and tried to go on a rampage of usurping authority and promoting their counterrevolutionary Rightist line. But in 1991, they were basically repulsed and beaten. Towards the end of 1991, the chief advocate of parliamentarism and urban insurrection prepared four long letters addressed to the general membership attacking the central leadership which by then was securely in the hands of the proletarian revolutionaries. The central leadership undertook a series of decisions to assert the proletarian revolutionary line and resolved to launch a comprehensive and thoroughgoing rectification movement in the Party.

In reaction to the rectification movement, the ringleaders of the "Left" and Right opportunists have thoroughly exposed themselves as a counterrevolutionary Rightist group, using anticommunist, anti-Stalin slogans and serving as special psy-war and intelligence agents of the U.S.-Ramos regime after trying in vain to decapitate, discredit, disintegrate and destroy the Party and the revolutionary movement through factional, splittist and wrecking activities. The most vicious counterrevolutionary Rightists who attack the rectification movement include those who have committed not only serious ideological, political and organizational errors but also serious criminal offenses against the Party and the people. They have thoroughly exposed themselves and are now the target of criticism and repudiation by the Party rank and file.

Despite the serious deviations and errors committed by the "Left" and Right opportunists for a long time without prompt correction and which are only now being comprehensively and thoroughly rectified, the all-round strength of the Party and the revolutionary movement remains formidable and in varying respects is equal to the level of 1983 or 1984. The Party has several tens of thousands of members both in rural and urban areas and is deeply rooted among the toiling masses of workers and peasants. There are millions of people in the armed revolutionary movement and the legal democratic movement under the leadership of the Party. Most of these people are covered by the organs of political power both in rural and urban areas. They are in the mass organizations of workers, peasants, youth, women, professionals and other people. There are the Party branches in factories, farms, schools and communities and the Party groups in institutions and mass organization.

The New People's Army is under the absolute leadership of the Party. The strength of the people's army includes several thousands of full-time Red fighters, with automatic rifles and other high-powered weapons. These weapons are nearly 100 percent seized from the enemy through tactical offensives. The Red fighters are augmented by part-time guerrilla squads, the militia and self-defense units. The Party is at the core of and leads the organs of political power and the rural-based mass organizations. The Party also leads the united front. This encompasses the organs of political power, the National Democratic Front and legal alliances based on class and sectoral interests and

V. Rectification Movement Under Marxism-Leninism-Mao Zedong Thought: 1992 Onward

A comparison between the period of 1968–77 and the subsequent period of 1978–91 shows that in the former period deviations, errors and shortcomings were promptly and thoroughly criticized and repudiated in the light of Marxism-Leninism-Mao Zedong Thought; while in the latter period the most serious deviations and errors arose, accumulated and hardened within central leading and staff organs without being promptly criticized and rectified, thus increasingly undermining and violating the theory and practice of Marxism-Leninism-Mao Zedong Thought. Subjectivism and opportunism ran rampant within the Party as a result of the slackening of ideological vigilance and militancy along the proletarian revolutionary line.

At the root of all the ideological, political and organizational deviations, errors and shortcomings within the Party was the diminution and in certain areas even disappearance of the study and conscious application of Marxism-Leninism-Mao Zedong Thought. When the ideological line is not correctly and clearly defined and followed, then all kinds of deviations, errors and shortcomings can thrive. Preoccupation with practical work from day to day, without the guidance of theory leads to unhealthy currents, degeneration and grave losses.

At the end of 1991, the proletarian revolutionary cadres and the entire Party membership recognized the urgent need for a comprehensive and thoroughgoing rectification movement. The first and main rectification document, Reaffirm Our Basic Principles and Rectify Errors was drafted and together with other rectification documents was processed by the Executive Committee, the Political Bureau and the Central Committee, one after the other in

1992. It is based on scores of major documents and hundreds of other documents over a period of several years, reflecting the democratic interaction of the central leadership with lower Party organs and organizations through direct investigations, consultations, reports and minutes of conferences and meetings at various levels of the Party.

The most important task in the rectification movement is theoretical education in Marxism-Leninism-Mao Zedong Thought. The rectification movement is mainly and essentially an education movement. After a long period of neglecting theoretical education, the Party is compelled to make a new start in accordance with the principle that there can be no revolutionary movement without a revolutionary theory. But this time, the Party is endowed with a far greater amount of revolutionary experience, both positive and negative, than that which the proletarian revolutionaries had in 1967 to 1969, during the first great rectification movement. There is also far greater confidence because there is now a far greater number of Party cadres and members and they are determined to overcome the deviations, errors and shortcomings.

In this education movement, the most important study materials are Reaffirm Our Basic Principles and Rectify Errors, the supporting document, General Review of Important Events and Decisions from 1980 to 1991 and Stand for Socialism Against Modern Revisionism. The first two documents focus on deviations, errors and shortcomings in the Philippine revolutionary struggle and the third document deals with the revisionist deviation, explains the phenomenon of modern revisionism and capitalist restoration, firms up the resolve to achieve the national-democratic and socialist stages of the Philippine revolution, combats the ideological offensive of the imperialists and their anticommunist petty-bourgeois camp followers and points to the bright socialist and communist future of mankind.

Even as these documents are the result of the study and analysis of accomplished facts and are based on democratic discussions within the Party, these are open and subject to the endless dialectical process of study and practice. So, the lower Party organs and organizations are being encouraged to further sum up and analyze their experience in the light of these documents, drawn by the central leadership in the exercise of its duty to provide ideological and political leadership to the entire Party organization and the revolutionary movement. In giving life to the principle of democratic centralism, the Party follows the dictum of Mao Zedong Thought, "from the masses to the masses" of the Party membership through the appropriate organs and units of the Party.

In view of the prolonged period in which theoretical education has been diminished or neglected in the entire Party, there is currently the drive to reproduce the classic works of Marxism-Leninism-Mao Zedong Thought and basic Party documents along the proletarian revolutionary line within the Party, promote immediately the reading and study of these by all Party collectives and to undertake a three-level program of study: basic, intermediate and advance. In the past, there was either a scarcity or complete lack of these Marxist-Leninist study materials. At the same time, where and when there were some studies, these were sporadic and either incomplete or lopsided. To correct such a situation, the cadres in charge of education are instructed to push the three-level program of study.

The basic Party course seeks to instill the spirit of serving the people, self-sacrifice, combating liberalism and proletarian internationalism and to provide an initial understanding of dialectical and historical materialism, a comprehensive grasp of Philippine history, the basic problems of Philippine society, the new-democratic revolution and the current rectification movement.

The intermediate Party course seeks to develop the ability of the Party cadres and members to analyze their own experience and the experience of their particular collectives and the entire Party organization in actual revolutionary struggle — in Party building, army building and united-front building, economic work and cultural work, in the light of the basic central and regional documents of rectification and, above all, in the light of Marxism-Leninism-Mao Zedong Thought. Comparative studies are also made within the framework of the national revolutionary struggle and of the world proletarian revolution, in accordance with Marxism-Leninism-Mao Zedong Thought. The main thrust is to study the experience of the Party and the essential and relevant works of Comrade Mao Zedong.

The advance Party course seeks to provide a thoroughgoing, comprehensive and deepgoing understanding of the three stages of Marxism, Leninism and Mao Zedong Thought in materialist philosophy, in the critique of capitalism and revisionism, in the grasp of socialist political economy, and the strategy and tactics of the proletariat in the new-democratic and socialist stages of the revolution and in continuing the revolution under proletarian dictatorship in socialist society until communism can arise. The objective of the advance Party course is to create a corps of senior and middle-level cadres capable of leading the Philippine revolution now and in the long future.

Theoretical education in the CPP is not formalistic. It is integrated with the concrete practice of the Philippine revolution. There is a wealth of experience and an accumulation of problems to solve in the ongoing revolutionary practice of the Party cadres and members. The living study of Marxism-Leninism-Mao Zedong Thought is most intense when confronting the long unrectified and deepgoing deviations and errors of the past and the current serious problems. The rectification movement is absolutely necessary. Otherwise, the Party cannot overcome the long-accumulated problems and the drive of the imperialists and the petty-bourgeois anticommunists to destroy it through ideological and psychological warfare in combination with the most brutal military means.

The current circumstances for pushing Marxist-Leninist theoretical education are exceedingly favorable. Firstly, the subjectivist and opportunist currents that have been pushed by unremoulded petty-bourgeois elements within the Party have been frustrated in actual revolutionary practice and have been basically defeated by the central leadership through its basic rectification documents and by the entire Party membership through further study and analysis of their experience. Secondly, the disintegration and collapse of the revisionist ruling parties have in a big way cleared the way for the advance of the proletarian revolutionary cadres who are armed with Mao Zedong Thought. Thirdly, the crisis of the world capitalist system is rapidly worsening and the imperialists and their retinue of petty-bourgeois anticommunists are now embarrassed by their own triumphalist propaganda about their "victory over socialism". Their straw-figure socialism is in fact modern revisionism and bureaucrat capitalism masquerading as socialism.

The old and new Filipino revisionists (Gorbachovites), bourgeois populists, liberals and neoliberals, the petty-bourgeois socialists, Christian-democrats, social-democrats, Trotskyites, insurrectionists and militarists who have hitched a ride on the anticommunist ideological and political offensive of the imperialists and who have separately and jointly mocked at Marxism-Leninism and at the CPP have dramatically exposed themselves as a small band of anticommunist counterrevolutionaries by their own proclamations and actions. They draw their slogans from the antiquated arsenal of the Cold War by declaring themselves as an anti-Stalinist alliance and by acting directly and indirectly in collaboration with and in support of the U.S.-Ramos regime.

Since the late 1970s, the most blatant attack on the line of the CPP has been on its analysis of Philippine society as semicolonial and semifeudal. It took the form of ceaseless questioning without respect for the facts. This was followed by the proposal to change the strategy and tactics of the new-democratic revolution, especially in the sphere of armed struggle, under the guise of innovating on, refining and adjusting strategy and tactics. Thus, the "Left" opportunist line of "regularization" and "strategic counteroffensive" as well as of combining urban insurrectionism and military adventurism; and the Right opportunist line of liquidationism, reformism, capitulationism and pacifism were pushed.

By way of rectification in the field of political education, such works as Philippine Society and Revolution, Specific Characteristics of People's War in the Philippines, Our Urgent Tasks, On the Mode of Production in the Philippines, Philippine Crisis and Revolution, Continuing Struggle in the Philippines are being put forward as study materials concerning the character of Philippine society, the character of the ongoing stage of the Philippine revolution, the motive forces, the targets, the tasks, the socialist perspective of the Philippine revolution.

To rectify the grave error of militarism, there is now a wide recognition of the need to develop extensive and intensive guerrilla warfare with a widening and deepening mass base in the entire stage of the strategic defensive of the people's war. There is now a clear recognition that the drive to form NPA companies and battalions interfered with and prevented the full development of platoon-size forces and operations and the multiplication and consolidation of the guerrilla fronts; unduly lessened the number of guerrilla squads and armed propaganda units as the horizontal forces for mass work and the sustainable guerrilla platoons and companies as centers of gravity of guerrilla fronts and regions, respectively; shallowed and narrowed the mass base; and resulted in intolerable logistical burden on the masses because of the top-heavy structure of the NPA.

Thus, a major point in the rectification movement is the redeployment of the forces of the NPA. The main thrust is to have only 25 to 30 percent of NPA personnel in platoons and companies serving as centers of gravity (rallying points and strike forces) from the level of the guerrilla fronts upward; and 70 to 75 percent of the personnel serving in local guerrilla squads, subdivisible into armed propaganda teams for mass work under favorable conditions (where enemy forces are not concentrated). The NPA retains the capacity to launch offensives involving various sizes (small teams, squads, platoons, companies and upward) according to the level of development and concrete circumstances.

Even the centers of gravity are to be in relative concentration when not in an offensive mode, so that they can also participate in mass work and other nonmilitary work. The center of gravity goes for absolute concentration only when conducting tactical offensives, politico-military training, security duty, tax enforcement, and other similar operations. A big number of guerrilla squads are now deliberately spread out in order to expand and consolidate the existing guerrilla fronts, recover lost ground and open and develop new areas of work. At the same time, these guerrilla squads can be drawn in like a net by the center of gravity to muster the superior strength for annihilating or disarming an enemy target.

The drive to prematurely build NPA companies and battalions in violation of the line of extensive and intensive guerrilla warfare has resulted in gross setbacks. There is therefore a return to the period before the full development of platoon-size forces and operations and multiplication and consolidation of the guerrilla fronts was aborted. It is wrong to form prematurely larger units, fight in the way that the enemy wants us to fight and thus play into his hands. Thus, the line of "strategic counteroffensive" and "regularization" and its worst application in the line of combining urban insurrectionism and military adventurism have been criticized and repudiated.

There is no mystery about the apparent success of the enemy with its offensive strategy or war of quick decision and its tactics of gradual constriction. Due to his far superior military forces, it suits him to deploy brigades in order to concentrate on a guerrilla front or a province and then tries to convert his strategic advantage into tactical advantage by using special operations teams for intelligence and psywar purposes and also well-informed and well-armed platoons, companies and battalions for specific offensive operations. He can be successful only if in the first place the NPA forces in his target area have given up the strategy and tactics of guerrilla warfare that is widely and deeply based among the people in a protracted people's war. The copy-cat special operations teams can be successful only insofar as the NPA has previously given up mass work and the expansion and consolidation of the mass base.

Through correct redeployment and mass work, the NPA can go back to the strategy and tactics which yielded the most weapons by launching only those offensives that can be won. It can disarm the paramilitary forces and the local police and wipe out small units of the regular enemy forces. It can evade the superior enemy forces that it cannot yet defeat. Instead of trying to hit the large forces or hard points of the enemy, it can wait for in ambush or lure in the small part of the enemy force that it can beat. The NPA can defeat the reactionary armed forces only piece by piece and thereby accumulate strength over time.

The CPP's revolutionary experience has proven again and again that people's war cannot be developed without the full and widespread realization of the minimum land reform program, consisting of rent reduction, elimination of usury, raising of farm wages, restitution of grabbed land, improving prices of farm products, increasing agricultural production and promotion of sideline occupations, and rudimentary cooperation through exchange of labor, work animals and tools. Land reform is undertaken along the antifeudal line, with the proletarian cadres relying mainly on the poor and lower middle peasants and farm workers winning over the middle peasants, neutralizing the rich peasants and taking advantage of the splits between the enlightened and despotic landlords in order to isolate and destroy the power of the latter. The antifeudal line is within the framework of the entire new-democratic revolution.

It is worthwhile to review and improve the Revolutionary Guide to Land Reform on the basis of the rich experience in the antifeudal struggle. The main content of the new-democratic revolution is the solution of the land problem, up to the confiscation of landlord property and free distribution of land in the maximum land reform program. But this program is best carried out after the realization of the minimum land reform program on so wide a scale that the potentially unified landlord class and the enemy troops can no longer effectively counter the confiscation of land with the massacre of the peasant leaders and masses. Undoubtedly the best time to carry out the maximum land reform program is when the enemy is defeated over extensive liberated areas or when the entire country is already liberated.

Without a comprehensively organized mass base, the Party and the people's army cannot thrive and advance. Thus, the organs of political power are necessarily set up. These are supported by the mass organizations of workers, peasants, women, youth, cultural activists and children. From these organizations, working committees to assist the organs of political power are created and put in charge of public education, mass organizing, self-defense, land reform, production, finance, health, cultural activities, arbitration and so on. Where there is a strong mass base, there can be a strong Party and deep reserves for the people's army through such augmentative forces as the self-defense units, militia and local guerrilla forces.

There is dual political power in the Philippines today. One is the revolutionary government in the guerrilla fronts. And the other is the reactionary government still entrenched in the cities. The revolutionary government can be expanded and consolidated only through the integral factors of revolutionary armed struggle, land reform and mass base-building. If the Party gives up any of these factors, the revolutionary movement begins to shrink and fail. When the territory of the revolutionary government grows, that of the reactionary government shrinks.

To prevent such phenomena as Ahos campaign and other instances of anti-informer hysteria from recurring, the system of law and justice in the revolutionary movement is being developed, with the proper legal and judicial code and trained personnel to apply these. Since the beginning, the Party and the revolutionary movement have been committed to the development of a democratic system of law and justice. There is an accumulation of decisions and rules pertaining to these. Since 1972, the Rules for Establishing the People's Revolutionary Government has laid down a bill of rights which guarantees the civil and political rights of the people.

There is a crying need for proletarian revolutionary cadres in the countryside because for a long period of time, there was a reverse flow of Party cadres and members (especially experienced ones) from the rural areas to the urban areas, propelled by the "Left" opportunist line of combining urban insurrectionism and military adventurism and by the Right opportunist line of reformism and parliamentarism. The Party is once more stressing the importance of revolutionary work in the countryside because it is here where the armed strength is accumulated and developed to overthrow the ruling system and because the guerrilla fronts are in dire need of certain competent personnel that only the cities can provide.

The urban-basing and repeated arrests in 1988 to 1991 of the former NPA "general command" in Metro Manila and certain regional commands are negative examples for the entire Party and the people's army. The rectification movement repudiates the previous practice of the "general command" and some regional army commands to base themselves in urban areas under such pretexts as operating radios, computers and other high-tech equipment, leading both the rural-based people's army and armed city partisans or waiting for a sudden turn of events in the urban areas. Certainly so-called special operations, which in fact deteriorated into gangsterism, is an impermissible reason for urban basing. The eventual control of town and provincial centers shall be the result of the wave-upon-wave advance of the revolutionary forces.

There is the Party organization that properly belongs to the urban areas. From the underground, it leads the legal democratic mass movement, which has a defensive character. The entire Party is repudiating the previous error of being carried away by the "Left" opportunist illusion which regards armed city partisan warfare and armed urban insurrections as the decisive factor for advancing or winning the revolution or by the Right opportunist illusion which regards reformism and parliamentarism or any combination of Right and "Left" opportunism or by a flip-flop from one to the other as likewise the decisive factor for advancing or winning the revolution. Any muddleheadedness in this regard is impermissible because it has proven to be very costly.

For a considerable period of time, the legal democratic mass movement will play an important role in the development of the revolutionary armed struggle but it shall be a role secondary to the revolutionary armed struggle being carried out in the countryside. It means that the legal democratic forces in the urban areas cannot by themselves overthrow or radically transform the ruling system even if on certain occasions the unarmed uprising of the people as in 1986 is capable of causing the downfall of one reactionary ruling clique and replacing it with another reactionary ruling clique. In a country like the Philippines, it takes more than an armed or unarmed urban uprising to defeat the entire reactionary armed forces, bring down the entire ruling system and make social revolution. Through the process of protracted people's war, the revolutionary forces develop the strength not only to overthrow the entire ruling system but also to basically complete the new-democratic revolution and start the socialist revolution.

The pull of both the "Left" opportunist line of urban insurrectionism and the Right opportunist line of reformism on Party cadres and members to stick to the urban areas even when they can no longer operate effectively in the urban areas have wrought serious damage to the urban-based Party underground and legal democratic mass movement as well as to the armed revolutionary movement in the countryside. The Party is systematically dispatching Party cadres and members and revolutionary activists to the countryside in order to help raise the level of revolutionary work in the countryside and not only to put into relatively safer conditions in the countryside those who can no longer work effectively in the urban areas. There is a lot of catching up to do in dispatching fresh revolutionary cadres and activists to the countryside in order to respond to the crying need for them there.

There are certain anticommunist elements who wish to induce the Party to take the road of counterrevolutionary reformism. They claim that the people have gotten tired of waging armed resistance against their oppressors and exploiters and that by implication prefer to suffer in silence the violence of oppression and exploitation indefinitely. They prate about deemphasizing the people's war or even altogether abandoning it. The best proof of the fallacy and chicanery of this counterrevolutionary line is that the pseudoprogressive petty-bourgeois groups like the revisionists, bourgeois populists, petty-bourgeois socialists, liberals and neoliberals, Christian democrats and the like have remained small, marginal and inconsequential. They seem to be larger than they are only when they are used as tools of anticommunist propaganda by the ruling system and by foreign anticommunist agencies. The legal mass movement that has a national democratic character is still led by the proletarian revolutionary party. Were the CPP to terminate or diminish the people's war, then it would become impotent and marginalized like these anticommunist petty-bourgeois groups.

Those who are pushing the counterrevolutionary reformist line also make a hue and cry about peace at any cost to the people and to the revolutionary cause. They wish pacifism to take hold of the revolutionary forces and thereby liquidate them. These reformist elements wish to appropriate the name of the people for their own counterrevolutionary purposes under the pretext of being the "third force" between the reactionary government and the National Democratic Front but they have exposed themselves completely by going so low as to provide intelligence briefings and psywar support to the U.S.-Ramos regime and collaborate with the agents of the regime in holding anticommunist rallies.

The Party and the entire revolutionary mass movement are systematically smashing the counterrevolutionary line being peddled by the alliance of the anticommunist petty-bourgeois that echo the anti-Stalin slogans of the U.S. imperialists and that actively assist the U.S.-Ramos regime, especially in intelligence and psywar. By unmasking these elements, all Party members and mass activists can raise the level of their consciousness and militancy. These anticommunist petty-bourgeois groups have incorporated into their ranks the frustrated ringleaders of urban insurrectionism and military adventurism and criminals who have engaged in bloody witchhunts, gangster activities and intelligence service to the enemy.

To further develop the urban-based legal democratic mass movement, the Party continues to do painstaking mass work among the workers, urban poor, poor fishermen, students, youth, women, the professionals, and the small and medium businessmen. The work in the trade unions, urban poor communities, student movement, institutions and so on results in solid mass organizations and secret Party branches and groups. And the masses are aroused, organized and mobilized along the national democratic line on the issues that most affect their lives.

The rectification movement combats and rejects the pernicious suggestion from various pseudorevolutionary quarters that the working class must give up its vanguard role or that the Party must be liquidated in favor of a united front at first dominated by petty-bourgeois groups but ultimately serving the imperialists, the big compradors and landlords. There would have been no revolutionary movement at all in the Philippines now if not for the leadership of the working class through its advance detachment, the Communist Party of the Philippines. Those who say otherwise have no other intention but to undermine, sabotage and destroy the revolutionary movement.

It is the CPP's continuing achievement that its organization is nationwide and deeply rooted among the masses of the workers and peasants. It is a Party with a cadre and mass character. The quantity and quality of the Party membership are examined. The ideological and political quality is examined first of all. Those who do not come up to the standards are given special attention to become truly qualified as Party members. Those who do not wish to raise the level of their qualifications through ideological and political studies and practical work are allowed to leave the Party.

There is a new resolve to increase the proportion of Party members with worker and peasant status to at least ninety percent and to reduce the proportion of those from the petty-bourgeois intelligentsia, not by turning away those who are willing to remould themselves but by positively accelerating the recruitment of members from the toiling masses. The all-round strength of the membership of the Party is drawn from and tested in the revolutionary mass moment. The advance elements in the revolutionary mass movement are invited to become candidate-members. Emphasis is on the recruitment of the advance elements from the working class movement, from the people's army and the peasant movement and from the intelligentsia.

Party leading organs and units take responsibility for and plan the systematic recruitment of candidate-members and their development into full Party members within the prescribed period of candidature. It is a long-running shortcoming of the Party that the mass activists of the national democratic movement are recognized and yet are not being invited to become candidate-members and that in the case of those invited as candidate-members, they are not developed to become full Party members within the prescribed period. An individual Party member can recommend a mass activist to become a candidate-member. It is subsequently the responsibility of the Party unit receiving the recommendation to see to it that a cadre verifies the personality and record of the recommendee and see to it that he or she becomes a full Party member by taking the basic Party course and fulfilling trial work.

The practice of assessing and evaluating work and making criticism and self-criticism is being reinvigorated and encouraged in every leading organ and in every unit. The leading organs are required to take responsibility for and take initiative in the promotion of criticism and self-criticism even after the successful end of the current rectification movement.

The principle of democratic centralism is upheld. It means that centralized leadership is based on democracy and the latter is guided by the former in accordance with the theory and practice of Marxism-Leninism-Mao Zedong Thought. Both bureaucratism and ultrademocracy are being combated. There is inner Party democracy but at the same time there is Party discipline. Exponents of ultrademocracy have recently exposed themselves as inveterate liquidationists and anticommunists.

To guard against bureaucratism, the leading organs consist of elected representatives of lower Party organs and organizations and are not cut off from but continuously interact with them in order to gather facts and recommendations from below, through direct investigation, reports, consultations, and study and work conferences. All leading organs up to the National Party Congress are required to meet as regularly as possible in accordance with the provisions of the Party constitution. Thus, the experience of the Party can be promptly summed up and the tasks can be defined.

At the same time, the phenomenon of independent kingdoms, factionalism or autonomism is being vigorously combated. The most rabid opponents of the rectification movement have tried to destroy the Party by whipping up ultrademocracy or anarchy. They wish to decapitate and disintegrate the Party and thereby preempt their grave accountabilities. The so-called "freedom of criticism" long ago criticized by the great Lenin is rejected. Any communist party, whether out of power or in power loses its proletarian revolutionary character when it admits into its ranks alien elements and allows them to promote petty-bourgeois and other antiproletarian ideas and actions within the Party.

While the ringleaders of the "Left" and Right opportunists were still formally in the Party, they sought to liquidate the leadership of the working class and the Party. The "Left" opportunists wanted to do away with the absolute leadership of the Party over the New People's Army. They demanded that the NPA have a separate machinery independent of the Party so that they could freely push their line of urban insurrectionism and military adventurism and conduct "special operations", including gangster activities. The Right opportunists wanted to liquidate the Party as the vanguard and center of the revolution, replace it with a bogus united front and reduce the Party to a member organization, giving up its independence and initiative and subordinating itself to a majority of petty-bourgeois groups and individuals that depict the Party as an unwelcome "authoritarian" entity. The Party has smashed both types of opportunists by issuing the directive on the Relationship of the Party with the NPA and the United Front.

The problem of security for the Party, especially in the urban underground, has become complicated and aggravated by the treachery of a handful of "Left" and Right opportunists who have become outright enemy agents, engaged not only in a campaign of slander and lies against the Party but also assisting the enemy in so-called keyhole operations. The Party is therefore reorganizing its personnel, shifting a number of them to the countryside and, most important of all, recruiting more Party members in order to render useless the previous information level of the renegades.

As a result of the current rectification movement, the Communist Party of the Philippines can be expected to become stronger ideologically, politically and organizationally. The rectification movement is guided by Marxism-Leninism-Mao Zedong Thought. It seeks to reinforce the foundation of the Party, enhance the victories already won, overcome deviations, errors and shortcomings and raise to a new and higher level the fighting will and capabilities of the Party and the people against the enemy. It is a method learned from Mao Zedong in strengthening the revolutionary party of the proletariat. It is a major component of Mao Zedong Thought.

VI. Prospects of the Philippine Revolution Under the Guidance of Marxism-Leninism-Mao Zedong Thought

So long as the ruling system in the Philippines remains semicolonial and semifeudal, there is the urgent need for the new-democratic revolution and there is the fertile ground for the growth in strength and advance of the armed revolutionary movement of the people. The chronic crisis of the system makes the protracted people's war possible and necessary. And this crisis is ever worsening.

The fundamental causes that gave rise to the Marcos fascist dictatorship persist. The shift from the rule of Marcos to that of Aquino and then to that of Ramos has entailed the aggravation and deepening of the crisis from one level to another. Foreign monopoly capitalism, domestic feudalism and bureaucrat capitalism still ride roughshod over the people and are intensifying the oppression and exploitation of the people.

The U.S. imperialists instigated Marcos to unleash the open rule of terror in 1972 in order to eliminate the newly-resumed armed revolutionary and to have a free hand in imposing neocolonial economic policies on the people. The result was nationwide expansion of the armed revolutionary movement and the aggravation of the Philippine agrarian backwardness and an insatiable addiction to foreign loans for anti-industrial purposes.

To preempt the rising hatred of the people and the surge of the armed revolutionary movement, the U.S. imperialists had to foment a big split in the reactionary armed forces in order to cause the downfall of its puppet. Under the Aquino regime, further splits within the reactionary armed forces occurred and the economy further slid down after a brief seeming recovery. Under the Ramos regime, the new chieftain of the reactionaries bases himself on only 23.5 percent of the vote and desperately flaps about to serve the greed of his imperialist masters and his own clique and to appease his political rivals within the exploitative system. The regime knows no way by which to maintain its rule but to beg for foreign investments and loans and escalate total war which combines utmost brutality and psychological warfare.

The chronic socioeconomic and political crisis is guaranteed to worsen by the internal laws of motion of the ruling system. These mean the relentless oppression and exploitation of the people by the exploiting classes of the comprador big bourgeoisie and the landlord class, the ceaseless contradictions among the reactionary factions and the irrepressible resistance of the people. The ultimate doom of the ruling system is ensured by the perseverance of the people in their armed revolutionary movement.

The current regime is at a loss as to how to draw from domestic and foreign sources the wherewithal for its maintenance. The people have been sucked dry of their sweat and blood for the benefit of the imperialists and the local reactionary classes. At the same time, it has become absurd for the imperialists to be further extending loans that can never be repaid. New loans are still being incurred to cover the chronic deficits and increasingly to pay the debt service.

After crowing about the triumph of neocolonialism and the triumph of capitalism over revisionist bureaucrat capitalism, the three centers of the world capitalist system (the United States, Japan and Western Europe) no less are conspicuously afflicted by the crisis of overproduction. The unprecedented development of high technology and abuse of finance capital in corporate speculation and neocolonialism in the period after World War II has deepened and aggravated the general crisis of capitalism, including the economic and financial devastation of the third world and former Soviet bloc countries. The field for maximizing profits has shrunk due to the ruin of the countries floundering in foreign debt. The Philippines is a prime example of the floundering loan-client.

The laws of capitalism continue to drive the winning monopolies in the industrial capitalist countries to adopt higher technology that raises their own profit and productivity rates but kills jobs of both blue and white collar workers and drives down the profit and productivity rates of their entire national economies. The abuse of finance capital since the sixties has brought about supermonopolies and has ravaged the neocolonies. Now, monopoly capitalism is at a loss as to how to dispose of surplus goods and services it produces amidst the wasteland of neocolonialism, bankrupt bureaucrat capitalism and the ongoing mass unemployment even in the centers of the world capitalist system.

All major industrial capitalist countries are now engaged in the reconsolidation of their national and regional positions and in the redivision of the global market, sources of raw materials and fields of investment. The trend among the supermonopolies is to restrain themselves from extending productive investments as well as loan capital for nonproductive purposes to countries like the Philippines.

Under these circumstances, the promise of the Ramos regime to turn the Philippines into a "newly-industrializing country" is a mere pipe-dream. Even the "tigers" of East Asia, including the coastal provinces of China, are now feeling the adverse effects of the contraction of the American consumer market and the impending shift to Mexico of the low value-added manufacturing-for-reexport under the North American Free Trade Agreement (NAFTA).

The gravity of the crisis of the world capitalist system can be seen not only in the conditions of economic depression in industrial capitalist countries and the priorly long-running economic and financial ravages of neocolonialism in the third world and the former Soviet-bloc countries but also in the rising and widescale rampages of nationalism, fascism, racism, ethnocentrism, religious fundamentalism and other blatant factors of political crisis in the wake of the global economic crisis.

The worsening crisis of the world capitalist system and that of the domestic ruling system converge, interact and help each other to generate an ever worse crisis in the Philippines and guarantee the favorable conditions for protracted people's war. The global crisis of capitalism now tends to draw simultaneously the attention of the imperialist forces to so many "trouble spots" (the former Yugoslavia, Central Asia, Somalia, Angola, Haiti, Kampuchea, and so on) of their own making even as they wish to focus on and mop up the remaining anti-imperialist states like the People's Democratic of Korea and Cuba and the armed revolutionary movements led by Marxist-Leninist parties.

For 25 years already, the United States, Japan and Western Europe have directly and indirectly poured resources into the armed counterrevolution in the Philippines. But this has proven futile. The armed revolution continues to exist and grow. The desire of the imperialist powers to extinguish the Philippine armed revolution is ever growing but their capability to do so is not limitless.

The Communist Party of the Philippines looks forward to the resurgence of the anti-imperialist and socialist movements as a result of the unprecedented crisis of the world capitalist system. It is the internationalist duty of the CPP to uphold the torch of armed revolution and wage protracted people's war self-reliantly in order to help bring about such resurgence on an unprecedented scale. There can be no better way than this for the Communist Party of the Philippines to carry out the principle of proletarian internationalism.

The Communist Party of the Philippines engages mainly in bilateral relations with parties, organizations and movements abroad on the basis of ideological-political understanding of Marxism-Leninism as well as on the basis of anti-imperialist political solidarity. The Party also participates in multilateral seminars and conferences that may forge agreements, resolutions or declarations as a result of consensus and unanimity.

In foreign relations, the Party upholds the principles of mutual respect for independence, equality, noninterference, cooperation and mutual benefit. The Party is interested in the international propagation of Marxism-Leninism-Mao Zedong Thought through ideological-political exchanges. It is also interested in broad anti-imperialist solidarity, irrespective of the ideological stand of those involved.

The perspective of the new-democratic revolution in the Philippines is socialist. In the first place, the new democratic revolution can be won only because the leading force is the working class, the main force is the peasantry and the additional basic revolutionary force is the urban petty bourgeoisie. The revolutionary forces are waging the new-democratic revolution, working hard, struggling fiercely and making sacrifices essentially because they want the current revolution to lead to socialism rather than to capitalism.

The theory of Marxism-Leninism-Mao Zedong Thought guides the Communist Party of the Philippines and the Filipino people in the struggle to achieve the new-democratic and socialist stages of the Philippine revolution. Moreover, this theory provides the basic principles and the foresight of continuing revolution under proletarian dictatorship in order to consolidate socialism, combat modern revisionism and prevent the restoration of capitalism in socialist society until imperialism is defeated on a global scale and communism becomes possible.

The disintegration of the revisionist ruling parties and revisionist-ruled social systems and the worsening crisis of the world capitalist system vindicate the full scope of Marxism-Leninism-Mao Zedong Thought, including Mao's successful practice of the new-democratic and the socialist revolution; his critique of imperialism, modern revisionism and neocolonialism; and his theory and pioneering practice in applying the theory of continuing revolution under proletarian dictatorship through the Great Proletarian Cultural Revolution. With a comprehensive and profound understanding of Mao Zedong Thought, the proletarian revolutionaries of the world cannot be assailed by doubts about the future of socialism and communism and cannot be misled by any kind of revisionism.

The time has come for the proletarian revolutionaries who uphold Marxism-Leninism-Mao Zedong Thought to seize the revolutionary initiative. They can grow in strength and advance on the fertile ground provided by the worsening crisis of the world capitalist system and by the proven bankruptcy of modern revisionism.

While the protracted people's war continues, the Party, the people's army and the organs of political power and the revolutionary mass organizations can continue to exist and grow in strength until they can seize the cities on a nationwide scale. On the way to total victory in the new-democratic revolution, the revolutionary forces and the people achieve definite and tangible victories and enjoy definite gains. The moment the revolutionary forces capitulate, they are reduced to small and inconsequential entities at the mercy of the imperialists and the exploiting classes; the organs of political power already established would disappear. The people under the leadership of the Communist Party of the Philippines cannot be any inferior to their ancestors who fought the colonialists for more than 300 years to reach the old democratic revolution.

It is a great victory that the revolutionary movement led by the Communist Party of the Philippines has already attained in a far shorter time a level of strength and a scale far greater than that reached by any previous revolutionary movement in the entire history of the Philippines. The accumulated strength and experience of the current revolutionary movement must proceed to a new and higher level.

The accumulated achievements and experience of the Party in the new-democratic revolution are abundant and rich. These are bound to become far more abundant and richer upon the basic completion of the new-democratic revolution and the start of the socialist revolution. The protraction of the people's war provides an ample opportunity for the wider and deeper development of the revolutionary forces and for more favorable conditions in the world.

The Filipino people have won brilliant victories in revolution because they are led by the Communist Party of the Philippines under the guidance of Marxism-Leninism-Mao Zedong Thought. Modern revisionism has become discredited and most revisionist regimes, including the Soviet Union, have collapsed. Soviet-sponsored regimes that arose by coup d'état in the 1970s have disappeared. So have been those regimes established by petty-bourgeois-led insurrection. Anticolonial movements dependent on Soviet social-imperialism have gone into neocolonial compromises, reminiscent of 1935 and 1946 in the Philippines. In contrast, the Philippine revolution continues to stand as a pillar of resolute armed revolution against imperialism and the local reactionaries.

But Filipino communists should not become conceited and complacent about their current position in the world proletarian revolution. They have no choice but to work harder, fight more fiercely and be prepared for further sacrifices because the imperialists and the reactionaries are now exerting more efforts to defeat and destroy the Philippine revolution by every foul means. At the same time, there is hope that the widespread social turmoil will lead to the resurgence of the anti-imperialist and socialist movement on a global scale.

In leading the Philippine revolution, the Communist Party of the Philippines consciously integrates the theory and practice of Marxism-Leninism-Mao Zedong Thought. When it follows the proletarian revolutionary line, the Party marches from victory to victory. But wherever and whenever this line is violated, the revolutionary movement suffers setbacks. Consequent to the rectification movement that is now being carried out, the Party is enhancing its ideological, political and organizational strength, overcoming deviations, errors and shortcomings and is raising to a new and higher level the fighting will and capabilities of all the revolutionary forces and the broad masses of the people against imperialism and the reactionaries.

www.ingramcontent.com/pod-product-compliance
Lightning Source LLC
LaVergne TN
LVHW021759060526
838201LV00058B/3153